SPAIN

AND THE WORLD TABLE

SPAIN
AND THE WORLD TABLE

The Culinary Institute of America

with text by Martha Rose Shulman

Photography by Ben Fink

LONDON, NEW YORK, MUNICH, MELBOURNE, AND DELHI

editor NASIM MAWJI

senior editor ANJA SCHMIDT

designer JESSICA PARK

managing art editor MICHELLE BAXTER

art director DIRK KAUFMAN

dtp coordinator KATHY FARIAS

production manager IVOR PARKER

executive managing editor SHARON LUCAS

photographer BEN FINK

Published by DK Publishing
375 Hudson Street, New York, New York 10014

07 08 09 10 10 9 8 7 6 5 4 3 2 1

SD313–April 2008

A catalog record for this book is available from the Library of Congress.

ISBN 978-0-7566-3387-5

DK Books are available at special discounts for bulk purchases for sales promotions,
premiums, fund-raising, or educational use. For details contact DK Publishing Special
Markets, 375 Hudson Street, New York, New York 10014 or SpecialSales@dk.com.

Color reproduction by Colourscan, Singapore
Printed in China by Toppan Printing Co., (Shenzen) Ltd.

Discover more at www.dk.com

contents

PREFACE

The paella pans were bubbling and steaming as the dry vine cuttings underneath crackled and popped. These were no ordinary pans, but gigantic four-foot-wide vessels, all oozing at the rim with rice, rabbit, and spices. As acclaimed Spanish paella expert Rafael Vidal walked through this outdoor kitchen, carefully stoking the fires and checking his delicacy, a crowd of hungry and eager chefs (many of whom had come from all over the world) watched intently. Nearby, Llorenç Petràs, owner of a much-loved mushroom shop in Barcelona's La Boquería market, was grilling hundreds of calçots, spring onions similar to small leeks.

Later, when the assembled chefs nibbled on tapas, peeled the charred layers off the calçots and dipped them in a rich, nutty romesco sauce, and then heartily savored the saffron-scented paellas, they all knew an inspiring and delicious culinary immersion had just begun.

It was yet another exciting day at The Culinary Institute of America (CIA) at Greystone. Like every other year in November, more than 700 chefs and food professionals had gathered for the college's flagship Worlds of Flavor International Conference & Festival, which this year featured Spain and all of its spectacular food, wine, and culinary traditions.

Indeed, the CIA's "Spain and the World Table: Regional Traditions, Invention, and Exchange," co-presented with The Spanish Institute of Foreign Trade, Foods from Spain, and Wines from Spain, together with a host of regional Spanish governments and private companies, was perhaps the largest and most comprehensive conference ever held in the United States on Spanish food and wine. It brought together an "A-list" of top Spanish gastronomic talent, from three-star Michelin chefs to distinguished regional cooks, from Spanish cheese and olive oil experts to wine authorities and ingredient specialists. More than fifty Spanish chefs made the trip to the Napa Valley conference from all across Spain.

The food and cooking at the event was exceptional, but the sense of history in the making was truly galvanizing: an unprecedented U.S. gathering of top Spanish culinary talent sharing what they do best with their American counterparts at this very moment in time when Spanish leaders in food and wine are at the "top of their game."

Greg Drescher affirms the vibrancy and passion that surround Spanish food today.

It is this kind of unique culinary experience that has made the CIA's Worlds of Flavor conference the most influential professional forum in the country for world cuisines and flavor trends and a "must attend" for chefs, corporate menu decision-makers, wine and other beverage specialists, suppliers, journalists, and other professionals. Each November the event transforms the Napa Valley campus into an amazing crossroads of world food and culture.

This book is the product of the conference on Spain and is designed to share all the vibrant and robust flavors as well as the knowledge and passion of the influential and talented Spanish chefs who presented there.

During the event, one could see within a few minutes the whole story of contemporary Spanish gastronomy—the ancient juxtaposed against the modern, the rustic against the refined, and all

José Andrés (right) enjoys calçots, a glass of wine, and the lively atmosphere at the Worlds of Flavor conference.

shaped by culinary influences from around the world. Legendary chef Ferran Adrià of El Bulli mesmerized the audience as he shared the imperatives of creativity and demonstrated his latest applications of food science. Outside, in one of the CIA's outdoor kitchens, chef Cándido López Cuerdo of Segovia patiently roasted his suckling pigs in a wood-fired oven, a tradition that reached back into medieval Spain.

Moments of intense concentration and delight ensued as Spanish cheese expert Enric Canut described the elements of quality of Spain's best artisanal cheeses. Then there were unexpected moments: Chef Dani García of Marbella displayed good-humored patience when he discovered that he couldn't demonstrate his frozen olive oil popcorn at the scheduled time because the liquid nitrogen had failed to arrive with that morning's routine milk delivery at the CIA. Such was the spirit of the conference.

Now, through this book, Martha Rose Shulman—who has authored many of our best Mediterranean cookbooks—has magically combined that very spirit and passion from the conference with savory recipes and in doing so transports us into a world that is part fantastic Spanish kitchen and part Spanish culinary "brain trust."

We invite you now to come into our kitchen; to feel the genius of these chefs, cooks, and food and wine experts; taste the results and really understand what a delicious proposition Spain is today.

JOSÉ ANDRÉS
Chef, television personality, author, and chairman of the CIA's "Spain and the World Table" conference

GREG DRESCHER
Executive Director of Strategic Initiatives, The Culinary Institute of America

INTRODUCTION

TRADITION, INVENTION, AND EXCHANGE

A Basque chef stands at the stove, creating alchemy. He is warming salt cod and olive oil in an earthenware *cazuela* over a low flame. As it starts to bubble, he takes the handles of the dish and begins to shake it gently. He shakes it slowly but continuously, the fish and the oil in constant motion. After about 20 minutes the olive oil and the protein- and gelatin-rich juices from the fish begin to emulsify, and soon the salt cod is coated in a thick, velvety sauce. This magical transformation of two ingredients is not a product of the "new" Spanish cooking, but a classic, much loved Basque dish called *bacalao al pil pil*.

A chef from Navarra stands at his cooking station, and he too is creating alchemy. He is thinking of *pil pil* as he heats salt cod with sautéed garlic for 2 minutes, then blends

Like a magician performing a conjuring trick, Ferran Adrià (left) prepares orange sorbet from freshly squeezed orange juice and liquid nitrogen at the Worlds of Flavor conference.

half of it with olive oil, lime zest, garlic, and hot cream mixed with agar agar and gelatin. He flakes the remaining cod and adds it to the mixture, then folds in whipped cream to make a mousse that is a riff on the Basque dish. This he pipes into small PVC tubes, inserts brochette sticks down the middle, and freezes. When the *pil pil* popsicles are frozen and ready to serve he will remove them from the tubes, wrap them in paper-thin ribbons of cooked Navarra asparagus, like barbershop poles, pull out the sticks, and dress the cylinders with a caramelized reduction of red wine vinegar, balsamic vinegar, and sugar.

All cooking is alchemy, of course, but lately Spanish chefs have been getting a lot of attention for the far-out creations, bordering on science fiction, that are coming out of their kitchens. They are at the forefront of contemporary haute cuisine, wowing diners with innovative food that is as revolutionary in the world of gastronomy as Picasso's *Les Demoiselles d'Avignon* was to the art world one hundred years ago. Yet every new creation has at its center a taste memory, be it a frozen *pil pil* mousse, a sphere of food turned inside out, a deconstructed paella bathed in an ethereal sea spray foam, an elusive olive oil "couscous," or a kernel of gazpacho "popcorn." Today's Spanish chefs are generating some of the world's best and freshest ideas about food, yet the new Spanish cooking is firmly rooted in Spain's strong gastronomic traditions.

There are many ways to look at *la cocina Española*: it can be defined by its ingredients, its techniques, its history, or its regionalism. To really understand this rich and diverse cuisine, one should look at all of these elements, because they overlap. Their roles are equally important in understanding traditional Spanish cooking as they are in comprehending the food being created by today's new wave chefs. We can better understand the ingredients—*los productos*—that are at the heart of all Spanish cuisine if we understand Spain's history and its regionalism, and we will understand the nature of Spain's signature dishes if we look at Spanish cooking techniques.

INGREDIENTS

Those of us who have never been to Spain can nonetheless taste some of its finest key ingredients, because Spain is sharing its products more than ever before. Its wonderful salt-cured hams, of which the renowned *jamón Ibérico* is arguably the best in the world, and its sausages; its juicy olives; the sweet, nutty olive oils from Catalonia and stronger picual olive oils from Andalusia; and its wines, which today are making their mark on the world market. Spain exports some of the world's finest canned and bottled foods—aged sherry vinegars, roasted piquillo peppers, cured anchovies, rich tuna packed in olive oil—and produces over one hundred kinds of cheese, several of which—*Cabrales, Manchego, Garrotxa, Roncal, Torta del Casar*—have made their way to cheese stores in America. Then there is Spanish saffron, that luxurious spice so essential for Valencia's golden rice dishes and savory stews; and the equally essential short-grain rices, Senia, Bomba, and Bahía, which can find no substitute when it comes to making paellas and other signature *arroces*.

These days it is not difficult to find classic Spanish cheeses such as Cabrales, Manchego, and Torta del Casar in American cheese stores.

Spain's quality ingredients are at the heart of the flavor and texture profiles that we associate with the cuisine. Saffron and almonds; sherry vinegar, garlic, and olive oil; the smoky Spanish paprika known as *pimentón*; juicy salt cod; locally grown fruits and vegetables; roasted sweet red piquillo peppers; and anchovies and tuna inspire cooks to create traditional dishes and invent new ones.

Sweet piquillo peppers are roasted and packed in their juices. They are available canned and in jars and add a distinctive flavor to many Spanish dishes.

HISTORY

The exchange of food and agricultural techniques has been taking place between Spain and the rest of the world for thousands of years. The country's complex history could be written around food, beginning with the Phoenicians, who came as early as the 9th century B.C.E. in search of the bluefin tuna, which still migrate into the Mediterranean in the spring, and salt, which they needed for curing the fish. The Romans brought vines, wheat, and olive trees. Agriculture flourished during the 800-year Hispano-Muslim period. The Arabs were responsible for vastly overhauling irrigation technology; they made water available for farming as it had never been before. Spain's small vegetable farms—*huertas*—and rice cultivation are their legacy. Many of the foods we associate with Spanish cooking—rice and almonds, oranges and melons, eggplant and artichokes, and sugar—were introduced into Spain by the Arabs.

The voyages of discovery in the 15th and 16th centuries had a great impact on the evolution of Spanish cuisine and, for that matter, on cuisines throughout the world (imagine

The classic Spanish omelet, tortilla Española, is served in tapas bars across the country. Would it have been as popular if it hadn't contained potatoes?

Indian food without chiles, Italian food without tomatoes). Tomatoes, potatoes, peppers, pumpkins, squash, maize, chocolate, and haricot beans were all foods from the New World. It took many years, in some cases more than a century, for New World foods to become established in Spain, but they eventually became essential to the cuisine. Spain would not have her national dish, the potato omelet called *tortilla Española*, were it not for potatoes. Without tomatoes, gazpacho would still be a simple soup made from water, garlic, bread, olive oil, and vinegar. The food exchange between Spain and the Americas took hold so completely that today Spain is renowned for many foods whose origins were in the Americas, like piquillo peppers and specific types of beans— the *fabe* that defines Asturian *fabadas* and the *garrofo* that many paellas cannot be without.

This exchange worked both ways: it would be difficult to imagine the Americas without wheat and onions, citrus and melons, radishes, grapes, and sugarcane. Yet these foods had never taken root on American soil before Columbus arrived with their seeds. Nor were Native Americans familiar with animal husbandry; pigs, sheep, and cattle were unknown in the New World. Pork and beef arrived with the Europeans.

History plays a role in the evolution of Spanish pork products as well. Pork took on significance during the period that followed the expulsion of the Moors and Jews from Spain at the end of the 15th century. Forbidden by both Muslim and Jewish law, eating pork was indicative of being a Christian and thus a true Spaniard. That Spain has for most of its history been an extremely poor country was also significant, because the pig is such an economical animal. Every bit of it can be used.

To comprehend the culinary explosion that has been taking place in Spain over the last twenty years it's important to understand the country's recent history. For nearly four decades following the end of the Spanish Civil War in 1939, Spain was cut off from the rest of the world by Franco's ultra-conservative government, and its strong creative spirit (think Picasso, Dalí, Gaudí) was nearly crushed. Regionalism was repressed, and many local foodways risked annihilation. The government went so far as to make it illegal to make artisanal cheeses!

Since the death of Franco and the restoration of democracy in Spain, there has been a cultural explosion that has found a voice in gastronomy as well as the other arts. Regional food traditions are being revived all over the country. In contemporary restaurants everywhere humble traditional dishes have attained cult status. There is a regional exchange going on that is very new in Spain. Today Andalusian specialties like gazpacho and salmorejo are served in trendy Barcelona restaurants, something you never would have seen twenty years ago. Local products are being recognized and protected by the government with Denomination of Origin status. And creative chefs, now unfettered, are pushing the envelope with a cuisine that borders on science, and blurs the lines between what has gone before and what is possible in the future, while never losing sight of its Spanish core.

REGIONALISM

Spain's seventeen regions provide a deep cultural diversity that can be looked at through a gastronomic lens. Catalonia, known for combining elements of the sea and the mountains (*mar y montaña*), and sweet and savory in its distinctive cuisine, has a startling array of salt cod dishes, and brings us *allioli* and grilled vegetable medleys (*escalivada*), *romesco* sauce, rice and vermicelli dishes (*fideos*), and a famous seafood and tomato stew called *suquet*. From the eastern Mediterranean regions of Valencia and Murcia come rice dishes, and from the southern region of Andalusia we get those wonderful vegetable and vinegar soups, gazpacho, *ajo blanco*, and

SPAIN consists of seventeen regions,
each one with its own distinctive
ingredients and culinary techniques.

FRANCE

ATLANTIC
OCEAN

A Coruña

Santiago

Lugo

GALICIA

Pontevedra

Ourense

PORTUGAL

Oviedo

ASTURIAS

Santander

CANTABRIA

San
Sebastián

Bilbao

BASQUE COUNTRY

Vitoria-Gasteiz

León

Pamplona

NAVARRA

Logroño

LA RIOJA

Huesca

Girona

CATALONIA

Palencia

Burgos

Soria

Zaragoza

Lérida

Barcelona

Zamora

Valladolid

CASTILE-LEÓN

ARAGÓN

Tarragona

Salamanca

Segovia

Ávila

MADRID

Madrid

Guadalajara

Teruel

Castellon de la Plana

BALEARIC ISLANDS

Cuenca

Toledo

Cáceres

EXTREMADURA

CASTILE-LA MANCHA

VALENCIA

Valencia

Badajoz

Mérida

Albacete

Alicante

Córdoba

Jaén

MURCIA

Murcia

MEDITERRANEAN SEA

Huelva

Seville

ANDALUSIA

Granada

Almería

Málaga

Cádiz

CANARY ISLANDS

MOROCCO

ALGERIA

Geography, climate, and history have all influenced Spain's cuisine. In the central region, bean and meat stews are popular.

salmorejo, as well as the best fried seafood in the world, mint-spiked meatballs (*albóndigas*), and sweet, rich confections. Many of these foods are legacies of the Arabs. Andalusia is the home of sherry and Jabugo ham, and tapas are thought to have their origins here.

The vast central regions of Spain, Castile-León, Castile-La Mancha, and Extremadura, are meat-eating regions, famous for their roasted lamb and suckling pig, and their rustic bean and meat stews. Acorn-eating Ibérico pigs from Extremadura are world renowned for their ham, and the smoked paprika that is used so widely in Spanish cooking comes from this region. La Mancha produces the saffron that is essential to many Spanish dishes.

From the landlocked northern regions of La Rioja, Navarra, and Aragón come hearty lamb and red pepper stews. Navarra and La Rioja are vegetable-growing regions, and are especially known for their red piquillo peppers, asparagus, artichokes, potatoes, and beans.

Then there are the northern coastal regions. The Basque country has long been famous for its cuisine, and is the seat of the revolutionary movement in Spanish cooking that was the beginning of *La Nueva Cocina Española*. The Basques are noteworthy fishermen, consequently some of the most famous Basque dishes are seafood dishes, such as *marmitako*, a tuna and potato stew, and hake with green sauce. They also have some signature cod preparations, such as *pil pil*, and *bacalao a la vizcaína*, cod in a red pepper sauce. Galicia, Asturias, and

Cantabria, the other northern coastal regions, also produce wonderful seafood dishes. Asturias is famous for its beans (*fabes*), the key ingredient in a hearty bean and sausage stew (*fabada Asturiana*), as well as clam and bean stew. Inland from the coast, Galicians enjoy a famous hearty bean and smoked meats stew called *caldo Gallego*.

There are also islands off both coasts of Spain that contribute to the regional gastronomy of the country. In the Atlantic, almost 1,000 miles from the mainland and only 70 miles from Morocco, the Canary Islands have belonged to Spain since they were conquered in the 15th century. They provided Spanish sailors en route to and from the Americas with an Atlantic base. Now they provide Spain with income from tourism, and with an exotic cuisine accented by spicy pounded sauces called *mojos*, fish dishes, potatoes and tomatoes, and tropical fruits. It was in the Canary Islands that many of the New World foods first took root.

The cuisine of the Balearic Islands of Mallorca, Menorca, and Ibiza is decidedly Mediterranean, full of olive oil and garlic, eggplant and tomatoes, fish and sweet local peppers. It's famous for a layered eggplant casserole called *tumbet*, and for thick bread and vegetable soups called *sopes*.

TECHNIQUES

Cooking techniques are another window through which we can look at and understand the flavors and textures in Spanish cuisine. Emulsions such as *allioli* and *pil pil*, pounded mixtures

Chef Joan Roca experiments with smoke and its ability to influence flavors. This creation is an interpretation of a classic Spanish dish with squid, potatoes, and smoked paprika.

such as *romesco* sauce and *picada*, puréed vegetable or almond soups thickened with stale bread and flavored with vinegar such as Andalusia's gazpachos, exist because of specific techniques that have been honed over the centuries. Spain has built a whole category of dishes, *migas*, around crumbled stale bread, and another, *fideuas*, around noodles that are cooked like rice in a paella. The need to preserve cooked fish, using vinegar and olive oil, gave rise to a category of dishes called *escabeches*. Egg yolks left over when the whites were taken to be used in sherry clarification were destined for rich egg pastries that the nuns perfected and that are still the realm of convent bakeries.

The revolution that is going on in Spanish restaurant cooking today is all about technique. Chefs are probing the limits of what they can do with food, often working hand in hand with scientists and lab technicians. They apply liquid nitrogen to foods to reduce their temperatures drastically, resulting in new forms, such as solid olive oil semolina; they thicken purées and make gels with xanthan gum and agar agar without having to heat them, and make foams using a siphon and CO_2 cartridges. They are turning foods inside out as they transform them into caviar-like liquid spheres by dropping purées into calcium chloride solutions. The chefs are mad about vacuum cooking; they cook foods of all sorts in vacuum packs at very low temperatures for long periods of time, with incredibly moist, tender results. They reduce foods to dusts using dehydrating techniques, capture aromas—sometimes aromas as ephemeral as dirt or sea spray—through distillation and send them back to the diner in the form of smoke. The boundaries between sweet and savory, dessert and entrée, break down, as a chef sends out a savory sorbet to begin a meal, wraps a piece of asparagus in a caramel veil, or encases an anchovy in a chocolate bonbon.

TRADITION, MODERNITY, AND EXCHANGE

But for all the new technology, there is a great deal of interplay between tradition and the avant garde. Creative Spanish chefs get their inspiration from the artisans who produce the basic ingredients, *los productos*, from home cooks, and from their mothers—those who have always made local dishes, and who today are recognized and appreciated more than ever before. The classic Spanish dishes are memorable because they have big Mediterranean flavors, because they are made with the freshest of ingredients, because they represent a country that has boundless energy and joie de vivre, and tremendous imagination. More than the fashionable scientific ingredients, the xanthan gum and the liquid nitrogen, the

The excitement and energy of Spanish food is inspiring chefs outside the country. Japanese chef Kiyomi Mikuni garnishes his sushi paella with shellfish typically found in a paella.

agar agar and the calcium chloride; and more than the fancy equipment—the Thermomixes and the vacuum cookers, the siphons and the stills—it's the imagination that is at the heart of this fusion of the old with the new.

Today Spanish chefs are communicating with one another and with chefs from all over the world as they have never done before. They come together annually in Madrid and in San Sebastián, and bi-annually in Barcelona, for international food conferences, where they share their ideas, sample new products, and exchange new techniques. Then they return to their own restaurants and put those new ideas to work. At tables from Tokyo to Lima, Miami to Paris, you will find the influence of Spanish food traditions and contemporary Spanish chefs.

And from around the world, food lovers are flocking to Spain. If they are seeking out the new, they will find it in restaurants from the Pyrenees to the Rock of Gibraltar. But in so doing, they will taste what has come before, and what—more than ever—is there to stay.

TAPAS

TAPAS
Small bites for Spanish and American tables

Throughout Spain, from tiny villages to big cities, people from all walks of life and of all ages congregate in lively tapas bars on a daily basis to have a drink, sample little bites and, most of all, to talk. They talk about everything under the sun, while sipping sherry or beer, Cava or *sidra* (cider), or Basque white wine poured into small glasses from a flask raised high in the air.

Simple finger foods such as these Manchego Croquettes served with a slightly tart quince sauce make the perfect accompaniment to a glass of wine.

A WAY OF LIFE

The Spanish tapas tradition is as much a social one as a gastronomic one. Traditional tapas bars are atmospheric places with tiled walls and dark wooden bars that fill with people from noon until 3 in the afternoon (before lunch), then again from 7 to 10 at night (before dinner). In Spain people do not embark on their *tapeo*—their tapas bar crawl—with the intention of dining on tapas (though that, in fact, is what sometimes happens). They go out to socialize, to have conversation, to flirt, to have a drink. People may stand at the bar, eating mussels and olives and dropping the shells and pits on the floor, or sit at a table with a group of friends. The barman yells orders out to the cooks, small plates of food are set out, and somehow the barman and the diners keep track of the tab.

One category of tapas, called *pinchos*, are so called because they are served with a toothpick (*pinchar* means "to prick"). The toothpicks, or skewers, are also known as *banderillas*, after the instrument used by the picadors in bullfighting. As you eat your tapas you leave the toothpicks on the plate, and the barman counts them up to figure out your bill. Spanish omelets are often cut into squares and served on toothpicks, as are little canapés. In the Basque country, many types of tapas are called *pintxos*, and they are almost always based on bread. Other categories of tapas include small finger foods (*cosas de picar*, or "things to nibble") such as olives and almonds; fried foods such as *croquetas*; and hot, saucy foods that come in small earthenware casseroles called *cazuelas*.

ORIGINS AND INFLUENCES

Tapas originated in Andalusia, where sherry is made. The word comes from the verb *tapar*, "to cover." Glasses of sherry would be covered with a piece of ham or cheese to keep the flies and the dust off, so it is said, and from there the snacks evolved. The fact that people needed to nibble on something while sipping the fortified wine, and that the intense heat of the long Andalusian summers made people less inclined to eat big meals, probably had just as much to do with it.

Today some of Spain's tapas bars are sleek, bright, and modern, their cutting edge tapas set out on specially crafted serving trays, in shot glasses, and on spoons and skewers. Patxi Bergara and his wife, Blanca Ameztoy, create contemporary *pintxos* such as "False Anchovy Lasagna" on pages 20–21 at their Bar Bergara in San Sebastián, Spain. In Madrid's Europa Decó restaurant in the Hotel Urban, Chef Joaquín Felípe is creating fanciful tapas such as Serrano Ham Cones with Migas and Quail Eggs (pages 40–41) and the fusion-inspired Red Tuna Bites on page 48. In the stratosphere of Spanish food science, dishes such as Chef Ferran Adriá's liquid olive "grapes," liquefied olives encased in a skin, are inspired by the simplest of tapas, marinated olives.

Tapas have provided Spanish chefs with a template for exploring the country's regional cuisines. Twenty years ago you would never find gazpacho or salmorejo

Slices of cheese or ham, which were originally intended to keep insects and dust out of one's drink, may have been a precursor to tapas as we know them today.

Gazpacho, the refreshing Andalusian soup that was once sustenance for workers in the fields, is now often served in shot glasses in stylish tapas bars.

outside of Andalusia. Now you'll find it in tapas bars in Barcelona, Madrid, and San Sebastián served in small shot glasses. What was once considered traditional and regional is suddenly contemporary and cosmopolitan.

In addition to the recipes in this chapter, there are other recipes featured in this book, particularly the cold soups, some of the seafood dishes, and some of the salads and vegetable dishes, which can be served as tapas. Ensaladilla Rusa (pages 94–95) and Garlic Potatoes (page 98), for example, are traditionally served in bars all over Spain. Contemporary chefs serve gazpacho and its variations, such as the Beet and Cherry Gazpacho on page 73 and the Cold Almond and Garlic Soup on pages 74–75 in small shot glasses.

TAPAS COMES TO AMERICA

Chefs in the United States have been greatly influenced by the tapas tradition, particularly in the last ten years, when we've seen a proliferation of restaurants with menus built around little dishes, shared at the table. The word is used rather loosely; the type of dish described as a tapa may not have its roots in Spain. The custom itself will never be the same here, simply because the Spanish *tapeo* is a social tradition that has evolved in a very different type of setting. In America, we dine early; we are used to finishing a meal at about the time a Spanish diner would be just beginning to think about where to go for dinner. So the idea of small dishes with exciting flavors and textures has taken hold as a meal concept, and American diners will happily sip wine by the glass while dining on a selection of them.

CLASSIC SANGRIA

THERE IS NOTHING MORE REFRESHING than a glass of cold sangria on a hot summer day. Classic sangria should not be too sweet, with only a moderate amount of orange juice. It should sparkle with hints of citrus, and the wine should be a fruity one. It's best to use organic fruit here.

SERVES 8

6 tablespoons sugar

6 tablespoons water

8 strawberries, quartered

1 cup raspberries

1 cup blueberries

1 cup blackberries

8 slices peeled oranges (about 1)

5 cups dry red wine

1½ cups orange juice

⅔ cup Grand Marnier

1½ cups sparkling water

1. **Combine** the sugar and water in a small saucepan and bring to a boil over medium heat, stirring to dissolve the sugar. Remove from the heat and allow to cool.

2. **Combine** the fruit gently in a bowl. Mix the sugar-water, wine, orange juice, and Grand Marnier in a large pitcher.

3. **Add** the fruit to the pitcher and stir gently to combine.

4. **Add** the sparkling water and serve immediately, or allow the mixture to sit refrigerated (for up to 12 hours) before finishing with the sparkling water and serving over ice. To serve, spoon ⅓ cup of the fruit into each of the glasses and pour the liquid over.

Recipe by THE CULINARY INSTITUTE OF AMERICA

WHITE SANGRIA

A LIGHTER VERSION of traditional sangria may use white instead of red wine. Peaches, cherries, and nectarines are added in this recipe to provide a sweet yet crisp flavor. Any white wine chosen for this recipe should not be too dry. It's slightly less alcoholic than the classic, but equally—maybe even dangerously—refreshing.

SERVES 8

¼ cup sugar

¼ cup water

1 cup diced ripe peaches

¾ cup diced plums

1 cup pitted cherries

1 cup diced nectarines

8 slices peeled oranges (about 1)

1 bottle (750 ml) white wine

6 tablespoons orange juice

6 tablespoons lemon juice

½ cup Amaretto

1 pint (480 ml) sparkling water

1. **Combine** the sugar and water in a small saucepan and bring to a boil over medium heat. Stir to dissolve the sugar. Remove from the heat and allow to cool.

2. **Combine** the fruit gently in a bowl. Combine the sugar-water, wine, orange juice, lemon juice, and Amaretto in a large pitcher.

3. **Add** the fruit to the pitcher and stir gently to combine.

4. **Add** the sparkling water and serve immediately, or allow the mixture to sit refrigerated (for up to 12 hours) before finishing with the sparkling water and serving over ice. To serve, spoon ⅓ cup of the fruit into each of the glasses and pour the liquid over.

Recipe by THE CULINARY INSTITUTE OF AMERICA

ANCHOVY AND PISTO
BOCADILLOS

CHEF PATXI BERGARA calls this dish "False Anchovy Lasagna," because he layers the toast, pisto (a cooked vegetable medley somewhat like ratatouille, made with peppers, onions, and zucchini), and anchovies like miniature lasagnas. The dish is a great showcase for anchovies, which accent the savory pisto.

SERVES 8

8 baguette slices, sliced on the bias ¼ inch (5 mm) thick

8 to 16 oil-packed boneless anchovies, rinsed

2 tablespoons sherry vinegar

10 tablespoons extra virgin olive oil, divided use

1½ cups small-dice yellow onion

1⅓ cups small-dice green bell peppers

1¼ cups small-dice red peppers

1½ cups small-dice zucchini

1½ cups finely chopped vine-ripened tomatoes (skin and seeds removed)

½ teaspoon salt, or as needed

½ teaspoon freshly ground black pepper, or as needed

2 teaspoons aged balsamic vinegar

1. Preheat the oven to 325°F (165°C). Toast the baguette slices on an ungreased baking sheet for 8 to 10 minutes, flipping halfway through, until crisp and dry on the surface but still a bit chewy and soft on the inside.

2. Toss the anchovy fillets with the sherry vinegar and 2 tablespoons of olive oil. Refrigerate for 6 to 8 hours.

3. Heat the remaining olive oil in a large, heavy skillet over medium heat and add the onions and peppers. Cook, stirring from time to time, until tender, about 10 minutes. Add the zucchini and tomatoes, season with the salt and pepper, and cook for another 15 minutes, or until the mixture is very tender and fragrant. Taste and adjust seasoning with salt as needed. Remove from the heat.

4. Dry the anchovies. Top each piece of toast with 2 tablespoons of the vegetable mixture (pisto). Lay 1 to 2 anchovy fillets, depending on size, on top of the pisto. Dress with ¼ teaspoon of balsamic vinegar and serve.

Adapted from a recipe by PATXI BERGARA

ANCHOVY AND PEPPER
BOCADILLOS

THIS TAPA IS EASY to put together with ingredients you can keep on hand. If you can't get piquillo peppers, substitute sweet red bell peppers. If you can find lipstick peppers at your farmers' market, they also make a perfect stand-in for the piquillos.

SERVES 8

16 small oil-packed anchovy fillets, rinsed

16 large salt-packed anchovy fillets, rinsed

¼ cup sherry vinegar

6 tablespoons extra virgin olive oil

4 roasted piquillo peppers, seeded and quartered lengthwise

8 garlic cloves, minced

1½ teaspoons salt, divided use

1 large green bell pepper, preferably a thin-fleshed, thin-skinned variety, seeded and cut into wide lengthwise strips

16 baguette slices, lightly toasted

32 potato chips

6 tablespoons Lemon Parsley Vinaigrette (page 231)

1. Place the oil-packed anchovies in one small bowl and the salt-packed anchovies in another small bowl. Add 2 tablespoons of sherry vinegar to each bowl, toss with the anchovies, cover with plastic, and refrigerate overnight.

2. Heat 3 tablespoons of the olive oil in a large heavy sauté pan over medium-high heat. Add the piquillo peppers and sauté, stirring often, until tender, about 2 minutes. Push the piquillo peppers to the outer edge of the skillet, add the garlic and continue to cook for another minute, until the garlic is fragrant and just beginning to color. Stir in ½ teaspoon of salt, remove from the heat, and transfer to a bowl.

3. Heat the remaining 3 tablespoons of olive oil in the skillet over medium-high heat. Add the green pepper and sauté, stirring often, until tender, 10 to 15 minutes. Add 1 teaspoon of salt or to taste and remove from the heat.

4. Top each baguette slice with one strip red and one strip green pepper. Drain and rinse the anchovies, then lay one fillet of the oil-packed anchovy and one fillet of the salt-packed anchovy over the peppers. Decorate each tapa with two potato chips, drizzle with about a teaspoon of the vinaigrette, and serve.

Adapted from a recipe by PATXI BERGARA

CHORIZO BOCADILLOS

HERE'S A GREAT SPANISH TWIST on hot dogs with relishes. You can get 2- to 3-inch (5 to 8 cm) mini chorizo sausages from LaTienda.com, and at some specialty grocery stores and Spanish markets. You can also serve larger sausages as a main dish.

SERVES 8

For the jalapeño relish

2 tablespoons extra virgin olive oil

⅓ cup medium-dice fire-roasted Anaheim peppers

⅓ cup small-dice red jalapeños

4 teaspoons finely diced onions

1¼ teaspoons chopped garlic

2 baby dill pickles, chopped

4 teaspoons sugar

¼ teaspoon salt, or as needed

Freshly ground black pepper, as needed

For the roasted onion marmalade

¼ cup extra virgin olive oil

1⅓ cups thinly sliced grilled onions

3 tablespoons tomato sauce

2 tablespoons sugar

Salt, as needed

Freshly ground black pepper, as needed

For the red bell pepper ketchup

¼ cup extra virgin olive oil

1⅓ cups small-dice red bell peppers

1 tablespoon chopped garlic

3 tablespoons sugar

3 tablespoons sherry vinegar

3 tablespoons tomato sauce

3 tablespoons red bell pepper purée

Salt, as needed

Freshly ground black pepper, as needed

For the bocadillos

16 mini Spanish chorizo sausages (2 to 3 inches (5 to 8 cm) long and dry-cured if available)

16 small sausage buns

1. Make the jalapeño relish. Heat the olive oil in a large heavy sauté pan over medium-high heat and sauté the peppers, onions, garlic, and pickles, stirring often, until soft, about 10 minutes. Add the sugar, salt, and a small pinch of pepper and sauté for another 5 minutes. Remove from the heat, transfer to a bowl, and allow to cool to room temperature. Clean and dry the pan.

2. Make the roasted onion marmalade. Heat the olive oil in the pan over medium heat and add the onions. Sauté for 15 minutes, stirring frequently, until golden brown and soft. Add the tomato sauce and sugar and cook, stirring often, until reduced to marmalade consistency, about 20 minutes. Season to taste with a small pinch each of salt and pepper. Transfer to a bowl and allow to cool. Clean and dry the pan.

3. Make the red bell pepper ketchup. Heat the olive oil in the pan over medium heat and add the peppers and garlic. Sauté, stirring often, until soft, about 10 minutes. Add the sugar and vinegar and continue to cook for 15 minutes, or until the vinegar has reduced and the mixture is thick. Add the tomato sauce and the bell pepper purée and cook, stirring often, for another 10 minutes. Season to taste with a small pinch each of salt and pepper. Remove from the heat and purée in a blender until very smooth, about 1 minute.

4. Grill the sausages over medium-high heat until cooked through, turning several times to sear the outside evenly, about 3 minutes. Place each sausage on a bun or serve on a platter. Set up the garnishes for guests to help themselves.

Adapted from a recipe by ROBERT PETZOLD

WINE AND SHERRY

WITH THE SAME INTENSITY that modernity has arrived on the gastronomic scene in Spain, so it has arrived in the Spanish *bodega*, or winery. Beginning in the 1980s and picking up steam in the 1990s, winemaking techniques as well as grape cultivation began to be updated. "Flying winemakers," young, freshly educated itinerant oenologists, arrived in droves, money came from the European Union, and private estates took over many of the regional cooperatives.

Different "improver" grape varieties were planted to add flavor and finesse to the established Spanish vines, and old varieties were revived. Irrigation and mechanization were introduced in some areas. As a result, Spanish wines today are making their mark on the international market. Spanish wine, like Spanish food, is creating a buzz.

SOME WELL-KNOWN WINES AND SHERRIES

Rioja: Wines from this region were the first to be recognized with the *Denominación de Origen Calificada* (DOCa), the highest legal designation for a wine in Spain. Rioja wines are typically made with about 80 percent Tempranillo blended with Garnacha Tinta (Grenache), Mazuelo, and Graciano. In recent years some bodegas have been producing single-vineyard wines with Tempranillo only, which have been well received in the international marketplace.

There are four basic Rioja designations—Guarantee of Origin, Crianza, Reserva, and Gran Reserva. Guarantee of Origin wines are young wines that have little or no oak, and are consumed as table wines. Crianza, aged for 24 months, at least 12 months of which are in oak barrels, is typically served in tapas bars and as a house wine in restaurants. Reserva is aged for 36 months, with at least 12 months in the barrel. Gran Reserva requires 24 months aging in the barrel and another 36 months minimum aging in the bottle before release. These are only made in exceptional years.

Penedès: The largest and most important *Denominación de Origen* (DO) in Catalonia, Penedès produces a range of wines, including most of the Cava made in Spain, which now has its own DO. The wines of Penedès began to gain prestige during the 1970s, when the winemaking family of Miguel Torres Carbo and his son Miguel A. Torres modernized their winemaking and introduced different grape varieties, such as Cabernet Sauvignon, Chardonnay, Sauvignon Blanc, Merlot, and Pinot Noir, which were blended with the native varieties.

Penedès is primarily a white wine-producing region, although some fine reds are produced by the Torres family and other small growers, using mainly Cabernet Sauvignon or Tempranillo grapes. White wines, made almost exclusively with the three local grapes, Xarel-lo, Macabeo, and Parellada, are light and fruity, and go well with the Mediterranean food of the region.

Priorat: This small, isolated DO zone in Catalonia makes some of Spain's most exciting red wines. They are made from primarily Garnacha (Grenache), with some Cariñena (Carignan), and small amounts of French varieties such as Cabernet Sauvignon, Merlot, Syrah, and Pinot Noir.

Ribera del Duero: This wine zone in Castile and León, in north central Spain, has only had DO status since 1982. Its rich red wines, made almost exclusively with a local variant of the Tempranillo grape called Tinto Fino or Tinta del Pais, or with a blend of Tinto Fino and Cabernet Sauvignon, compete well both locally and internationally with Rioja reds. One of Spain's most prestigious and expensive red wines is produced here by Vega Sicilia.

Rueda: Also in Castile and León, this zone is about halfway between Madrid and León and is a major producer of white wine. The industry here was revolutionized in the 1970s, when winemakers began to see the potential of the local Verdejo grape for making quality white wine. Rueda Superior must contain at least 85 percent Verdejo. Rueda also produces a 100 percent Sauvignon Blanc varietal (Rueda Sauvignon). The wines from Rueda are light, fruity, and dry.

Rías Baixas: This is the major DO wine zone in Galicia. It produces some of Spain's finest white wines, made primarily with the white Albariño grape, which pair exquisitely with seafood.

Jerez: This DO is in Andalusia around Cadiz, on the Atlantic side of the tip of Spain and is famous for sherry. Production is centered in Jerez de la Frontera, Sanlúcar de Barrameda, and Puerto de Santa María. The Palomino Fino grape is used for most types of sherry.

There are two principal types of sherry: pale, dry *fino* (called *manzanilla* in Sanlúcar de Barrameda) and dark, full *oloroso* (also dry). The grapes grown on older vines on the best soils are used for finos; grapes grown on heavier clay soils are used for olorosos. The purer juices are also selected for finos. A second selection takes place after the first fermentation, when the sherry is fortified to between 15.5 and 22 percent with a grape spirit called aguardiente. Wines that develop a veil of yeast (flor) are classed as finos and are not fortified beyond 15.5 percent. Olorosos do not develop flor and are fortified to about 18 percent. Finos that are fortified beyond 15.5 percent and lose their flor evolve into darker, richer amontillados.

CRISPY CABRALES
AND PHYLLO SANDWICHES

THESE CRISPY PHYLLO TAPAS—filled with a creamy mixture of pungent Cabrales, cream cheese, and Manchego—are simple to make and yet dramatic in appearance. The phyllo is baked until brown and crispy, then the cheese filling is sandwiched between two phyllo triangles. You can stand the sandwich constructions on their sides to serve them.

SERVES 8

¼ cup grated cured Manchego or Manchego-style goat cheese

¼ cup crumbled Cabrales

⅓ cup cream cheese

½ cup plus 1½ tablespoons heavy cream, divided use

¼ cup sugar

1 teaspoon soy sauce

4 sheets phyllo dough

1. **Bring** the cheeses to room temperature.

2. **Combine** ½ cup of the heavy cream with the sugar and stir gently with a whisk until the sugar has dissolved. Set aside.

3. **Mash** the grated Manchego, the Cabrales, and the cream cheese together in a mixing bowl with the remaining heavy cream and the soy sauce.

4. **Preheat** the oven to 375°F (190°C). Line a baking sheet with parchment. Transfer a sheet of phyllo carefully to the parchment-lined baking sheet. Brush lightly but thoroughly with the cream mixture and place another sheet on top. Brush the top phyllo sheet with the cream mixture. Cut the phyllo into 3-inch (8 cm) triangles, using a pizza cutter. Separate the triangles slightly. Place the sheet pan in the oven and bake for 6 to 7 minutes, until light to medium brown and crisp. Remove from the oven. Repeat with the remaining phyllo.

5. **Top** 16 of the triangles with 1 to 2 tablespoons of the mashed cheeses. Then place another phyllo triangle on top of each one to form sandwiches.

Adapted from a recipe by PEDRO MORÁN

PIQUILLO- AND ANCHOVY-STUFFED
OLIVES

THERE'S NO BETTER TAPA than a good stuffed olive. But the ones you usually find in the supermarket are filled with poor-quality peppers and even poorer anchovies. One of the best appetizers for a lunch or dinner is to take a good olive and stuff it with the real thing. Simple ingredients prepared in a simple way— that's the best way to take your everyday cooking to a higher level. Buy large unpitted olives for this dish. It's more work for you, but the olives are usually better quality and have meatier flesh. Piquillo peppers come in 8-ounce (225 g) (or larger) jars. They are available at specialty markets and from online sources.

SERVES 8

16 extra-large unpitted imported green olives
8 oil-packed anchovy fillets
4 canned piquillo peppers
2 medium garlic cloves, unpeeled
6 tablespoons extra virgin olive oil
2 teaspoons grated orange zest
2 tablespoons sherry vinegar
Sea salt, as needed

1. **Pit** the olives, using an olive pitter if possible. If you must pit them manually, put your hand on top of the widest part of the flat side of a knife, and press down on the side of each olive. Apply steady pressure until the olive flattens slightly and you feel resistance from the pit. Give the olive a quarter turn and use the knife as before to gently press down, steadily increasing pressure until you meet resistance from the pit once again. At this point, the pit should be mostly freed from the flesh of the olive. Make a lengthwise slit in the olive from end to end, stopping at the pit. Gently pry any adhering olive flesh from the pit, using a paring knife, if necessary, to free the pit. Be careful not to split the olive in half.

2. **Cut** the anchovy fillets lengthwise to create sixteen long slices, removing any long or stiff bones. Cut the piquillo peppers into sixteen ½-inch- (1 cm) wide strips.

3. **Place** one anchovy slice and one pepper strip in each olive. You can be generous with the filling, allowing the anchovy and pepper to spill out of the olive.

4. **Split** open the garlic cloves by placing them on a chopping board and pressing down hard with the base of your hand or with the flat side of a knife. Discard the peels.

5. **Mix** together the garlic, olive oil, orange zest, and vinegar in a small bowl. Place the stuffed olives in a separate shallow, wide bowl, pour the dressing over them, and marinate at room temperature for 30 minutes. Remove the olives from the dressing, sprinkle with sea salt, and arrange on a plate with toothpicks for serving.

Adapted from a recipe by JOSÉ ANDRÉS

MISSION FIGS
STUFFED WITH SPANISH BLUE CHEESE

SHARP SPANISH BLUE CHEESES, such as Cabrales or Picón, contrast wonderfully with the soft, subtle, sweet flesh of fresh, ripe figs. Enjoy these stuffed figs with a glass of Oloroso sherry, another perfect partner for a fig. The cocoa nibs, pressed into the cheese, are a surprise ingredient that adds a little bitter depth and crunch to the mixture. If fresh figs are unavailable, large dried, soft Calimyrna figs can be substituted. Simply slice the figs in half and place 1 teaspoon of cheese on each fig half and ½ teaspoon of cocoa nibs on top.

SERVES 8

12 large ripe but firm fresh figs

7½-ounce (215 g) wedge of tangy Spanish blue-veined mixed milk cheese, such as Cabrales, Picón, or Valdeón

¼ cup cocoa nibs

1. Cut the stem end of each fig about ¼ inch (5 mm) from the top using kitchen scissors. Press the tip of a spoon into the opening to make a ½-inch- (1 cm) deep indentation for the cheese in the soft center of the fig.

2. Trim the outer rind off the wedge of cheese. Gently crumble with a fork in a medium bowl until the largest pieces are the size of a small marble. Do not overmix.

3. Press a level teaspoon of cheese into the center of each fig.

4. Press ¼ to ½ teaspoon of cocoa nibs into the cheese. Serve.

Adapted from a recipe by MARIE SIMMONS

SPANISH CHEESE

SPAIN PRODUCES SOME OF THE WORLD'S FINEST CHEESES, and many of them are now available in the United States. Yet it wasn't too long ago that regional, artisanal cheese production was illegal in Spain. During the Franco years, when the government was highly centralized and regionalism was repressed, only 10,000 liters of milk per day were authorized to be made into cheese. In 1968 a report by the Ministry of Agriculture described forty-two cheeses; thirty of them were illegal.

Government decrees notwithstanding, go to the central market in Barcelona, Valencia, Madrid, or Malaga, and the enticing displays of cheeses from all over the country will tell you that the Spanish have always been cheese makers and cheese eaters.

The first Cheeses of Spain poster was published in 1986. On it were forty-eight cheeses, nearly half of them still illegal under Spanish law. That same year the first Spanish artisanal cheese fair was held, drawing over 100,000 visitors. Regional cheeses began to be promoted in stores, markets, and in cooking magazines.

By the 1990s the laws had caught up with the times, and artisanal cheese makers were recognized by the government, which began to distinguish and protect regional cheeses with the Denomination of Origin (DO) status, and, in 1992, published the first official catalog of Spanish cheeses. Spain was designated The Country of 100 Cheeses in 1996; a book entitled *100 Cheeses* followed in 1998, and then a poster entitled *Spain, the Land of 100 Cheeses*.

Today cheese is among the many traditional Spanish ingredients that inspire chefs. You can find Spanish cheeses at good cheese stores and from online sources (see page 263).

SOME FAVORITE SPANISH CHEESES

Cabra al Vino, Murcia al Vino: These are two different wine-bathed goat's milk cheeses from the Murcia region. The rind is bathed in red wine for up to three days during ripening, which tints it a deep purplish red. Inside, the cheese is white, mild, and smooth, with a distinctly floral bouquet and a bold flavor.

Cabrales: One of Spain's best known cheeses, from the mountainous northern Asturias region, this is a blue cheese made from a mix of cow, goat, and sheep's milk. It matures in caves for at least three months and develops its own natural blue veins. It's a sharp, rich cheese that can be used as you would use any other blue cheese.

Garrotxa: This is a semisoft goat's milk cheese from Catalonia. Production was begun in the early 1970s by a group of Catalan professionals who wanted to revive cheese making in the region.

Ibérico: A Manchego-style cheese with the same sort of cross-hatched pattern on its rind, Ibérico is made from pasteurized cow, goat, and sheep's milk. It is firm, oily, and aromatic.

Idiazabal: This is a handmade Basque cheese made in the Spanish Pyrenees from unpasteurized sheep's milk. One of the country's most popular cheeses, it has a smoky flavor, a legacy of the Basque tradition of aging their cheeses in chimneys. Today the rich, buttery cheese is lightly smoked.

Mahon: Spain's second most popular cheese after Manchego, this 100 percent cow's milk cheese is produced exclusively in the Balearic island of Menorca. It is a complex cheese, with a buttery/nutty/tangy flavor. In Spain it's served sliced, drizzled with olive oil, and sprinkled with black pepper and herbs.

Majorero: This cheese, made from unpasteurized goat's milk, was awarded Best Hard DO Cheese at the 2005 World Cheese Awards. It's made on the island of Feurteventura in the Canary Islands, and pressed in palm fronds, which leave an attractive imprint on its ocher-colored rind.

Manchego: Spain's best known cheese, Manchego is made in the central region of La Mancha from 100 percent sheep's milk. It can be aged from two months to more than a year. Manchego Reserve is a sharper, nuttier, more brittle cheese that is aged for over 12 months.

Murcia: This satiny goat's cheese from Murcia has a distinctive lemony-peppery flavor.

Roncal: One of Spain's most highly esteemed cheeses, this is produced in the Roncal Valley, in the Navarra region of the Spanish Pyrenees. Made from unpasteurized sheep's milk, it has a moist, smooth texture similar to Manchego except a little drier, and with a rustic, nutty flavor. It's often served with *membrillo* (quince paste).

Tetilla: From Galicia comes this famous semisoft cow's cheese, whose name means "nipple." The cheese is shaped like a woman's breast. It has a waxy yellow rind, an elastic, creamy interior, and a mild, buttery flavor. It's an excellent melting cheese.

Torta del Casar: This luxurious, semisoft sheep's cheese is from Extremadura. It is disk-shaped with a thin, soft rind. As it ripens, the inside remains semi-liquid, causing the cheese to sink in the middle and giving it its cakelike shape (hence the name). Traditionally, it is warmed slightly in the oven before serving, then the top rind is cut off and the runny insides are eaten with a spoon. The flavor is herbal and slightly bitter, due to the use of wild thistle to coagulate the milk.

MANCHEGO CROQUETTES
WITH QUINCE SAUCE

FOR THE BEST FLAVOR, use true Manchego made from ewes' milk, and preferably cured, for these savory croquettes. Cured Manchego is drier than semi-cured and easier to grate. Croquettes can be fried up to 4 hours in advance and kept at room temperature. Place them on a baking sheet and reheat them in a preheated 400°F (200°C) oven until hot, about 10 minutes. Fried croquettes can be frozen for up to 1 month. Remove them from the freezer 15 minutes before heating. Simply place them on a baking sheet and bake in a preheated 375°F (190°C) oven for 15 minutes.

SERVES 8

1 pound 4 ounces (575 g) russet potatoes, scrubbed
¾ teaspoon salt, or as needed
2 teaspoons extra virgin olive oil
1⅔ cups grated Manchego (loosely packed)
2 teaspoons minced green onions
3 tablespoons finely chopped flat-leaf parsley
Pinch thyme
Pinch hot pimentón or cayenne
3 large eggs, divided use
¾ teaspoon red wine vinegar
⅔ cup dry breadcrumbs
1 quart (1 liter) olive oil, for frying
⅔ cup Quince Sauce (page 220)

1. **Place** the unpeeled potatoes in a medium saucepan and cover with 8 cups of water. Add ¼ teaspoon of salt and bring to a gentle boil over medium-high heat. Cover partially and cook until tender, about 30 minutes. Remove the pot from the heat. Drain the potatoes, return to the pot, cover tightly, and let sit for 5 minutes.

2. **Hold** the potatoes with a dishtowel so you don't burn your hands, and cut in half, using a spoon to scrape out the flesh into a small bowl. Discard the skins. Add the olive oil and mash the potatoes with a fork or potato masher until smooth, 1 to 2 minutes.

3. **Stir** the cheese into the potatoes. Add the green onions, parsley, ½ teaspoon of salt, thyme, and hot pimentón or cayenne.

4. **Separate** two of the eggs. Place the whites in a medium clean, dry bowl. Stir the yolks into the potato mixture.

5. **Beat** the egg whites to stiff peaks at medium-high speed, about 2 minutes. Beat in the vinegar until just combined. Fold half of the beaten whites into the potato mixture until thoroughly combined, then fold in the remaining whites.

6. **Beat** the remaining egg in a shallow bowl. Spread the breadcrumbs on a 10- by 13-inch (25 by 33 cm) baking sheet or baking dish.

7. **Scoop** tablespoonfuls of the potato mixture onto a second baking sheet, then use your hands to shape the portions into balls or ovals. Drop the croquettes one at a time into the beaten egg and roll them to coat all sides. Lift them out with the spoon and a fork, allowing the excess egg to drain off. Transfer the drained croquettes to the breadcrumbs. When you've dipped 6 of these, roll in the breadcrumbs to coat all sides, then place on a parchment-covered 11- by 16-inch (28 by 40 cm) baking sheet. Repeat this process with the remaining potato mixture until all the croquettes are dipped and breaded.

8. **Heat** the oil in an 8-inch (20 cm) wide deep skillet to 360°F (180°C). Fry the croquettes in batches of six, turning them once, until golden brown, about 1½ to 2 minutes. Remove from the oil with a slotted spoon and transfer to a 10- by 13-inch (25 by 33 cm) baking sheet lined with paper towels. Hold the finished croquettes in a warm oven until ready to serve (up to 15 minutes). Serve with the quince sauce.

Adapted from a recipe by JANET MENDEL

CASTELLANO
WITH QUINCE PASTE

Quince paste (*membrillo*) and cheese, particularly Castellano and Manchego, are a classic Spanish combination. Thin slices of the sweet/acidic *membrillo* contrast beautifully with the firm, dense but moist cheese. These little "sandwiches" make the perfect accompaniment to a glass of wine.

SERVES 8

8-ounce (225 g) wedge semi-mature Castellano or Manchego

8 ounces (225 g) quince paste

1 cup olive oil

6 slices sandwich bread

3 tablespoons pine nuts or macadamia nuts, toasted and finely chopped

1. **Cut** the cheese crosswise into twenty-four ⅛-inch- (3 mm) thick slices. Clean the knife and dip in warm water, then cut the quince paste into 12 slightly thicker slices, nearly ¼ inch (5 mm) thick.

2. **Heat** the oil in a large, heavy skillet over medium-high heat until it shimmers slightly and fry 3 slices of the bread on both sides until golden, about 1 minute per side. Remove from the oil and drain on paper towels briefly. Repeat with the remaining 3 slices of bread.

3. **Place** 2 slices of cheese in a single layer and in alternating directions on each piece of bread. Top with a single layer of the sliced quince paste (this may require more than one slice, depending on the dimensions and shape of the quince paste before you slice it). Top the quince paste with another 2 slices of cheese as before. Cut each topped bread slice into quarters to create 4 triangles, and arrange all of the triangles on a platter or 8 small plates. Sprinkle each triangle with a heaping ¼ teaspoon of finely chopped nuts before serving.

Adapted from a recipe by Jesús Ramiro

PADRÓN PEPPERS
PAN-FRIED WITH SERRANO HAM

PADRÓN PEPPERS are a famous, rare green pepper from the region around Santiago de Compostela. Villagers from the village of Padrón harvest only the small young peppers, because the more mature peppers are quite spicy, but a few spicy peppers always make it into the mix. At tapas bars they are sautéed in olive oil and sprinkled with sea salt, and you never know when you'll bite into a hot one. They can also be served as an accompaniment to grilled meat, fish, or poultry. Chef/author Maricel Presilla adds Serrano ham to the mix and serves this at her Cucharamama Restaurant in Hoboken, New Jersey.

SERVES 8

15 to 20 Padrón peppers, depending on the size
¼ cup extra virgin olive oil
¼ pound Serrano ham, cut into ½-inch (1 cm) dice
¼ teaspoon coarse sea salt, or as needed

1. Place the peppers in a medium colander and rinse under cold running water. Dry thoroughly with paper towels.

2. Heat the oil in a large, heavy sauté pan over high heat until it is sizzling. Add the ham and sauté for 40 seconds, or until the surface has darkened, the fat has turned golden brown and begun to crisp, and the meat smells fragrant. Add the peppers and cook, stirring, until they are blistered and softened but have not turned brown, 5 to 8 minutes.

3. Transfer to an attractive serving platter, sprinkle with sea salt, and serve immediately.

Adapted from a recipe by MARICEL E. PRESILLA

CHORIZO-STUFFED MUSHROOMS

To make a savory filling for stuffed mushrooms, sausage and ham are added to the chopped stems, along with onions and garlic. The mushrooms are then topped with breadcrumbs or a combination of grated cheese and crumbs. For even cooking, quickly sauté the mushroom caps in olive oil or butter to brown and soften them a bit before stuffing. These can be assembled ahead of time, then baked just before serving.

SERVES 8

24 large white button or cremini mushrooms, wiped clean with a damp towel or brush

6 tablespoons plus 1 teaspoon extra virgin olive oil, divided use

6 tablespoons (¾ stick) butter, plus extra melted butter for basting as needed

¾ cup finely chopped onions

2 tablespoons minced garlic

½ cup minced Serrano ham

½ cup dry-cured chopped chorizo sausage

¼ cup chopped parsley, thyme, marjoram, or a combination of these

½ cup toasted breadcrumbs

½ teaspoon freshly ground black pepper, or as needed

2 tablespoons grated Manchego or Parmesan (optional)

1. Remove the stems from the mushrooms and chop them finely. Reserve the caps and 1 to 1⅓ cups of the chopped stems separately.

2. Heat 6 tablespoons of the olive oil in a large sauté pan over medium-high heat and brown the mushroom caps, about 8 minutes, turning halfway through. Set aside.

3. Melt the butter in a small sauté pan over medium heat and cook the onions until soft, about 5 minutes. Add the garlic and the mushroom stems and cook until the stems have wilted, about 3 minutes. Add the ham and chorizo and cook for 2 to 3 minutes, or until lightly browned. Stir in the herbs and breadcrumbs. Season to taste with ⅛ teaspoon of pepper. Remember that the ham will give off more salt as it heats.

4. Preheat the oven to 400°F (200°C). Oil or butter a 13- by 9- by 2-inch (33 by 23 by 5 cm) baking dish with about 1 teaspoon of oil. Spoon a scant tablespoon of the mixture into each of the mushroom caps. Place in the baking dish and bake in the preheated oven for 15 minutes, or until golden brown, basting with a little melted butter, if desired. Sprinkle each cap with ¼ teaspoon of grated cheese, if using. Serve hot or warm.

Adapted from a recipe by Joyce Goldstein

SERRANO HAM CONES
WITH MIGAS AND QUAIL EGGS

THESE ATTRACTIVE CONES are made with crisp ham and filled with breadcrumbs and more diced ham. You can find cream horn cones to shape the ham in pastry supply stores. Arrange the cones artfully on a platter, or look for a tray with small holes to set the cones in for serving. Ibérico ham is what was called for in the original recipe and should be used if available.

SERVES 8

Eight 1/16-inch- (2 mm) thick slices Serrano ham (about 5½ ounces or 150 g)

3 tablespoons extra virgin olive oil

2⅓ cups crumbled country-style bread, crusts removed

¼ cup diced Serrano ham (about 1½ ounces or 40 g)

1 teaspoon minced garlic

8 quail eggs

1. Preheat the oven to 350°F (175°C). Wrap the ham slices around 4½-inch- (12 cm) long by 1½-inch- (4 cm) wide cream horn or cone molds, overlapping the edges by about ½ inch (1 cm) and leaving some of the ham extending about 1 inch (2.5 cm) beyond the length of the mold. Place the cones seam side down on a cooling rack and bake until the ham is crisp, about 15 minutes. Pull the cooling racks out of the oven, cool to room temperature, then remove the molds. Handle the crisp edges carefully to avoid breaking them.

2. Heat the olive oil in a heavy sauté pan over medium-high heat and add the breadcrumbs and diced ham. Cook, stirring continuously, for 2 minutes, then add the garlic. Continue to stir until the breadcrumbs begin to crisp and the garlic begins to brown, about 3 minutes. Remove from the heat.

3. Fill the cones with 1 to 2 tablespoons of the breadcrumb mixture and transfer to a serving platter. When all of the cones are filled, spoon 1 tablespoon of the remaining filling on the platter at the mouth of each cone. Hold in a warm oven while preparing the eggs (but for no longer than 5 to 10 minutes).

4. Bring a small saucepan of water to a simmer over medium-high heat and add the quail eggs. Simmer for 1 minute, remove from the heat, and rinse briefly under cold water until the eggs are no longer hot but still warm. Break open each egg over a cone, letting the yolk run out over the filling. Serve warm.

Adapted from a recipe by JOAQUÍN FELÍPE

TORTILLA ESPAÑOLA

SPANISH OMELET, the classic potato and onion frittata, is one of Spain's best known dishes. It can be cut into squares and served as a tapa, or cut into wedges for a first course or light meal. The omelet turner is a useful piece of equipment when preparing this. It resembles a pan lid with a knob on top. You hold onto this when you flip the omelet from the pan and slide it back into the pan to cook the second side.

SERVES 8

9 Yukon gold potatoes, peeled and sliced ⅛ inch thick (about 2 pounds or 900 g)

1¾ teaspoons salt, divided use

½ cup plus 2 tablespoons extra virgin olive oil, divided use

1 cup chopped yellow onions

⅓ cup chopped red bell peppers

⅓ cup chopped green bell peppers

½ cup diced chorizo sausage

1 cup diced Serrano ham

10 large eggs

1. **Toss** together the sliced potatoes and 1 teaspoon of salt in a medium bowl. Heat ½ cup of the olive oil in a large, heavy nonstick or well-seasoned cast-iron skillet over medium heat and add the potatoes. Cook, stirring occasionally, until the potatoes start to soften but not brown, about 5 minutes. Add the onions, peppers, sausage, and ham. Continue to cook, stirring often, until the potatoes are tender, the chorizo is cooked through, and the ingredients are well blended, another 5 to 10 minutes. Transfer the potato and onion mixture to a colander placed over a large bowl and drain. Clean the pan.

2. **Beat** the eggs in a large bowl until smooth, then stir in the potato mixture. Season with ¾ teaspoon of salt.

3. **Return** the pan to medium heat and add 2 tablespoons of olive oil. When the oil is very hot, add the egg mixture to the pan. Tilt the pan so that the eggs run over the bottom of the pan in an even layer, then turn the heat to low. Cook, shaking the pan from time to time, until the omelet has set, about 8 minutes.

4. **Cover** the pan with an omelet turner or flat-bottom pot lid, and flip the omelet onto the omelet turner or lid. Then carefully slide the inverted omelet back into the pan. Return to the heat and cook on the other side until lightly browned, about 5 minutes. Slide the omelet out onto a plate. Allow to cool to room temperature, cut into 8 wedges, and serve.

Adapted from a recipe by CHEFA GONZÁLEZ-DOPESO

TORTILLA ESPAÑOLA
WITH LAMB SHANKS

THIS IS A HEARTY TWIST on the traditional potato and onion Tortilla Española (page 43). First you braise lamb shanks in red wine, then you shred the savory meat into the omelet. The reduced broth from the lamb shanks serves as a delicious sauce for the omelet, which can be enjoyed as a tapa, cut into small squares, or as a first course, cut into wedges.

SERVES 8 AS A FIRST COURSE, OR 16 AS A TAPA

For the lamb shanks

2 lamb shanks (about 2 pounds 3 ounces or 1 kg)

2 teaspoons salt

1 teaspoon freshly ground black pepper

2 tablespoons extra virgin olive oil

2 cups diced yellow onions

1 cup diced carrots

⅔ cup diced celery

¼ cup minced garlic

4 cups Spanish red wine, preferably Tempranillo

2 teaspoons cayenne

4 teaspoons smoked paprika

3 thyme sprigs

2 cups water, or enough to cover the meat

For the tortilla

1½ cups extra virgin olive oil, or as needed

5 medium Yukon gold potatoes, peeled and sliced ⅛ inch (3 mm) thick (about 1 pound 8 ounces or 680 g)

2 cups minced yellow onions

8 eggs

1 teaspoon salt

¼ teaspoon freshly ground black pepper

1. Preheat the oven to 350°F (175°C). Season the lamb shanks with the salt and pepper. Heat the olive oil in a large heavy soup pot or Dutch oven over high heat. Add the lamb shanks and brown well on all sides, 5 to 7 minutes. Remove from the heat and transfer to a bowl. Return the pan to medium-high heat and add the onions, carrots, celery, and garlic. Cook, stirring often, until the vegetables caramelize, about 10 minutes. Add the wine to the hot pan and deglaze, stirring and scraping the bottom of the pan with a wooden spoon.

2. Return the lamb shanks to the pot, add the cayenne, paprika, thyme sprigs, and enough water to just cover the meat and bring to a simmer. Cover and place in the oven for 2 hours, or until the lamb is fork tender and falling away from the bone. Remove from the oven and allow the meat to cool in the liquid for 1 hour, or until cool enough to handle.

3. Remove the lamb shanks from the liquid and shred the meat, discarding all of the fat and sinew. Set the shredded meat aside. Strain the liquid. Use a gravy separator to remove the fat, or chill the broth and skim the fat off the surface. Return the broth to the pot, bring to a boil over high heat, and reduce by half, about 25 minutes. Set aside to use as a sauce. Keep the oven at 350°F (175°C).

4. Make the tortilla. Heat all but 2 tablespoons of the olive oil in a large heavy skillet over medium heat. Add the potatoes and onions and cook, stirring frequently, until they are tender, about 10 minutes. Remove the potatoes and onions from the oil.

5. Beat the eggs in a large bowl and season with salt and pepper. Add the potato-onion mixture and stir together. Heat the remaining 2 tablespoons of olive oil in a large nonstick skillet over medium-high heat. When the oil is hot, add half the egg and potato mixture. Shake the pan, lifting the edges of the omelet with a spatula and tilting the pan so that egg runs underneath to set the omelet. Layer the shredded lamb over the egg mixture, then top with the remaining egg and potato mixture. Cook, shaking the pan gently, for 4 minutes, or until the bottom is browned. Place in the oven. Bake for 30 minutes, or until set. Slide the omelet onto a plate and flip back into the pan to brown the top for 3 minutes (or brown under the broiler). Remove from the heat and allow to cool for 30 minutes. Cut into 1½-inch (4 cm) squares, or into 8 wedges, and serve with ¼ cup of the sauce.

Adapted from a recipe by KEVIN MARQUET

SPICY FRIED POTATOES

THESE CLASSIC SPICY FRIED POTATOES with allioli, or Spanish garlic mayonnaise, make a delicious, rich hot tapa. They can also be served as a side dish with grilled meat or fish.

SERVES 8

For the potatoes
7 Yukon gold or Russet potatoes, peeled and cut into 1-inch (2.5 cm) cubes

1 quart (1 liter) water

¼ teaspoon saffron threads

1 teaspoon salt

For the pimentón oil
¼ cup extra virgin olive oil

2 teaspoons Spanish sweet paprika

1 teaspoon cayenne

For the allioli
2 medium garlic cloves

1½ teaspoons salt, divided use

1 large egg

1½ cups extra virgin olive oil

½ teaspoon lemon juice

1 teaspoon saffron water from the potatoes

¼ teaspoon freshly ground black pepper

4 cups extra virgin olive oil, for frying, or enough to fill the pan 3 inches (8 cm) deep

1. Place the potatoes and water in a medium saucepan and bring to a boil over high heat. Add the saffron and salt, reduce the heat to medium, cover partially, and boil gently until the potatoes are barely tender, about 10 minutes. Remove 1 teaspoon of the cooking water to add to the allioli, and drain the potatoes. Return to the pot, cover tightly, and allow the potatoes to steam for 5 minutes, until dry. Spread the potatoes out on a baking sheet to cool before frying.

2. Make the pimentón oil. Heat the olive oil in a small frying pan over low heat and add the paprika and cayenne. Just when the paprika looks like it is about to sizzle, after 20 to 30 seconds, remove it from the heat and allow the oil to infuse while you make the allioli, or about 10 minutes.

3. Make the allioli. Mash the garlic and ½ teaspoon of salt together in a medium mortar and pestle or on a cutting board. Combine the garlic with the egg in a food processor fitted with the steel blade and turn on the machine. Slowly drizzle in the oil to make a thick mayonnaise, about 2 minutes. Add the lemon juice and 1 teaspoon of saffron water from the potatoes and blend well. Taste and adjust the seasoning with the salt and pepper.

4. Heat 3 inches (8 cm) of the olive oil in a large, wide, heavy skillet over high heat to 325°F (160°C). Add the potatoes and fry until golden, 10 to 15 minutes. Remove from the heat with a slotted spoon or a spider and drain on paper towels. Serve ⅓ cup of the potatoes with a drizzling of 1½ teaspoons of the pimentón oil and 3 tablespoons of the allioli.

Adapted from a recipe by CHEFA GONZÁLEZ-DOPESO

ZARANGOLLO RAVIOLI
WITH HERRING ROE

THE RAVIOLI IS MADE BY STUFFING thinly sliced strips of zucchini with gently cooked onions. This dish can also be dressed with Ñora-Infused Oil (page 232). The sweet red pepper purée may also be lightened by adding olive oil. If you can't find wine cheese from Murcia, substitute drunken goat cheese. The wine-washed rind of the drunken goat cheese is reminiscent of the wine cheese from Murcia.

SERVES 8

4 zucchini

2¾ teaspoons salt, divided use

2¾ cups very finely diced spring onions

5 tablespoons extra virgin olive oil, divided use

½ teaspoon freshly ground black pepper, divided use

2 sweet red peppers, roasted and seeded

¼ cup grated Murcian wine cheese or drunken goat cheese

8 quail eggs

3 tablespoons herring roe

1 tablespoon sea salt crystals

1 tablespoon crushed white peppercorns

1 tablespoon crushed pink peppercorns

1 tablespoon chives

1. **Wash** the zucchini, trim the ends, and slice lengthwise into ¹⁄₈-inch (3 mm) thick slices using a mandoline or a sharp knife. Bring 3 quarts (3 liters) of water and 2 teaspoons of salt to a rolling boil in a large pot over medium-high heat. Blanch the zucchini strips for 3 minutes, or until soft and pliable. Transfer carefully to a bowl of ice water to stop the cooking. Drain well and pat dry with paper towels.

2. **Cook** the onions in a large sauté pan with ¼ cup of olive oil over medium heat until soft, about 10 minutes. Raise the heat to medium-high and sauté the onions, stirring frequently, until lightly caramelized, 5 to 7 minutes. Season with ½ teaspoon of salt and a pinch of pepper and reserve until needed.

3. **Purée** the red peppers in a blender on high speed until smooth, about 1 minute. Season with a pinch each of salt and pepper.

4. **Cross** two pieces of zucchini over each other to make an X. Place 1 tablespoon of the onions where the two pieces cross and fold each of the four ends of the zucchini over the onions to create the ravioli. Flip the ravioli over so that the seam is on the bottom. Repeat with the remaining zucchini and onions and transfer carefully to a lightly oiled baking sheet.

5. **Top** each ravioli with 1 teaspoon each of cheese and bake in a 350°F (175°C) oven for 10 minutes, or until heated through. Meanwhile prepare the eggs.

6. **Fry** the quail eggs in a large nonstick pan with 1 tablespoon of olive oil over medium heat for 3 minutes, or until the whites are completely white and the yolk is still bright orange. Season with a pinch each of salt and pepper.

7. **Top** each ravioli with a quail egg and 1 teaspoon of the roe. Decorate each plate with 2 tablespoons of the sweet red pepper purée and a small pinch each of the salt, peppercorns, and chives. Place a ravioli on each plate and serve.

Adapted from a recipe by JUAN ANTONIO PELLICER

RED TUNA BITES

THIS IS A FUSION of Japanese and modern Spanish culinary styles and ingredients. The sashimi-cut tuna is layered with paper-thin slices of desalted salt cod and anchovies and served sashimi style, with a mayonnaise-based sauce. The little bites are served on spoons. Note that the salt cod needs to be desalted beforehand, which takes a minimum of 36 hours.

SERVES 8

4 ounces (115 g) salt cod, sliced paper-thin

1 tablespoon soy sauce

4 oil-packed anchovy fillets, rinsed and very thinly sliced

1 pound 2 ounces (510 g) tuna loin, cut into sashimi-style slices about ³⁄₁₆ inch (5 mm) thick

2 tablespoons mayonnaise

2 tablespoons toasted or fried almonds

1 tablespoon extra virgin olive oil

Water, as needed

1 ounce (30 g) cooked Spanish chorizo sausage, crumbled

1. Desalt the salt cod by placing it in a bowl with enough fresh cold water to cover it. Soak, refrigerated, for 36 to 48 hours, changing the water at least four times. Drain well.

2. Pour the soy sauce into a widemouth bowl. Spread the cod out on a cutting board and layer the anchovies evenly across the top of the cod. Top with a layer of tuna slices, overlapping the slices if necessary, to cover the cod evenly. Cut into 1¼- by 1¼-inch (3 by 3 cm) bite-sized pieces, dip in soy sauce, and place on spoons.

3. Blend together the mayonnaise, almonds, oil, and enough water to make a smooth sauce. Strain and spoon a scant teaspoon over each of the tuna bites. Sprinkle ½ teaspoon of the chorizo on each piece and serve.

Adapted from a recipe by JOAQUÍN FELÍPE

RIAS ALTAS BITES

THIS IS A RIFF on a classic Spanish *croqueta*, fried croquettes made with stiff breaded béchamel. These crispy squares are made with a thick béchamel into which shrimp are stirred. The mixture is cooled until stiff enough to cut into squares, then coated with breadcrumbs and fried in olive oil.

SERVES 8

¼ cup (½ stick) butter

½ cup all-purpose flour

2 cups whole milk

¾ cup peeled, deveined, and minced shrimp (21 to 25 count)

½ teaspoon salt

¼ teaspoon freshly ground white pepper

Pinch freshly grated nutmeg

2 large eggs, beaten

½ cup olive oil, for frying

2 tablespoons minced green onions

1. Line a 2-quart (2 liter) baking dish with plastic, leaving a 1-inch (2.5 cm) overhang. Melt the butter in a small, heavy saucepan over medium heat and add the flour. Cook, stirring constantly for 3 minutes, until the roux is just beginning to color, then slowly whisk in the milk. Stir with a wooden spoon, scraping the bottom and sides of the pan to prevent sticking, until the mixture thickens, about 4 minutes. Turn the heat to low and simmer, stirring often, for 15 minutes, or until the mixture holds a swirl.

2. Stir the shrimp into the sauce. Season to taste with the salt, pepper, and nutmeg. Simmer for 1 minute, or until the shrimp turns pink. Remove from the heat and scrape into the plastic-lined baking dish, spread evenly, and smooth the top over. Cover and chill until the mixture is cool and stiff, about 3 hours.

3. Dampen your knife with warm water and cut the chilled sauce mixture into 1-inch (2.5 cm) squares. Beat the eggs in a medium shallow bowl and place the breadcrumbs in another slightly larger shallow bowl. Dip the squares in the egg, then into the breadcrumbs.

4. Heat the oil in a 10-inch (25 cm) skillet over medium-high heat to 350°F (175°C). Fry the squares until golden brown, about 1 minute per side. Remove from the pan, drain briefly on paper towels, and serve hot, garnished with minced green onions.

Adapted from a recipe by CHEFA GONZÁLEZ-DOPESO

COLD MUSSEL ESCABECHE
WITH VINEGAR AND PIMENTÓN

THIS TAPA is one of those dishes that you'll find in most bars in Spain, made with canned mussels. But don't fool yourself. Sometimes those cans are very expensive, filled with the highest-quality mussels that have been perfectly cooked. You can re-create this very popular tapa right at home, without opening an expensive Spanish can. Simply scald fresh mussels for a mere few seconds and cook them just enough to be edible but not so much that they become chewy. This technique can be used for any bivalves.

SERVES 8

2 pounds (900 g) Prince Edward Island mussels, thoroughly cleaned and debearded

1 cup extra virgin olive oil

6 medium garlic cloves

1 teaspoon orange zest

1 tablespoon Spanish hot paprika (pimentón)

½ cup sherry vinegar

1 teaspoon black peppercorns

2 rosemary sprigs

2 thyme sprigs

2 bay leaves

½ teaspoon salt

1. Bring 1½ quarts (1½ liters) of water to a boil in a small saucepan over medium-high heat. Place 10 mussels in a sieve and immerse them in the boiling water for 5 seconds, or just until the mussel shells open. Transfer the mussels from the sieve to a colander and place the colander over a medium bowl to catch any juices from the mussels. Repeat until you have cooked all of the mussels.

2. Open the mussels and remove them from the shells. Transfer them to a medium nonreactive bowl, being careful to keep them whole. Reserve under refrigeration. Strain the liquid in the bowl through a cheesecloth or fine mesh strainer into a small saucepan (there should be roughly 1 cup of the mussel liquid). Bring the liquid to a boil over medium heat, and reduce to about ¼ cup, 6 to 8 minutes. Set aside.

3. Heat the oil in a small sauté pan over medium heat. Split open the garlic cloves by placing them on a chopping board and pressing down hard with the base of your hand or with the flat side of a knife. Slice off the tough root end of each clove and discard the skins. Add the split garlic to the oil and brown it on all sides, about 2 minutes.

4. Remove the pan from the heat and add the reduced mussel water, orange zest, pimentón, vinegar, peppercorns, rosemary, thyme, bay leaves, and salt. Allow the escabeche to cool to room temperature, then pour it over the mussels. This dish usually tastes even better the day after you cook it. To serve individual portions, place approximately 8 mussels on each small plate, then stir the oil-vinegar mixture just before spooning it over the mussels. Garnish with marinated herbs and garlic cloves. Alternatively, place the mussels back in their shells and spoon the oil-vinegar mixture over them.

Adapted from a recipe by JOSÉ ANDRÉS

MUSSELS WITH OLIVES

MUSSELS ON THE HALF-SHELL, embellished with a pungent mixture of tomatoes and olives, make a beautiful hors d'oeuvre or tapa. Serve them on a platter or on individual plates. This particular tapa is popular in the seafood-abundant region of Cantabria, but you'll find variations throughout coastal Spain. You may use any variety of mussel for this dish. Smaller mussels are easier to handle if you are serving this from a platter to standing guests.

SERVES 8

¼ cup dry white wine

1 cup sliced Spanish onions

½ bay leaf

2 teaspoons salt, divided use

16 mussels, thoroughly cleaned and debearded

1 tablespoon extra virgin olive oil

1½ teaspoons minced shallots

¾ teaspoon minced garlic

3 plum tomatoes, peeled, seeded, and cut into small dice

2 tablespoons black olives, pitted and chopped

1½ teaspoons anchovy fillets, chopped

Pinch freshly ground black pepper

1. **Combine** the wine, onions, bay leaf, and 1 teaspoon of salt in a medium saucepan. Bring to a boil over medium-high heat and add the mussels. Cover and steam for 1 to 2 minutes. Remove the mussels from the pan as they open. Reserve about ¼ cup of the cooking liquid.

2. **Remove** the mussels from their shells and place one mussel inside each of the halved shells.

3. **Heat** the oil in a large sauté pan over medium heat. Sauté the shallots and garlic in the oil until translucent, about 30 seconds. Add the tomatoes, olives, anchovy fillets, and the mussel liquid. Cook over medium heat until reduced by half, about 2 minutes. Season with 1 teaspoon of salt and the pepper. Spoon 1 teaspoon of the sauce over each mussel and serve 2 mussels per portion.

Recipe by THE CULINARY INSTITUTE OF AMERICA

SHRIMP IN GARLIC

A QUICK FIX FOR GARLIC LOVERS, *gambas al ajillo*, as it is known in Spanish, is a classic tapa. It has been adopted in several Latin American countries where it is common to see variations under the name *camarones al ajillo*. Be sure to keep a few breath mints handy after enjoying these treats.

SERVES 8

6 tablespoons extra virgin olive oil

¼ teaspoon red pepper flakes

10 garlic cloves, sliced very thin

16 shrimp (26 to 30 count), peeled and deveined

2 teaspoons salt, divided use

⅛ teaspoon freshly ground black pepper

10 tablespoons white wine or lemon juice

¼ cup roughly chopped flat-leaf parsley

1. Heat the oil in a very large sauté pan over medium-high heat. Sauté the pepper flakes and garlic for a minute, then add the shrimp and sauté for another 1 to 2 minutes. Add 1 teaspoon of salt and a pinch of pepper. Quickly take the shrimp out of the pan with a slotted spoon when they are just cooked through. Remove the fried garlic just as it starts to brown and set aside.

2. Add the white wine or lemon juice to the pan (keeping the heat at medium high), and reduce by three-quarters, shaking the pan frequently to emulsify the sauce, 4 to 5 minutes.

3. Season with 1 teaspoon of salt and a pinch of pepper. Finish the sauce with the chopped parsley. Place the shrimp on a platter and spoon the sauce and fried garlic over the shrimp.

Recipe by THE CULINARY INSTITUTE OF AMERICA

CHICKEN CHILINDRON

THIS COLORFUL RECIPE incorporates a touch of a staple Spanish spice, pimentón, and the cured flavor of Serrano ham. When a dish is prepared *al chilindron*, it generally includes tomatoes and peppers. Enjoy this moist chicken stew over crunchy toasted bread.

SERVES 8

¼ cup extra virgin olive oil, divided use

1 pound 2 ounces (510 g) boneless, skinless chicken thighs, cut into large dice

4 teaspoons salt, divided use

2 tablespoons brandy

1 cup minced Spanish onions

¾ cup small-dice green peppers

1 cup small-dice red peppers

¼ cup Serrano ham, julienne

2 tablespoons minced garlic

4 plum tomatoes, peeled, seeded, and cut into small dice

1 teaspoon Spanish hot paprika (pimentón)

½ cup chicken stock

¼ teaspoon freshly ground black pepper

1 teaspoon chopped parsley

16 slices toasted bread (optional)

1. Heat 2 tablespoons of the olive oil in a medium sauté pan over medium-high heat. Add the chicken and season with 2 teaspoons of salt. Sauté the chicken in the oil until the outside is just cooked, about 2 minutes, then add the brandy and flambé it. Remove the chicken and reserve until needed.

2. Put the pan back on the heat and add the remaining 2 tablespoons of oil. Add the onions, peppers, and ham to the pan. Cook, stirring frequently, until browned, 5 to 7 minutes. Add the garlic and cook for another 2 minutes, or until the garlic begins to brown. Stir in the tomatoes, pimentón, chicken stock, and the reserved chicken.

3. Cover and stew over low heat for about 15 minutes. Adjust the seasoning with 2 teaspoons of salt and the pepper, if needed. Garnish with parsley and serve with slices of toasted bread, if desired.

Recipe by THE CULINARY INSTITUTE OF AMERICA

THE MEDITERRANEAN

THERE IS NO ONE MEDITERRANEAN CUISINE; there are many. They include not only the cuisines of the dozen or so countries with shorelines on the Mediterranean Sea but within those countries, the cooking of specific regions. Spain is a case in point, with distinctive culinary traditions emanating from Catalonia, Andalusia, Asturias, Galicia, La Mancha, and the rest of the seventeen regions in this large and varied country.

◄ **Eggs and potatoes** come together in the Spanish omelet, or *tortilla Española*. Here, it is cut into bite-sized pieces, as it is served in tapas bars across the country.

► **A typical Mediterranean market** overflows with a huge variety of fruit and vegetables. Including a good range of fresh produce in your diet has been shown to have dramatic health benefits.

SIMPLE, FRESH INGREDIENTS

Despite all of this variation, one generality applies: the Spanish table reflects a way of eating that we refer to collectively as the "Mediterranean Diet," an olive oil–based diet that is inherently healthy and very long on big flavors. Every Spanish cook is also a Mediterranean cook, someone who knows instinctively how to bring out the most flavor in a food. No matter where you go in Spain, cooks know how to make eating a pleasure. They do it simply, with olive oil, garlic, and salt, with herbs and spices, tomatoes and eggplant, peppers and squash, and other seasonal fruits and vegetables; with great cheeses, fish, wine, cured pork products, rice, and beans. They know what their food should taste like because they've been eating the same dishes for centuries. Recipes have been passed down from mother to daughter, from one generation to the next.

THE INFLUENCE OF THE MOORS

Spain is a paradigm for the cuisines of the Mediterranean. Of all of the European Mediterranean countries, the Arab influence is most pronounced here, because Spain was occupied by Arabs and muslimized Berbers (who collectively came to be known as the Moors) from the 8th century to the end of the 15th century. The Arabs brought with them tremendous advances in agriculture. It was they who introduced rice cultivation to the low-lying region around Valencia, and intensive vegetable gardening to the regions of Murcia

and El Levante. These gardens—*huertas*—still exist today, and many of the local dishes are their legacy. The Arabs also brought with them new varieties of olives and advanced olive-farming techniques. At a time when olive production in the rest of Europe was in decline, after the fall of the Roman Empire, it was on the rise in Spain. Today, Spain is still the largest producer of olives in the world.

WEATHER AND POVERTY

Culinary traditions throughout the Mediterranean have also been shaped by severe weather and great poverty, and Spain is certainly no exception. The olive groves and fruit orchards that you see when you drive through Spain are deceiving: Mediterranean land is dry land, and water is precious. There have been great famines throughout Spain's history, as there have throughout the Mediterranean. Hunger lurked constantly among the poor. As Sancho Panza's mother told him in *Don Quixote*, "Hunger is the best sauce in the world, and as the poor have no lack of it, they enjoy their food."

Hunger also breeds ingenuity. Stale bread became a staple, used for *migas* (a sort of breadcrumb hash that was originally eaten for breakfast), for thickening soups like gazpacho, and for stretching meat in the little meatballs called *albóndigas*. The egg, one of the few reliable sources of protein that was available if you had a chicken, took on a major significance, as evidenced by the many

wonderful *tortillas* (frittatas) in the cuisine. The problem of starvation was greatly alleviated after the arrival of the potato from the New World in the latter part of the 16th century. It joined forces with the egg in what many consider Spain's national dish, the *tortilla Española* (pages 42–43).

Mediterranean lands are dry and rocky, not well suited for grazing cattle. Sheep and goats do much better, which is why the cheeses that come from central and southern Spain are made from goat's and sheep's milk.

All of Spain does not border on the Mediterranean, of course. The verdant northern regions of Galicia and Asturias, Cantabria, País Vasco, and Navarra have a more Atlantic climate. Goats and sheep graze here, but so do cows. Rain is abundant. Yet the food is still influenced by the flavors of the Mediterranean that pervade the southern and eastern regions of Catalonia, El Levante, Murcia, the Baleares, and Andalusia.

THE MEDITERRANEAN DIET

In July 2006, Spanish researchers found that people following a Mediterranean diet that included a relatively high amount of fat from olive oil and nuts had lower levels of cholesterol, blood pressure, and blood sugar than those following a low-fat diet. The Mediterranean diet has been the focus of many studies, going back to the late 1950s. Findings consistently show that Mediterranean

groups have lower mortality rates from all causes with respect to men from control groups, and in particular there is a striking difference in mortality and incidence of coronary artery disease. Further studies have determined that the monounsaturated fat that occurs in olive oil plays an important role in reducing serum cholesterol levels (total cholesterol levels in the bloodstream).

The widespread use of olive oil is only one of a number of characteristics that link the Mediterranean diet with longevity. Just as significant is the fact that this is a diet that is rich in fresh fruits and vegetables. We don't yet fully understand why, but many studies have shown that fresh fruits and vegetables have a protective role against a variety of illnesses, including several types of cancer, atherosclerosis, Alzheimer's, and other chronic diseases.

Moderate consumption of red wine (that is no more than one glass a day for women and two for men) has also been associated with a lowered risk of coronary artery disease and heart attack. The way in which wine is consumed in the Mediterranean is significant; it is taken at meals, thus it has an association with food and with friends and family.

The health benefits of the Mediterranean diet are no doubt also related to lifestyle. The Spanish people know how to slow down and take pleasure in a shared meal. Enjoying food in the presence of other people, at a table, with a glass of good Spanish wine and the pleasure of company, has got to be good for your health.

SOUPS

SOUPS
Light and refreshing to robust and hearty

At The Culinary Institute of America's 2006 Worlds of Flavor conference on Spain and the World Table, Marbella-based chef Dani García prepared his signature cherry gazpacho topped with a scoop of savory/sour *queso de Ronda* sorbet. His soup was as contemporary as a soup could be, but the flavors he was playing with, he told the audience, reminded him of his childhood. The gazpacho tasted first of tomato, then of cherry; and the garnish provided a salty/savory contrast, the type of contrast Andalusians love (think melon and Serrano ham).

Robust soups such as this Rosh Hashanah Seven Vegetable Soup are packed with beans and vegetables and make satisfying meals in themselves.

REGIONAL FAVORITES

Soups in Spain are intensely regional. Not long ago you would have been hard pressed to find gazpacho outside of its native Andalusia, or *sopa de ajo* (thick, creamy garlic soup) far from the plains of Castile and La Mancha. Now peripatetic chefs and tourism have created an interest in the various Spanish regional cuisines, so you can find gazpacho in Barcelona and garlic soup in San Sebastián. Still, the most authentic versions are best sought out in their native regions.

Spanish soups fall into two categories. One group consists of hearty fare that constitutes a meal and would never be served as a first course. These soups contain beans, potatoes, fatty meats such as oxtail, ham hocks, and slab bacon, and nourishing vegetables such as Swiss chard. There is a fine line between these robust soups and the meat and bean stews known as *cocidos*, recipes for which can be found in the Meats chapter. The other category, represented by the recipes in this chapter, consists of lighter soups (though the Rosh Hashanah Seven Vegetable Soup on pages 84–85 could certainly make a filling meal) that are served as a first course. With the modern evolution of Spanish restaurants, these soups are gaining in importance.

According to food writer and historian Clifford Wright, gazpacho is the mother soup of all of the lighter bread-thickened Spanish soups. Even the thick, warming paprika-laced garlic soups of Castile-La Mancha are part of the gazpacho family that originated with the Hispano Arabs of Andalusia. They all evolved from the simple combination of bread, water, and garlic.

In Andalusia, where summers are scorching, refreshing cold soups prevail. Classic gazpacho Andaluz evolved as a way for peasants to transport meager lunch rations—stale bread, salt, water, and olive oil—to the fields. They would pound together the bread and garlic in a mortar, add salt, water, and olive oil, and that would be the midday meal. Vinegar was added for flavor, and after the New World tomato had been accepted as a food, it found its way into the mix, eventually becoming its most important ingredient. Chef Dani García, who devotes an entire section of the menu to cold soups (traditional and interpretive) at his restaurant, Calima, says that gazpacho Andaluz should be 90 percent tomatoes and the rest aromatics. He adds as little water as he can, blending the tomatoes a day ahead of making the gazpacho to draw out their own water. Then he adds salt, sherry vinegar, and high-quality, mild-tasting extra virgin olive oil.

MODERN INTERPRETATIONS

Chef García takes his gazpacho base in new directions, adding cherries, beets, or both. (An adaptation of this delicious soup appears on page 73.) He is one of several modern chefs making gazpachos with unexpected

Cold Almond and Garlic Soup, a refreshing Andalusian creation, is traditionally garnished with grapes. Here, sliced almonds have also been added.

Salmorejo is a close relation of gazpacho. This light and cooling soup is a perfect choice on a hot summer day.

ingredients, such as watermelon, mango, anchovies, and sardines. But he insists that if the soup does not contain tomatoes, it should not be called gazpacho.

Other cold Andalusian soups include the Malaga specialty *ajo blanco*, a tangy bread-thickened almond and garlic soup that is traditionally garnished with green grapes, which provide a sweet contrast to the bitter/sour flavors in the soup. Contemporary Spanish chefs such as Carles Abellán, chef owner of Commerç 24 in Barcelona, take the concept of the sweet with the pungent farther. Chef Abellán garnishes his garlic soup with a fragrant vanilla oil; other chefs make the soups sweet and the garnishes savory.

Salmorejo (pages 80–81) is another classic cold soup of Andalusia. A specialty of Cordoba, salmorejo is gazpacho's first cousin. It has a higher proportion of bread to tomatoes, and usually no water at all, so it is thick and should have a satiny texture. The simplest of soups, its only ingredients are tomatoes, garlic, bread, olive oil, and salt. Its classic garnishes are chopped hard-boiled egg and diced ham. However, modern chefs such as Kisko García, of Choco in Córdoba, continue to play with the old classics, and he garnishes his soup with marinated bacalao.

Soup is revered throughout the Mediterranean, and it always goes hand in hand with bread. But in many Spanish soups the bread is not an accompaniment, it is the basis of the soup itself. It's impressive how Spanish housewives have transformed these humble ingredients into such satisfying signature dishes; and, equally, how today's modern chefs are taking them into a new stratosphere altogether.

CHICKEN STOCK

ALTHOUGH MANY OF THE SOUPS in this chapter are made with water rather than stock, chicken stock is an important element in Spanish cooking, especially when it comes to rice. At the heart of any good paella Valenciana is a great chicken stock. You can keep this chicken stock on hand in the freezer for use in various recipes in this book. Freeze it in small quantities, and thaw as needed. You may need more or less water to cover the chicken bones, depending on the shape and size of your pot.

MAKES 2 QUARTS (2 LITERS)

4 pounds (1.8 kg) chicken bones

3 quarts (3 liters) cold water, or more or less as needed to cover the chicken bones by 2 inches (5 cm)

1 large onion, finely chopped

1 medium carrot, finely chopped

1 celery stalk, finely chopped

1 bay leaf

1 to 2 parsley sprigs

1 to 2 thyme sprigs

2 black peppercorns

¼ teaspoon salt

1. Rinse the chicken bones, place them in a large stockpot, and add enough water to cover them by 2 inches (5 cm). Bring to a boil over low heat. As the mixture comes to a boil, skim the foam and scum that come to the surface. Continue to skim regularly until the water has reached a boil.

2. Turn the heat to low and simmer slowly for 3 to 4 hours, until the stock smells very fragrant. Add the onion, carrot, celery, bay leaf, parsley, thyme, peppercorns, and salt. Simmer for another hour.

3. Strain the stock through a fine wire mesh sieve or a large strainer lined with cheesecloth into a bowl or another pot. Chill over an ice bath for about 30 minutes, stirring frequently. Skim off any fat that accumulates on the surface of the stock and discard. Use immediately, refrigerate for up to 3 days, or freeze for up to 6 weeks.

Recipe by THE CULINARY INSTITUTE OF AMERICA

FISH STOCK

UNLIKE OTHER STOCKS, fish stock is not long simmering. Indeed, if you cook the fish bones for too long the stock can become bitter. When making fish stock, use bones and heads from white-fleshed fish, and avoid salmon, mackerel, and other strong-tasting, fatty fish. Mahi is not a good fish for stock because it's acidic. Soak the bones in salt water for an hour beforehand. This will make the stock clearer and prevent it from tasting overly fishy. Most supermarket fish departments fillet their fish before displaying them, and you can usually call ahead to order bones and heads.

MAKES 2 QUARTS (2 LITERS)

4 to 6 pounds (1.8 to 2.7 kg) fish bones and heads

3 quarts (3 liters) cold water, or more or less as needed to cover the fish bones and heads by 2 inches (5 cm)

½ large onion, finely chopped

½ medium carrot, finely chopped

1 celery stalk, finely chopped

¾ cup mushroom trimmings (optional)

¼ teaspoon salt, or as needed

1. Combine all of the ingredients in a large pot, making sure that the water covers the fish bones and heads by 2 inches (5 cm). Bring slowly to a simmer, and skim off any scum and foam that rise to the surface. Simmer, without boiling, for 30 to 60 minutes.

2. Remove from the heat and strain through a fine wire mesh sieve or a large strainer lined with cheesecloth into a bowl. Chill over an ice bath for about 30 minutes, stirring frequently. Use immediately, refrigerate for up to 3 days, or freeze for up to 6 weeks.

Recipe by THE CULINARY INSTITUTE OF AMERICA

BROWN PORK STOCK

WHEN SPANISH RECIPES call for "ham stock," this dark, smoky pork stock will do just fine. You can use additional herbs in the sachet, such as oregano stems, crushed red pepper, caraway seeds, or mustard seeds. Note that to ensure a rich flavor, this stock must simmer for 6 hours.

MAKES 2 QUARTS (2 LITERS)

2 tablespoons vegetable oil

4 pounds (1.8 kg) fresh or smoked pork bones, including knuckles and trim

1 gallon (3.8 liters) cold water

2 tablespoons extra virgin olive oil

1 cup large-dice onions

½ cup large-dice celery

¼ cup large-dice carrots

5 tablespoons tomato paste, or as needed

1 sachet d'épices with 2 parsley stems, 3 cracked peppercorns, ½ teaspoon dried thyme, and a bay leaf

1 teaspoon salt

1. Preheat the oven to 450°F (230°C). Add enough vegetable oil to a large, deep roasting pan to film the bottom lightly. Heat the pan in the oven for 10 minutes. Add the bones to the pan and roast, stirring and turning from time to time, until they are a deep brown, about 35 minutes.

2. Transfer the bones to a 10-quart (10 liter) stockpot and add all but 1 cup of the cold water. Deglaze the roasting pan with the remaining 1 cup of water and add the released drippings to the stockpot. Bring the stock to a simmer slowly over low heat. Adjust the heat if necessary to establish an even, gentle simmer and continue to cook, skimming the surface as necessary, for 5 hours.

3. Heat a large sauté pan over medium-high heat. Add enough olive oil to film the pan. Add the onions, celery, and carrots, and cook, stirring occasionally, until the onions are a deep golden brown, about 10 minutes. Add the tomato paste and continue to cook, stirring frequently, until it takes on a rusty brown color and gives off a sweet aroma, 1 to 2 minutes. Add a few ladles of the stock and stir well to release the drippings; add this mixture to the stock along with the sachet d'épices and the salt.

4. Continue to simmer the stock, skimming as necessary and tasting from time to time, until it has developed a rich flavor and a noticeable body, about 1 more hour.

5. Strain the stock through a fine wire mesh sieve or a large strainer lined with cheesecloth into a bowl. Degrease by skimming the fat with a spoon or ladle, or use a gravy separator, or rapidly chill the broth, then skim the fat off the surface after it cools. Use immediately, refrigerate for up to 3 days, or freeze for up to 6 weeks.

Recipe by THE CULINARY INSTITUTE OF AMERICA

CONSOMMÉ WITH SAFFRON

María José San Román has been working for several years with the University of Madrid, studying the properties of saffron. She has found that saffron loves lots of time; the longer you simmer it, the more flavor it will impart. This intensely saffrony yet delicate consommé can be served as a first course, or you can serve it in demitasse cups as a tapa. The saffron gives it a beautiful color and a very special flavor.

SERVES 8 AS A FIRST COURSE, 16 AS A TAPA

10 ounces (285 g) beef chuck, cut into
    2-inch (5 cm) cubes

2 hen or chicken legs (about 5¾ ounces or 160 g each)

3 chicken legs (3½ to 4 ounces or 100 to 115 g each)

11 ounces (310 g) pork ribs (about 5 ribs)

1 beef shank bone (about 10½ ounces or 300 g)

1 ham hock, split (about 7 ounces or 200 g)

2⅔ quarts (2⅔ liters) water, preferably bottled water

2½ medium carrots, peeled and quartered

1½ medium parsnips, peeled and quartered

1½ medium beets, peeled and quartered

2½ Swiss chard leaves, with stalks

3½ cups coarsely chopped cabbage

½ teaspoon saffron threads, divided use

4 teaspoons salt, divided use

10¾ ounces (310 g) duck foie gras, partially frozen

Small pinch white pepper

1 tablespoon clover or other vegetable sprouts

2 teaspoons thinly sliced chives

1. Place the meats in a large soup pot or Dutch oven and add the water. Bring to a boil over medium-high heat, reduce the heat to medium-low, cover partially, and simmer for 1 hour. Skim off any foam that rises to the surface.

2. Add the vegetables and ¼ teaspoon of saffron to the pot with 2 teaspoons of salt, bring back to a gentle simmer, and continue to cook, partiallly covered, for another 2 hours, or until the level of the liquid in the pot has reduced to about half of the original amount.

3. Dice the foie gras into ¼-inch (5 mm) cubes while the broth simmers. Arrange the cubes in 1-tablespoon portions on a plate, then cover and refrigerate until thawed.

4. Strain the broth through a fine-mesh or cheesecloth-lined strainer into a 2-quart (2 liter) glass measuring bowl. If the broth has reduced to less than 6 cups, add enough water to bring the level to 6 cups. If the broth measures more than 6 cups, you may further reduce it, if desired, before adjusting the seasoning. Refrigerate until the fat solidifies on the top of the broth, 2 to 3 hours. Use a spoon to skim off as much of the fat layer as possible.

5. Return the broth to a clean soup pot or Dutch oven, taste the soup, and adjust seasoning with up to 2 teaspoons of salt and a small pinch of white pepper (or more or less of each as needed). Bring the soup back to a gentle simmer over medium heat and cook for 5 more minutes, or until the seasoning flavors have blended.

6. Place 1 tablespoon of the diced foie gras into each of 8 heated soup bowls, then ladle ¾ cup of the consommé into each bowl. Garnish each serving with a small pinch each of clover or vegetable sprouts, chives, and 2 to 3 threads of the remaining saffron.

Adapted from a recipe by María José San Román

SAFFRON

WHEN YOU TAKE A PINCH OF SAFFRON between your fingertips to add to your paella, potatoes, or soup, you are holding the dried stamens of the *Crocus sativus*, a low-growing crocus with small mauve blossoms that blooms every fall, blanketing the fields of La Mancha in purple. Seventy percent of the world's saffron grows on this high plateau just south of Madrid.

HARVESTING SAFFRON

When the first blooms appear between October 25 and November 5 (depending on the rains and weather), there is no time to sit and admire the flowers. This is the beginning of the harvest, the *manto*, and picking must start at once. The crocuses must be harvested in the early morning, after the dew has evaporated but before the petals open. Once they are warmed by the sun, the flowers become limp, making it difficult to pick them without damaging the stamens.

The pickers begin work shortly after dawn. Workers move down the rows of crocuses, bending low to the ground, plucking the flowers and putting them into esparto baskets, which are emptied into crates. As soon as the crates are filled, they're transported to the nearest village, where women—*las roseras*, or *mondadoras* (petal strippers)—sit at long tables heaped with the flowers, opening the petals with one hand while deftly and quickly pulling out the three amber red stamens with the other. They are paid by the weight of the stamens, so the quicker these pile up the better. Once the stamens are weighed, they're transferred to a sieve and dried over electric heating elements or braziers. All of this must be done in a day; if the stigmas are not plucked from the flowers on the day they are picked, they will be lost as the flowers quickly become pulpy.

It takes about 70,000 hand-harvested crocuses to produce a pound (450 g) of hand-plucked threads. Each acre of land yields only 5 to 7 pounds (2.3 to 3.2 kg). This is why saffron is the world's most expensive spice by weight. It has always been precious, valued for its aromatic properties since ancient times.

ESSENTIAL SPANISH INGREDIENT

The Moors brought *az-safran* (the word means "yellow") to Spain over one thousand years ago. Like so many of the foods they brought and cultivated, it became vital to the Spanish table, revered and utilized as in no other cuisine. Saffron is the spice that gives paella its unforgettable color and flavor. Like salt, it brings out the flavor of the foods that it seasons, adding its own special scent and unmistakable yellow hue in the process.

So great is the passion for saffron among Spanish cooks that the government funds studies about its applications. At the University of Castilla-La Mancha, Chef María José San Román and her colleagues have discovered that if you infuse 1 gram (0.035 ounces) of lightly toasted saffron for 4 hours in 1 quart (1 liter) of water that has been heated to approximately 150°F (65°C) , you obtain an intensely flavored broth that will transform a plain pot of potatoes or rice into an unforgettable dish. As Chef María José San Román says, saffron is a "slow food." It likes time, and time and the quality of the saffron, as opposed to the amount of saffron you use, is what matters.

QUALITY IS IMPORTANT

Spanish chefs are emphatic about the importance of using quality saffron. The Spanish government also recognizes the importance of saffron quality, and has certified saffron grown in La Mancha that meets quality specifications with a numbered DO (denomination of origin) label picturing a stylized crocus with Don Quixote superimposed on it. By certifying quality saffron, the government is helping to maintain the customs and foodways of the small La Mancha saffron producers, whose livelihood has been threatened in recent years by the influx of cheaper, lower-quality saffron from other countries. If you use cheaper, poor quality saffron, which is often cut with turmeric, you will end up with bitter, acrid flavors. It may give your rice a nice amber color, but the unmistakable aromatic flavor of saffron will not be a lasting one. One way to avoid being duped is to buy saffron threads rather than powder, which is more likely to be cut with other ground spices of similar color.

Saffron may be dear—an ounce (28 g) of the best Spanish saffron can cost $200—but it does not take much to flavor a dish. Spanish saffron is usually sold in 1-gram (0.035 ounce) quantities, which is enough for several large paellas or ten recipes of saffron rice for four. If it is infused in water as described above, it will go even farther. You can obtain good quality saffron in the United States from www. LaTienda.com and from Penzeys Spices (www.Penzeys.com).

STORING AND USING SAFFRON

Whether you buy saffron in the 1-ounce tins offered by LaTienda. com, Penzeys Spices, and through gourmet retailers, or in the 1-gram quantities sold in Spanish markets, it will keep best if stored in the freezer. Make sure that it is first well sealed in a plastic bag, then keep it in a tin or jar. Use it by the generous pinch (rub it gently between your fingers first to release the aroma). Saffron will keep in the freezer for a year or more.

GARDEN GAZPACHO
WITH HAZELNUT AND PEAR FRITTERS

DEEP-FRIED, hazelnut-coated pear balls make an unconventional garnish for this spicy gazpacho. Serve it in bowls for a first course, or in small glasses as a tapa (with the pear balls skewered on small wooden skewers).

SERVES 8 AS A MAIN COURSE, 16 AS A TAPA

10 heirloom tomatoes, of assorted colors and sweetness, cored, blended, and strained (about 12 cups purée)

1½ medium red bell peppers, cored and seeded

1½ large yellow bell peppers, cored and seeded

1½ medium poblano peppers, cored and seeded

½ English cucumber

⅛ medium habanero chile

2 tablespoons chopped cilantro

4 teaspoons lime juice

1 cup lobster stock or chicken stock

1 tablespoon kosher salt

Pinch freshly ground black pepper

½ cup shelled hazelnuts

1 egg

2 tablespoons water

Eight ¾-inch (2 cm) pear balls, scooped from 4 ripe but firm pears with a melon baller, or sixteen ¾-inch (2 cm) pear balls, scooped from 8 pears if serving as a tapa

¼ cup Wondra flour

6 cups vegetable oil

1. Place the tomato pulp in a large bowl. Finely dice half the peppers and cucumber and stir into the tomatoes. Place the remaining peppers, cucumber, and habanero in a food processor fitted with the steel blade and process to a pulp, 1 to 2 minutes. Stir into the tomatoes with the cilantro, lime juice, and stock. Taste and adjust seasoning with the salt and a pinch of pepper. Chill for 1 hour or longer, preferably overnight.

2. Prepare the hazelnuts. Preheat the oven to 250°F (120°C). Bake the nuts on a cookie sheet for 20 to 30 minutes, or until the skins begin to crack and the interior is lightly browned. Transfer the nuts to a terrycloth towel, gather the towel around them, twist tightly, and set aside for 5 minutes. Then vigorously rub the nuts through the towel for 2 to 3 minutes, or until most of the skin is removed. Discard the skin and grind the nuts in a food processor until finely chopped.

3. Make the pear balls. Beat the egg with the water in a small bowl. Roll the balls in Wondra flour, then in the egg wash. Shake off the excess egg and roll in the ground hazelnuts. Place on a parchment-lined half-sized baking sheet and place in the freezer for 1 hour or longer, or until they are frozen.

4. Heat 2 inches (5 cm) of vegetable oil (about 6 cups in an 8-inch-(20 cm) wide pan or deep fryer) over medium-high heat to 350°F (175°C). Deep-fry 5 pear balls until golden brown, about 2 minutes, flipping them halfway through cooking. Drain briefly on paper towels. Repeat with the remaining pear balls. Place 1½ cups of the cold gazpacho in a bowl, rest a warm fritter on top, and serve. If serving as a tapa, place ¾ cup of the gazpacho in a small glass, gently skewer a pear ball with a wooden skewer, and stand in the glass to serve.

Adapted from a recipe by VICTOR SCARGLE

GAZPACHO GARBANZOS

FRESH JALAPEÑO PEPPER, Tabasco, and cayenne pepper heat up this hearty addition to the family of cold Spanish soups. The roasted garbanzos are added as a garnish at the end and give an interesting texture and flavor to the soup. This is an excellent option for the vegetarians at your table.

SERVES 8

For the soup

12 ounces (340 g) Spanish onions, peeled and sliced ½ inch (1 cm) thick

1 pound (450 g) green peppers

1 pound (450 g) red peppers

1 jalapeño

1 pound (450 g) eggplant, peeled and sliced ½ inch (1 cm) thick

2 pounds (900 g) tomatoes, halved

2 tablespoons vegetable oil

4 teaspoons salt, divided use

½ teaspoon freshly ground black pepper

¼ cup roasted garlic

8 ounces (225 g) seedless cucumbers, peeled and sliced ½ inch (1 cm) thick

2 tablespoons chopped cilantro

¼ cup lime juice

¾ cup extra virgin olive oil

½ cup red wine vinegar

2 cups tomato juice

1 teaspoon Tabasco sauce

For the chickpea garnish

1 cup chickpeas, soaked overnight and drained

1 teaspoon extra virgin olive oil

⅛ teaspoon cayenne pepper

1 teaspoon saffron

¼ teaspoon hot paprika

¼ teaspoon dried thyme

1 teaspoon salt

1. Make the soup. Brush the onions, peppers, eggplant, and tomatoes with the vegetable oil and sprinkle with 1 teaspoon of salt and the pepper. Grill the vegetables until softened and browned, about 15 minutes for the green peppers and red peppers, 10 minutes for the onions, 9 minutes for the jalapeño, 6 minutes for the eggplant, and 4 minutes for the tomatoes. Peel and seed the peppers.

2. Blend the grilled vegetables, garlic, and cucumbers to a purée in a food processor.

3. Add the cilantro, lime juice, olive oil, red wine vinegar, tomato juice, and Tabasco. Adjust seasoning with 3 teaspoons of salt. Stir well and reserve in the refrigerator.

4. Make the chickpea garnish. Roast the chickpeas in a 375°F (190°C) oven for 35 minutes, or until golden brown. As soon as they come out of the oven, toss them with the olive oil and cayenne pepper, saffron, paprika, thyme, and salt. To serve, ladle 1 cup of the soup into a bowl and garnish with 2 tablespoons of the roasted and spiced chickpeas.

Recipe by THE CULINARY INSTITUTE OF AMERICA

BEET AND CHERRY GAZPACHO

THIS BRIGHT, GLISTENING SOUP is very similar to Dani García's cherry and beet gazpacho, a new wave gazpacho if there ever was one. And yet even with beets and cherries, the essence of classic gazpacho—tomatoes, bread, olive oil, vinegar, and onions—is there.

SERVES 8

1 medium beet, stemmed

3½ cups seeded and coarsely chopped plum tomatoes (about 6)

2 cups pitted Bing cherries

1 medium Spanish pepper, cored, seeded, and chopped

1 cup peeled and diced European cucumbers

3 tablespoons chopped red onions

2 garlic cloves, crushed

1 tablespoon coarse salt, divided use

1¾ cups cubed day-old country-style bread, crusts removed

2 cups chilled water

½ cup plus 2 teaspoons extra virgin olive oil, divided use

6 tablespoons sherry vinegar

Freshly ground black pepper, as needed

Spring water, as needed

¼ cup coarsely chopped green pistachios

¼ cup peeled small-dice peeled cucumbers, for garnish

4 teaspoons finely sliced mint leaves, for garnish (about 12 leaves)

1. **Preheat** the oven to 400°F (205°C).

2. **Wrap** the beet in aluminum foil, place it on a small baking sheet, and bake until it feels tender when pierced with a skewer, about 1 hour 20 minutes. Unwrap the beet and rinse it under cold running water, being careful not to burn yourself. Slip off and discard the skin; let the beet cool completely, then coarsely chop and reserve.

3. **Place** the chopped beet, tomatoes, Bing cherries, pepper, cucumbers, onions, and garlic in a medium bowl and toss until combined. Sprinkle 2 teaspoons of salt over the beet mixture and let stand for 10 to 15 minutes.

4. **Place** the bread in a separate bowl, add about 2 cups of chilled water to cover, and soak for 5 minutes. Drain the bread, squeeze out the excess liquid, then add the bread to the beet mixture.

5. **Place** half of the beet mixture in a blender with ¼ cup of olive oil and blend until it is finely puréed. Transfer the mixture to a mixing bowl. Repeat with the remaining beet mixture.

6. **Add** the vinegar, whisk to mix, and adjust seasoning with 1 teaspoon of salt and a pinch of pepper. Add spring water until the soup has the consistency of a smoothie.

7. **Refrigerate** the gazpacho, covered, until well chilled, about 2 hours. Serve ½ cup of the soup with 1½ teaspoons of the chopped pistachios, 1½ teaspoons of diced cucumbers, a pinch of mint, and ¼ teaspoon of olive oil.

Adapted from a recipe by ANYA VON BREMZEN

COLD ALMOND AND GARLIC SOUP

THIS IS THE TRADITIONAL *ajo blanco* soup, a marvelously refreshing cold soup made with almonds, garlic, and water. Also known as white gazpacho, *ajo blanco* is a perfect cold summer soup: easy to make, healthful, and distinctive. The Arabs who ruled Andalusia for almost 800 years introduced almonds to the Iberian Peninsula, and this dish probably originated with their reign. Though highly popular in Andalusia, it is little known in the rest of Spain and virtually unknown in the United States. Here it is served with its traditional grape garnish and toasted slivered almonds. Sliced apples are also traditional as a garnish.

SERVES 8

2 cups loosely packed day-old country-style bread
    or fresh bread, torn into 1-inch (2.5 cm) pieces

6⅔ cups water, or as needed, divided use

1 tablespoon coarsely chopped garlic

2 cups blanched almonds

2½ teaspoons salt, divided use

½ cup sherry vinegar

½ cup extra virgin olive oil

16 medium green grapes, halved and seeded, for garnish

⅔ cup toasted sliced almonds

1. Soak the day-old bread in 1⅓ cups of water in a medium bowl for 10 minutes. If using fresh bread, there is no need to soak it.

2. Process the garlic and almonds in a food processor fitted with the steel blade for 1 minute, or until finely ground. Stop halfway through the process to scrape down the sides of the bowl. Add the soaked bread and any soaking water (or the fresh bread), 2 teaspoons of salt, vinegar, and oil, and blend for 2 minutes, or until a smooth paste forms. Add 2 cups of the water and blend for 2 minutes longer, or until smooth.

3. Transfer to a medium nonreactive bowl and stir in the remaining 3⅓ cups of water (use 4⅓ cups if using fresh bread). Cover and refrigerate for at least 4 hours, or until well chilled.

4. Stir the soup well, reaching to the bottom of the bowl, just before serving. Taste and adjust seasoning with ½ teaspoon of salt, or more if desired. Ladle 1 cup of soup into each chilled soup bowl, garnish with the grapes and toasted sliced almonds, and serve.

Adapted from a recipe by TERESA BARRENECHEA

LAS PEDROÑERAS
HOT GARLIC SOUP

LAS PEDROÑERAS, in the Castile-La Mancha region of southwestern Spain, is known as the garlic capital of the country. Manolo de la Osa, chef-owner of Las Rejas restaurant in Las Pedroñeras, uses smoked black pudding, or morcilla (see page 183), and choricero pepper, in his version of the regional garlic soup. Choricero peppers, also known as ñora peppers, are small, round, intense, and sweet-fleshed red bell peppers that are always used dry, to add flavor to stews or soups. They are also an ingredient in chorizo sausages.

SERVES 8

2 garlic heads

3 tablespoons plus 2 teaspoons extra virgin olive oil, divided use

2 tablespoons salt, divided use

¼ teaspoon freshly ground black pepper

2 bay leaves

2 smoked ham hocks

2 morcillas

2 teaspoons Spanish sweet paprika

6 tablespoons tomato paste

4 quarts (4 liters) unsalted beef stock, divided use

2 choricero peppers, roasted, cut into thin strips

2 tablespoons minced oil-packed sun-dried tomatoes

8 slices country-style bread or baguette

6 large garlic cloves, peeled, 2 cut in half, 4 very thinly sliced

1 cup small-dice ham

8 eggs

1 cup sherry wine vinegar

1. Separate one garlic head into cloves and peel them. Separate the other garlic head into cloves, peel them, and crush them lightly with the side of a chef's knife.

2. Coat the uncrushed garlic cloves in 2 teaspoons of oil and a pinch of salt and the pepper. Roast the cloves in a 350°F (175°C) oven until soft, about 7 minutes. Allow to cool to room temperature.

3. Heat 1 tablespoon of the oil in a medium saucepot over medium-high heat. Sauté the bay leaves with the crushed garlic until the garlic is lightly browned, 1 to 2 minutes. Add the ham hocks and morcillas and sauté until golden brown, about 4 minutes.

4. Add the sweet paprika and tomato paste and sauté for another 3 minutes, stirring vigorously, then cover with 2 quarts (2 liters) of the beef stock. Add the choricero peppers and sun-dried tomatoes. Bring to a boil over medium heat, add the roasted garlic, season with the remaining salt, then lower the heat and allow to reduce until thickened, about 50 minutes. Remove the ham hocks and bay leaves, and reserve warm. Trim the meat out of the ham hocks, dice it, and add it to the soup pot.

5. Brush the slices of bread with 1 tablespoon of the oil. Toast in a 375°F (190°C) oven until golden brown, about 15 minutes. Rub with a cut garlic clove and cut into 1½-inch (4 cm) wide sticks.

6. Heat 1 tablespoon of the oil over medium-high heat in a medium sauté pan. Fry the diced ham and garlic shavings until lightly browned, about 3 minutes.

7. Poach the eggs. Heat the remaining 2 quarts (2 liters) of beef stock over medium heat until it reaches 160°F (70°C), then lower the heat to as low as possible and stir in the sherry wine vinegar. Break an egg into a cup and tip one at a time into the stock, cooking 4 eggs at a time. Poach the eggs for 4 minutes, or until the whites are set and the yolks are still runny. Skim the stock if necessary. Remove the excess stock by blotting the eggs briefly on paper towels and reserve until needed.

8. Serve ½ cup of the soup piping hot in a bowl with a poached egg, 1 tablespoon of diced ham and garlic shavings, and 2 pieces of toasted bread.

Adapted from a recipe by MANOLO DE LA OSA

BASQUE FISH SOUP

THIS RECIPE offers a great way to get the most out of a whole fish, such as snapper, and to use the last pieces of bread remaining from a loaf. Traditionally, Spanish cooks have found creative ways to make flavorful and satisfying dishes out of every part of the fish and every crumb of bread in the kitchen. In Basque Euskadi, this fish soup is known as *arrain salda*. Note that the fish heads or bones need to be soaked overnight before use.

SERVES 8

6 pounds (2.7 kg) fish heads or bones from cod, hake, or snapper

½ cup extra virgin olive oil, divided use

⅔ cup medium-dice Spanish onions

½ cup medium-dice carrots

4¾ teaspoons salt, divided use

1 bay leaf

¼ cup white wine

4 to 5 quarts (4 to 5 liters) water

⅔ cup minced leeks

1 teaspoon minced garlic

⅓ cup tomato purée

½ cup day-old country-style bread, broken into small pieces

1 tablespoon chopped parsley

1. Remove any remaining gills from the fish heads, using a boning knife or kitchen scissors. Soak the heads or bones in cold water overnight. Drain and rinse the heads or bones before using.

2. Heat ¼ cup of the oil in a very large stockpot over medium heat. Add the onions and carrots with ¼ teaspoon of salt and "sweat" the vegetables, stirring frequently for about 2 minutes, or until they begin to soften and release some of their liquid.

3. Add the fish heads or bones, bay leaf, and wine. Raise the heat to medium-high and reduce the wine by half, about 3 minutes. Add enough of the water to cover the heads or bones, along with 2 teaspoons of salt, and bring to a boil over medium-high heat. Reduce the heat to medium and simmer for about 1 hour, skimming the surface as needed to remove any foam or other impurities.

4. Strain the stock through a fine-mesh or cheesecloth-lined strainer and save the fish heads or bones. Let them sit for a few minutes, then when they are cool enough to handle, separate the meat from the bones very meticulously and reserve.

5. Heat the remaining olive oil in a large pot over medium heat. Add the leeks and garlic with ½ teaspoon of salt and cook for 8 to 10 minutes, stirring frequently, or until the leeks are tender and beginning to simmer in their own liquid. Stir in the tomato purée and cook until aromatic and slightly rust colored, about 5 minutes.

6. Mix in the bread. Add the fish fumet, bring to a boil, then reduce the heat to medium low and simmer for about 30 minutes.

7. Purée the soup in several batches in a blender, filling the blender only about halfway each time. Blend until smooth, about 1 minute, transferring the purée into a mixing bowl. Clean the pot, add the purée, and bring it back to a simmer over medium heat. Season with 2 teaspoons of salt, or more or less as needed. Finally, add the reserved meat to the soup and add the parsley just before serving.

Recipe by THE CULINARY INSTITUTE OF AMERICA

COD AND POTATO PURÉE
WITH CAVIAR

Manolo de la Osa, chef/owner of the Michelin-starred Las Rejas in Las Pedroñeras, Spain, serves this elegant purée in glasses, topped with a spoonful of herring roe. At the restaurant, he makes confit of mushroom oil, which is replaced here with truffle oil. Note that the salt cod needs to be desalted beforehand, which takes 36 to 48 hours.

SERVES 8

2½ ounces (70 g) salt cod (see page 139)

¼ cup extra virgin olive oil

2 cups chopped leeks, white parts only

3 garlic cloves, peeled

1 cup roughly chopped spring onions

⅔ cup peeled and roughly chopped starchy potatoes, such as Yukon gold or russets

4 ounces (115 g) smoked cod

1 quart (1 liter) Chicken Stock (page 64)

1 cup heavy cream

1 tablespoon truffle oil

2 teaspoons salt

½ teaspoon white pepper

1 tablespoon Green Parsley Oil (page 232)

4 teaspoons herring roe

8 chervil leaves, for garnish

1. Desalt the salt cod: Soak it in fresh cold water, refreigerated, for 36 to 48 hours, changing the water at least four times. Drain well.

2. Heat the oil in a medium saucepan over medium heat and add the leeks, garlic, and spring onions. Sauté until tender, 5 to 8 minutes, and add the potatoes. Cook, stirring, for a few minutes, until coated with oil, then add the smoked and desalted cod. Cook, stirring, for about 5 minutes until well incorporated, making sure not to brown the fish. Add the stock. Simmer until the potatoes are fork tender, about 20 minutes.

3. Remove from the heat and add the cream. Let stand for a few minutes, then transfer to a blender (it's best to do this in batches). Don't blend hot! Blend the mixture until smooth, about 30 seconds per batch, while drizzling in the truffle oil. Season lightly with salt. Taste and adjust seasoning with the pepper.

4. Serve ½ cup of the purée in small glasses or bowls. Top with a few drops of parsley oil and ½ teaspoon of herring roe. Decorate with chervil and serve.

Adapted from a recipe by Manolo de la Osa

CORDOBAN SALMOREJO

SALMOREJO, a thicker first cousin of gazpacho, can be served as a sauce or as a soup. The word comes from the Latin *salmuera*, which means salt water or salty water. Like gazpacho, it was a mixture of water, vinegar, and olive oil until the tomato arrived from the New World. This one is a simple mixture of tomatoes, bread, and olive oil. Its success depends entirely on the quality of your tomatoes and oil. Note that this soup needs to be left overnight to marinate before serving.

SERVES 8

5 pounds (2.25 kg) very ripe plum tomatoes

½ day-old baguette, cut into ½-inch (1 cm) dice

2 tablespoons coarsely chopped garlic

2 cups extra virgin olive oil

4 teaspoons salt

½ cup cooked, diced Ibérico or Serrano ham

1. Bring a large saucepan of water to a boil. Make an X in the bottom of the tomatoes with a sharp paring knife and then dip them in the boiling water for 10 to 15 seconds. Transfer the tomatoes to a bowl or sink full of cold water. Remove from the cold water and peel. Cut in half, remove the cores, and coarsely chop the tomatoes.

2. Combine all of the ingredients except the ham in a large bowl and toss together. Cover and marinate overnight in the refrigerator.

3. Blend one-third of the mixture at high speed until homogeneous, about 5 minutes. Repeat with the remaining soup. Chill for 2 hours. Serve 1¼ cups of the soup in a shallow bowl, garnishing each bowl with a tablespoon of diced ham.

Adapted from a recipe by KISKO GARCÍA

SOPA DE ALBÓNDIGAS

A WELL-SEASONED BROTH, this meatball soup is packed with hearty potatoes and chickpeas. The meatballs, made of ground beef and pork, provide a full rich flavor. Chopped egg and parsley top off the soup and add contrasting texture and freshness. This filling soup is a great starter, but it will also make a satisfying full meal in a bowl.

SERVES 8 AS A FIRST COURSE, 4 AS A MAIN COURSE

For the meatballs

½ cup ground beef (about 3 ounces or 85 g)
½ cup ground pork (about 3 ounces or 85 g)
5 teaspoons grated yellow onions
3 tablespoons dried breadcrumbs
1 large egg, lightly beaten
2 tablespoons chopped flat-leaf parsley
1½ teaspoons finely minced garlic
¼ teaspoon ground cinnamon
¼ teaspoon ground cumin
½ teaspoon salt
¼ teaspoon freshly ground black pepper

For the soup

1 tablespoon extra virgin olive oil
⅔ cup small-dice yellow onion
⅛ teaspoon crushed saffron threads
1½ quarts (1½ liters) chicken broth
1½ cups chickpeas, soaked overnight and drained
½ cup medium-dice potatoes
1 cup peeled, seeded, and diced tomatoes
½ teaspoon salt
¼ teaspoon freshly ground black pepper
2 tablespoons chopped flat-leaf parsley
1 hard-cooked egg, peeled and chopped

1. Make the meatballs. Combine the beef, pork, onions, breadcrumbs, egg, parsley, garlic, cinnamon, cumin, salt, and pepper in a medium bowl.

2. Knead with your hands until all the ingredients are fully incorporated and evenly distributed throughout the mixture, about 3 minutes. If you have time, cover and refrigerate the mixture for 1 hour to make forming the meatballs easier. Shape the mixture into tiny ½-inch (1 cm) meatballs with your hands and refrigerate.

3. Make the soup. Heat the oil in a large heavy pot over medium heat and sauté the onions until translucent, about 5 minutes. Add the saffron and broth and bring to a boil for 5 minutes. Add the chickpeas and cook until three-quarters of the way done, about another 1 hour 10 minutes. Add the potatoes and cook until tender, about 15 minutes.

4. Add the tomatoes, then slip the uncooked meatballs into the broth and simmer gently until cooked through, about 20 minutes. Season the soup with the salt and pepper.

5. Transfer 4 of the meatballs to a warm soup bowl using a slotted spoon. Ladle ½ cup of the hot soup stock and ¼ cup of the vegetables over the meatballs. Sprinkle with ¾ teaspoon of the parsley and 2 teaspoons of the chopped eggs.

Recipe by THE CULINARY INSTITUTE OF AMERICA

VALLADOLID BREAD SOUP
WITH HAM CAVIAR

THE HAM "CAVIAR" that garnishes this soup is a typical playful invention of the new Spanish chefs. When tapioca is cooked in a broth made from ham bones, it takes on the flavor of the ham, and it has the texture of caviar. It makes a delightful, fun garnish for this classic bread soup. Regular ham bones can be substituted for the Serrano ham bones.

SERVES 8 AS A FIRST COURSE, 16 AS A TAPA

For the soup
1 pound Serrano ham bones

2½ quarts (2½ liters) water

1¼ teaspoons salt, or as needed

¼ cup plus 1 tablespoon extra virgin olive oil, divided use

4 cups day-old baguette, cut into ½-inch (1 cm) dice

2 teaspoons minced garlic

1 teaspoon paprika

For the ham caviar
2 tablespoons fine tapioca pearls

2 teaspoons Paprika Oil (page 233)

3 tablespoons finely chopped Serrano ham

1 tablespoon chopped chives

1. **Make** the soup. Combine the ham bones and water in a medium stockpot and bring to a boil over high heat. Reduce the heat to medium low, cover partially, and simmer for 2 hours or until the meat is fork tender, skimming often. Remove from the heat and strain through a fine strainer. Season to taste with the salt and set aside.

2. **Heat** ¼ cup of the oil in a large, heavy soup pot or Dutch oven over medium heat and add the bread. Cook, stirring often, until lightly browned, 7 to 9 minutes. Meanwhile, heat 1 tablespoon of oil in a small skillet, add the garlic, and cook until it is fragrant, about 30 seconds, stirring often. Stir in the paprika, cook for 30 seconds more, and remove from the heat. When the bread is lightly browned, add the garlic and paprika to the pan and stir well. Continue to cook for 1 minute, stirring frequently.

3. **Add** 4 cups of the ham bone stock and bring to a simmer over medium-high heat. Reduce the heat to medium low and cover and simmer for 30 minutes. Remove from the heat and purée in two batches in a food processor fitted with the steel blade. Thin with 1 to 1½ cups of stock as needed to achieve a cream soup consistency. Return the soup to the pot and keep warm until ready to serve.

4. **Prepare** the ham "caviar." Bring 2 cups of the ham stock to a boil over medium-high heat in a small pot. Add the tapioca and boil for 25 to 30 minutes, or until the tapioca pearls are tender and clear. Add hot water as needed to maintain about 2 cups of liquid in the pot throughout the cooking time. Once the tapioca is cooked, drain well with a strainer, and rinse with cool water to stop the cooking. Set aside or refrigerate until ready to use. If the tapioca sticks together, rinse and drain briefly before using, stirring to separate any pearls that have clumped together.

5. **Spoon** the soup into glasses or bowls. Top with about 2 teaspoons of the ham-flavored tapioca, about ¼ teaspoon of paprika oil, about a teaspoon of chopped Serrano ham, and about ¾ teaspoon of chives.

Adapted from a recipe by JESÚS RAMIRO

ROSH HASHANAH
SEVEN VEGETABLE SOUP

THIS IS A TRADITIONAL JEWISH SOUP from Morocco, but it is very much like an Andalusian soup called *olla gitana*, or "gypsy stew," which uses pears instead of quince. The "gypsy" title was probably added as a cover, after the Jews had left Spain and the recipe remained in the culinary pipeline. Today in Spain they add ham to flavor the stock, but in pre-Inquisition days the soup was most likely made with beef. You may add diced cooked brisket to the basic vegetable soup for a more filling soup.

SERVES 8

⅔ cup chickpeas, soaked overnight and drained

5 cups chopped onions

6 cups beef broth or vegetable stock

8 cups large-dice peeled butternut squash

1 turnip or rutabaga, cut into wedges about ¼ inch by 1 inch (5 mm by 2.5 cm) thick

1 teaspoon ground cumin

½ teaspoon ground cinnamon

2½ teaspoons salt, or more as needed

3 medium zucchini, diced small

2 cups large-dice apples, quinces, or pears

1 bunch Swiss chard, greens only, cut into ½-inch (1 cm) strips (6 cups)

1 teaspoon freshly ground black pepper

2 tablespoons sugar

1. **Combine** the chickpeas, onions, and beef broth or vegetable stock in a large stockpot and bring to a boil over medium-high heat. Reduce the heat to low and simmer until the chickpeas are just tender, about 1 hour 15 minutes.

2. **Stir** in the butternut squash and turnip or rutabaga with the cumin, cinnamon, and 2 teaspoons of the salt and simmer until almost tender, about 10 minutes. Stir in the zucchini and apples, quinces, or pears and simmer for 5 more minutes, or until almost tender. Stir in the chard and simmer for another 5 minutes, or until the chard is tender.

3. **Season** with ½ teaspoon of salt, the pepper, and sugar, more or less to taste, and serve.

Adapted from a recipe by JOYCE GOLDSTEIN

ANDALUSIA

MANY OF THE THINGS WE ASSOCIATE WITH SPAIN—flamenco, bullfighting, sherry, gazpacho—have their origins in Andalusia, the vast southernmost region that stretches from the Mediterranean coast across the tip of the Iberian peninsula to the Atlantic. Its name is derived from *Al Andaluz*, the name that was given to Spain by its Moorish occupiers. It is a breathtakingly beautiful region of red earth and olive groves, of whitewashed villages and Moorish architectural masterpieces such as the Alhambra in Granada, the Mezquita or great mosque of Córdoba, and the Alcazar in Seville.

◄◄ **Gazpacho**, the most famous Spanish soup, originated in Andalusia. There are several different varieties, including white gazpacho which contains no tomatoes.

◄ **Fried foods** are popular in this region. At the Worlds of Flavor conference, small anchovies were deep-fried with impressive results.

▶ **Olive groves** stretch as far as the eye can see. Andalusia is the largest olive-producing region in the world.

THE MOORISH INFLUENCE

Walk down the narrow streets of cities such as Seville and Cádiz and behind wooden doors you'll find magical tiled courtyards with fountains, arched porticos, and lush gardens—all reminders of the presence of the Moors many centuries ago. But the Moors left more than their architecture behind when they were expelled from Spain in the 15th century. Signature dishes such as the little Spanish meatballs known as *albóndigas* (from the Arabic *al-bunduq*, meaning hazelnut, the size they are meant to be) are vestiges of the Muslim era. They evolved as a way to stretch meat with breadcrumbs. The famous white gazpacho of Granada, made with almonds, bread, and garlic, is another legacy of the Moors. There are countless others, such as the famous ratatouille-like eggplant and vegetable ragout called *albornía*; eggplant balls with cheese; and squash stuffed with a filling that includes raisins, green olives, and meat.

NECESSITY BREEDS INVENTION

As rich as it has been culturally, Andalusia has always been one of Spain's poorest regions. The great Andalusian dishes are simple ones, whose success is a function of the quality of the few ingredients that go into them. This is where cooks took stale bread and water, and with garlic, vinegar, olive oil, and eventually what became the most important ingredient, tomatoes, fashioned the refreshing concoction we know as gazpacho.

WHO SAID THE FRENCH INVENTED FRIES?

There is an old Spanish saying that the north stews, the center roasts, and the south fries. Andalusian cooks are renowned for their fried foods—it's said that "an Andalusian housewife can deep-fry the sea spray." This being the largest olive-producing region in the world, it comes as no surprise that they use extra virgin olive oil to do it. Miguel Palomo, chef-owner of the bar-restaurant Sanlúcar La Mayor in Seville, is emphatic about the quality of the oil and seafood he uses for his highly regarded fried fish. "The fish I use on Wednesday must come off the boat on Tuesday night and be cleaned as soon as it reaches the restaurant. The olive oil must be the best virgin olive oil from Jaén (the center of Spain's olive-growing industry), an oil that is also good for salads and for roasting peppers. We use a special flour (a fine semolina) milled in Seville to coat the fish, and we always use a deep fryer with a thermostat so that we can control the temperature."

ANDALUSIAN WINES

The wines produced in Andalusia go effortlessly with that fried food, cutting through the richness with cooling, mineral flavors. The sherries of Jerez are the most famous. Dry Fino and Manzanilla sherries pair beautifully with fried fish, as well as with the many other tapas they traditionally accompany. In fact, it is widely believed that the tapas tradition originated in Andalusia; people needed food to accompany the strong fortified wines.

As in other Mediterranean regions, the cooking of inland Andalusia differs from the coastal cuisine. It's heartier, earthier fare; as in other inland regions of Spain, you will find many bean and meat stews here. Chickpeas (the Spanish call them garbanzos) are particularly popular; they're cooked with tripe; with chorizo sausage; with greens; and with slab bacon or cured ham.

REGIONAL CHARACTERISTICS

The region has many protected products, including fine cured Jamón de Trevélez from Grenada, and Los Pedroches and Jamón de Huelva, both hams made from Iberian pigs. Cured ham is a typical garnish for salmorejo, a thick gazpacho made in Córdoba.

The people of Andalusia, the Andalusí, love to combine sweet with salty and savory flavors, another legacy of the Moors, and so on summer menus all over the region it is common to find sweet, juicy green melon served with salty cured ham.

The Arabs had a fondness for sweets, whose production was taken up by nuns in convents throughout the region after the Moors were expelled from Spain in the 15th century. They are unspeakably rich, sugary confections made with lots of egg yolks—the word for the confections and for egg yolks is one and the same, *yemas*. You'll also find fried pastries (*pestiños*) dripping with honey and coated in sesame seeds. The variety of pastries is impressive, as each convent has its own specialty. Commercial pastry making is a small industry in over 200 convents in Spain, and many of them are in Andalusia.

The Andalusí are known for their gaiety and passion. They enjoy life with an attitude and character that is much more devil-may-care than that of their more cerebral northern neighbors. Their cuisine is a reflection of this character—simple and straightforward, with big, easy-to-understand flavors that are also easy to love.

SALADS AND VEGETABLES

SALADS AND VEGETABLES

Fresh, seasonal produce

Travelers to Spain often find themselves hungry for salads and vegetables. If they have trouble finding these items, it's probably because they're looking in the wrong places—on restaurant menus. There is no shortage of salads and vegetable dishes in Spain—you can tell that just by peering down the colorful aisles of any produce market—but you need to go to a tapas bar (or a home) to find them.

Ensaladilla Rusa, the classic boiled vegetable and mayonnaise salad, can be found in most tapas bars in Spain. Variations abound, depending on the vegetables available.

SOME TYPICAL VEGETABLE DISHES

Go to a tapas bar in any Spanish city and you're likely to find the ubiquitous Ensaladilla Rusa (pages 94–95), a potato, vegetable, and tuna salad bound with mayonnaise; and vegetable dishes such as Garlic Potatoes, or *patatas al ajillo* (page 98), and Tortilla Española (pages 42–43). If you're in Andalusia you will no doubt stumble across the Andalusian version of potato salad called *papas aliñas*, and a marinated roasted pepper salad called *pimientos aliñados* in this region and *zorongollo* in others. *Cojongo*, a chopped vegetable and bread salad that resembles an unpuréed gazpacho, is a standard tapa in Extremadura.

This is not to say that Spanish restaurant chefs have nothing to offer when it comes to fresh vegetables. Most menus have an *ensalada mixta*, and although this can be insipid, if it happens to be summer you will not go wrong with a simple mix of quartered hearts of leaf or romaine lettuce and ripe tomatoes, dressed with nothing more than extra virgin olive oil, sherry vinegar, and sea salt. Catalonia's version of *salade*

Niçoise is called *xató*, and given the amazing quality of the Spanish tuna canned in olive oil, and the abundance of it, this salad is in a league of its own. The "dressing" is a tangy romesco sauce, a textured mix of roasted sweet and hot peppers and tomatoes, almonds and/or hazelnuts, toasted bread and olive oil, vinegar and garlic. The romesco clings to the salad greens (usually sturdy greens such as frisée) and other ingredients (tuna, anchovies, desalted salt cod, olives). The salad is eaten as a first course or as a main dish.

There are festivals planned around vegetables throughout Spain. South of Barcelona in the Penedes area, there is a *xató* festival at Carnival time called the *Xatonada*. One of the great rituals in Catalonia is the *Calçotada*, a feast of grilled calçots, exceedingly tender green onions that are planted in the spring, harvested in August, then replanted deep in the soil so that they produce five to six tender white shoots. These are harvested and grilled on large frames set over burning vines until they turn black on the outside. They are then wrapped in newspaper so that they continue to steam until very tender (twice harvested, twice cooked). They're traditionally served on terra-cotta roof tiles. Only the inner heart, squeezed from the charred outer layers, is eaten, with plenty of romesco sauce. Some say the whole exercise is merely an excuse to eat lots of romesco sauce.

NEW DIRECTIONS
Salads and vegetables are finding their way onto the menus of contemporary restaurants. Chef Joaquín Felípe of the Europa Decó

Calçots, or Spanish green onions, are placed on metal frames and blackened over a high flame.

Fish Tartare with Tomato and Crushed Potato—this innovative salad was created by Catalonia-based chef Nando Jubany and is typical of the new direction that Spanish food is taking.

restaurant at the Urban Hotel in Madrid builds a napoleon with paper-thin layers of tuna carpaccio and potato (pages 108–109), setting it atop a salad of seaweed and edamame topped with a delicate white asparagus dressing. Chef Nando Jubany has created a fish tartare and vegetable tower (pages 110–111). Tuna tartare has also arrived in Spain. Here it is prepared with Japanese influences by Kiyomi Mikuni (pages 112–113). Enrique Martínez of El Hotel Restaurante Maher in the Navarra region of Spain, the center of the country's piquillo pepper production, reduces the juice from roasted peppers and with the help of sugar, pectin, and a thermomix creates an intense membrillo-like pepper paste that he serves with curdled sheep's milk, a modernist version of the classic Spanish combination of sheep's milk cheese with membrillo.

The new wave chefs of Spain are fascinated by vegetables. They cook them in vacuum packs and use their juices to make vitamin-rich broths that they serve as appetizers. They turn them into ethereal foams, serving, for example, a white asparagus foam with a poached egg, asparagus, and truffle oil. They turn them inside out, reducing them to purées, then transforming them into liquid spheres. The great Ferran Adrià himself pinpoints one dish that symbolizes his philosophical quest for the new and different, his commitment to creating dishes that are never a copy of something that has come before. That dish is a *menestra de verduras*, a mix of vegetables, each one with a different texture and presentation, but each one an expression of itself.

JAMÓN AND ARUGULA SALAD
WITH CABRALES AND HAZELNUT VINAIGRETTE

BLUE CHEESE, SALAD GREENS, AND BACON are a classic salad combination. This one is a particularly Spanish rendition, with the famous pungent Cabrales standing in for the blue cheese, and Serrano ham standing in for the bacon. Hazelnuts are used almost as much as almonds in Spanish cooking. Here hazelnut paste forms the base for a rich salad dressing that pairs nicely with the other ingredients, and chopped toasted hazelnuts make a crunchy, nutty garnish.

SERVES 8

¼ cup hazelnut paste

2 tablespoons champagne vinegar

½ teaspoon minced shallots

½ cup grapeseed oil

½ teaspoon kosher salt

Large pinch freshly ground black pepper

8 cups arugula, cleaned, washed, and patted dry (1 large bunch)

8 slices Serrano ham (about 7 ounces or 200 g)

½ cup crumbled Cabrales

½ cup finely chopped toasted hazelnuts

1. Make the dressing. Place the hazelnut paste in a small mixing bowl and whisk in the vinegar and shallots. Slowly whisk in the oil and season with the salt and pepper.

2. Toss the arugula with ¼ cup of the dressing. Place a slice of ham on each plate and place about 1 cup of the greens on top. Garnish each plate with 1 tablespoon of the cheese and 1 tablespoon of the chopped toasted hazelnuts.

Adapted from a recipe by VICTOR SCARGLE

ENSALADILLA RUSA

THIS CLASSIC COOKED VEGETABLE salad is bound with mayonnaise, and can really be only as good as the mayonnaise you use. That's why it's important here that it be homemade. The quality of the tuna is also very important as it lends a lot of flavor to this dish.

SERVES 8

2 to 3 medium red potatoes, scrubbed and peeled (about 1 pound or 450 g)

2 medium carrots, peeled

1 cup fresh or thawed frozen peas

¼ cup chopped flat-leaf parsley, plus a few sprigs to garnish

1½ cups small-dice, hard-cooked eggs

¼ teaspoon salt

¼ teaspoon freshly ground black pepper

1½ cups Mayonesa (page 225)

1¾ cups loosely packed olive oil-packed canned tuna, drained (about 2 cans)

1. Bring 8 cups of salted water to a boil in a medium saucepan over medium-high heat. Add the potatoes and carrots and bring back to a gentle boil. Remove the carrots when just tender, after about 15 minutes. Cook the potatoes 10 to 15 minutes longer, or until just tender. If using fresh peas, bring 2 cups of salted water to a boil in a small saucepan and cook until just tender, 5 to 10 minutes. If using frozen peas, cook according to the package instructions.

2. Drain the vegetables and let cool to room temperature on a plate or cookie sheet. Cut the potatoes and carrots into ½-inch (1 cm) dice.

3. Toss the potatoes and carrots with the peas, parsley, and diced eggs in a large bowl. Season with the salt and pepper. Fold in the mayonnaise and adjust seasoning to taste. Fold in the tuna and serve.

Adapted from a recipe by JOSÉ ANDRÉS

SPAIN'S VEGETABLE KITCHEN

IF YOU HAVE ONLY EATEN IN TRADITIONAL SPANISH RESTAURANTS, you may wonder how far the Spanish vegetable repertoire goes beyond the tortillas Españolas, gazpachos, and red peppers that you see on menus everywhere. But one visit to a central market in any Spanish city will change this notion. Here you'll find crates packed to bursting with squash and beans, greens and herbs, eggplants and tomatoes, cauliflowers and radishes, lettuces, spring onions, potatoes, mushrooms, and asparagus, and there will be no doubt in your mind that Spain has a vibrant vegetable kitchen that is at the center of every home cook's repertoire.

THE HUERTAS

Intense vegetable and fruit cultivation in Spain is a legacy of the Arabs, who brought significant agricultural advances to the country. They established vast systems of irrigated vegetable gardens called *huertas*, which still exist today, particularly in the regions of Murcia and El Levante, but in all the other regions as well. There is a whole family of dishes in Spain called *hortalizas*, made with vegetables harvested from the *huertas*. Eggplants, spinach, winter squash, artichokes, cabbages, onions, garlic, asparagus, and fava beans were all cultivated by the Arabs. Some of the vegetables that we most associate with Spanish cooking—tomatoes, peppers, potatoes, lima beans—entered *huerta* production later, in the post-Columbian era. These foods were native to the Americas, and it took decades for them to be accepted as viable foods in Spain, unbelievable as this may seem now.

REGIONAL VEGETABLE DISHES

Several of Spain's favorite regional vegetable dishes are classic Mediterranean ragouts or medleys made with eggplants, onions, peppers, tomatoes, and squash simmered slowly in olive oil. In Andalusia, this dish, seasoned generously with paprika, is called *alboronía*. In Mallorca, the vegetables are layered and potatoes are added to the mix. The preparation, called *tumbet*, is Mallorca's most famous dish. Each vegetable is cooked separately, then layered and baked in a casserole with an intense tomato sauce. The Catalan vegetable medley, *escalivada*, is made with the same mix of vegetables, but they are roasted first. The Catalans also make *samfaina*, using the same vegetables and abundant olive oil in a ragout that is cooked down to an almost jamlike consistency and used as much as a sauce—with chicken, rabbit, and fish—as it is as a vegetable dish. In La Mancha, zucchini, onions, peppers, and tomatoes are cooked together in a dish called *pisto manchego*, which sometimes contains potatoes and bacon, and is traditionally served with eggs and/or chorizo. There are many recipes for pisto; zucchini, tomatoes, garlic, and onions are the common denominator.

Greens, particularly spinach and chard, are much loved in Spain, as they are throughout the Mediterranean. The Catalans claim the famous mixture of spinach, pine nuts, and raisins as their own, though you can find this dish all along the Mediterranean coast, from Spain to Italy.

One of Spain's most highly regarded vegetables is the piquillo pepper, a small, thin-skinned, intensely sweet red pepper that is grown in the north, in the Navarra region. Every September the air in this region is fragrant with the aroma of roasting peppers, as a huge percentage of the crop is grilled right in the fields immediately after being harvested. Canned Spanish piquillo peppers are high quality and increasingly available abroad. In restaurants, the peppers are roasted in the oven with a little olive oil. You'll find them on menus, tossed with tomatoes, sherry vinegar, and olive oil in a salad called *zorongollo* or *pimientos aliñados*. Other typical preparations include roasted peppers with anchovies, roasted peppers sautéed with garlic and served as a side dish with meat or poached eggs, and stuffed roasted peppers.

INNOVATIVE APPROACHES TO VEGETABLES

Spain's famous contemporary chefs revere vegetables. They link them to both the landscape and the culture of their country, and many grow the produce they use in their restaurants. "We are trying to reconcile ourselves with our landscape," says San Sebastián–based chef Andoni Luis Aduriz. He takes vegetables and herbs from his garden and cooks each one in a specific way, some with steam, some vacuum packed; winter squash is cooked in brown butter, whereas a wild mushroom is cooked in olive oil.

Navarra-based chef Enrique Martínez also grows his own produce and employs different cooking techniques for different vegetables. He uses condensation to unite vegetables, herbs, and purified water in nutritious, flavorful vegetable broths that he serves as an appetizer.

These intricate, often minimalist, restaurant creations are a far cry from the traditional rustic dishes. Yet they too express a deep respect and understanding of the wonderful vegetables that Spain produces.

GARLIC POTATOES

PATATAS AL AJILLO is one of Spain's most beloved vegetable dishes. Serve these as a tapa or as a side dish with meat or fish. Be sure to use thin-skinned potatoes or the final texture will not be the same.

SERVES 8

6 medium thin-skinned white potatoes, preferably Kennebec, scrubbed and cut into 1-inch (2.5 cm) cubes

4 teaspoons salt, divided use

3 tablespoons sunflower or canola oil

½ cup finely sliced garlic

6 tablespoons extra virgin olive oil

¾ teaspoon crushed red pepper

2 tablespoons chopped flat-leaf parsley

¾ teaspoon freshly ground black pepper

8 cups canola oil, or enough to fill the pan 3 inches (7 cm) deep

1. Place the potatoes, 6 quarts (6 liters) of cold water, and 2 teaspoons of salt in an large saucepan. Bring to a boil over high heat, reduce the heat to medium low, and simmer for 12 to 15 minutes, or until about half cooked—just tender but still very firm.

2. Heat the sunflower or canola oil over medium heat in a medium sauté pan and add the garlic. Cook the garlic, stirring, until it just begins to brown, 2 to 3 minutes. Remove from the heat and immediately add the olive oil, red pepper, parsley, pepper, and 1½ teaspoons of the salt. Stir together and keep in a warm oven or on very low heat, taking care not to cook the garlic any further.

3. Heat 3 inches (7 cm) of oil over medium-high heat in a deep, medium-size skillet to 350°F (175°C). Fry the potatoes until golden brown and crisp, 13 to 15 minutes. Remove from the heat, drain on a rack, then place in a mixing bowl. Stir in the remaining ½ teaspoon salt. Finally, add the garlic sauce and gently toss together. Serve immediately.

Adapted from a recipe by DANIEL OLIVELLA

POTATOES FROM THE BAKERY

BEFORE OVENS WERE STANDARD in home kitchens, it was common for people to take dishes like this potato gratin to the local bakery. Once the day's bread was baked, bakers would slide gratins and pies into their still-hot ovens, where they would bake and then be ready in time for the afternoon meal. This potato gratin is a simple one, without cheese or milk. The potatoes are thinly sliced and layered with onions in a gratin dish, and seasoned with salt and pepper, and various other herbs and spices. Finally, they're moistened with beef or veal stock, and all of these flavorful ingredients are absorbed by the potatoes as they bake.

SERVES 8

6 large Russet potatoes, peeled and sliced ¼ inch (5 mm) thick

2½ cups very thinly sliced onions

1 tablespoon salt, divided use

1½ teaspoons freshly ground black pepper, divided use

¼ cup extra virgin olive oil

½ cup (1 stick) butter, melted

4 large garlic cloves, slivered

1 bay leaf

¾ teaspoon crushed dried thyme

1 teaspoon sweet paprika

1¼ cups beef or veal stock

1. Preheat the oven to 375°F (190°C). Oil a 3-quart (3 liter) baking dish. Layer the potatoes and onions in four layers in the dish. Season each layer with ½ teaspoon of salt and ¼ teaspoon of pepper.

2. Stir together the oil and melted butter with the garlic, bay leaf, thyme, paprika, and 1 teaspoon salt and ½ teaspoon pepper. Drizzle evenly over the potatoes.

3. Pour the stock slowly down the side of the dish so it does not disturb the seasoning.

4. Cover with foil and bake for 60 to 75 minutes in the preheated oven, or until the potatoes are tender when pierced with a fork. For a crisp top, remove the foil after 50 minutes and bake uncovered for the last 20 to 25 minutes, or until lightly browned. Serve hot or warm.

Adapted from a recipe by DANIEL OLIVELLA

POTATOES LA RIOJA STYLE

THIS SAUCY POTATO DISH is served as a first course. La Rioja cooks say you shouldn't cut the potatoes with a knife, but rather cut them slightly, then break them into pieces. This is supposedly because the rough broken surface releases more potato starch, which is what thickens the cooking liquid.

SERVES 8

1 pound 14 ounces (850 g) Russet potatoes, peeled (7 to 8)

3 tablespoons extra virgin olive oil

1½ cups chopped onions

1 small green pepper, diced small

¾ teaspoon pimentón

1 bay leaf

1½ teaspoons salt, divided use

1 cup water

8 ounces (225 g) soft Spanish chorizo, cut into 8 pieces

1. Cut the potatoes by inserting the tip of the knife at one end of a potato and then carefully using it as a wedge to break off roughly 1½-inch (4 cm) pieces.

2. Heat the oil in a 12-inch (30 cm) earthenware cazuela or a large, heavy nonstick skillet over medium heat. Add the onions and cook until softened, about 5 minutes. Add the potatoes and cook, stirring and turning them in the oil, for another 5 minutes, or until they're hot and beginning to soften.

3. Add the green pepper, pimentón, bay leaf, ¾ teaspoon of the salt, and the water. Bring to a boil, lower the heat to medium-low or low heat, and cook the potatoes at a gentle simmer for 10 minutes.

4. Add the chorizo and continue to cook, stirring occasionally, for another 25 minutes, or until the potatoes are tender. Taste and adjust seasoning with ¾ teaspoon of salt, or more or less to taste. Remove from the heat and let stand for 10 minutes. The liquid in the pan should have thickened to a sauce consistency.

Adapted from a recipe by JANET MENDEL

POTATOES

IT TOOK MORE THAN A HUNDRED YEARS for the potato to be accepted as a food after it was brought to Spain from the New World in 1569–1570. A native of the Andes, the knobby tuber was considered more of a curiosity than a viable food, shunned partly because it is in the nightshade family. But once it was discovered to be rich in calories and nutrients, and easily grown in rocky soil, the potato began to catch on. By the end of the 17th century, potatoes were being used extensively in Spain and in Naples, which was then under the rule of the Spanish Bourbons. Today, Spain rivals Ireland in its reverence for this vegetable. Potatoes are fried and baked, stewed, and boiled. They are served as tapas, side dishes, soups, and hearty meals. They are at the heart of the country's national dish, the *tortilla Española*, or Spanish potato omelet.

Some potato dishes are eaten throughout Spain, others are regional. Galicia is particularly well known for its potatoes—is it a coincidence that this is the heart of Celtic Spain? The Canary Islands, which are the stopping off point between Spain and the New World, are also famed for their potatoes. Many of the dishes listed here have evocative names that refer to their humble nature, while others denote their region of origin.

SPAIN'S FAVORITE POTATO DISHES

Tortilla Española (pages 42–43): Not just Spain's favorite potato dish, her favorite dish altogether. A flat omelet filled with a generous quantity of sliced potatoes cooked in copious amounts of olive oil with onion and a little chorizo and/or Serrano ham, there is probably not a tapas bar in Spain that does not offer tortilla Española. When friends decide to go out, they often make a date by saying, "Let's go out to nibble on some tortilla."

Patatas fritas: Literally "fried potatoes," these are a standard side dish throughout the country and are Spain's answer to the French fry. But these are fried in olive oil.

Patatas pobres: Known as "poor man's potatoes," this is a simple dish of sliced potatoes cooked in olive oil and seasoned with salt, garlic, and parsley. Eggs can be broken over the finished potatoes to transform the dish into a meal.

Patatas bravas: The name means "fierce potatoes." These fried potatoes with a spicy tomato sauce are a favorite in Madrid tapas bars.

Patatas picantes: Another fried potato dish with a spicy tomato sauce, this dish is served with an added garlicky layer of allioli.

Patatas panaderas (page 104): A sliced potato gratin that was traditionally baked in the bread oven of the local bakery, after the bread was finished; sometimes served with allioli.

Patatas al ajillo: Potatoes fried with garlic and parsley. The potatoes are usually parboiled before being cooked with garlic in olive oil.

Patatas a la Riojana: A potato stew in which the potatoes are cut into chunks and stewed with onions, peppers, garlic, and chorizo.

Papas arrugadas: Literally "wrinkled potatoes," these are a specialty of the Canary Islands. The potatoes are cooked, unpeeled, in heavily salted water (traditionally it was seawater) until dried and the skins are wrinkly. This dish is always served with a spicy sauce (mojo) made with pounded chiles, herbs, cumin, and vinegar.

Patatas en salsa verde: A Basque specialty, this saucy dish is served as a first course or lunch. Parsley gives the sauce its green color.

Patatas viudas: This translates as "widowed potatoes." It is a simple potage of potatoes, onions, olive oil, and garlic.

Patatas revolconas: Mashed potatoes with smoked sweet Spanish paprika (pimentón), olive oil, onions, and garlic. A specialty of Extremadura and Castile.

Trinxat de la Cerdanya: A potato and kale cake that is a specialty of the Catalan Pyrenees.

Marmitako (page 145): A Basque fisherman's stew of potatoes, tuna, and olive oil.

Atascaburras: From La Mancha, a purée of potatoes, salt cod, olive oil, and garlic, garnished with chopped walnuts.

Patatas cazuela en ajopollo: A specialty of Andalusia, potatoes are cooked in an earthenware casserole with ground almonds, garlic, olive oil, and saffron.

Zorongollo: The word refers to a mixture of roasted peppers and tomatoes, here combined with sautéed potato slices and served warm or at room temperature. A specialty of Extremadura.

Patatas con judías verdes: In this potato and green bean dish, the potatoes are cut into chunks and boiled, then when they are nearly done, the beans are added. They're cooked together until the potatoes begin to fall apart. In Extremadura, the potatoes and green beans are cooked slowly in olive oil in a covered pot with onions, tomatoes, green peppers, garlic, and a bay leaf until the vegetables are tender.

PATATAS PANADERAS

SIMPLE AND DELICIOUS, these moist potatoes can be eaten as a tapa or as an accompaniment to meat, fish, or poultry dishes. There is no added butter or stock here, just potatoes, garlic, olive oil, and seasonings, tossed together in a baking dish, covered tightly, and baked—traditionally in the baker's oven after the bread was done. Be sure to use Yukon gold potatoes as they retain their moisture when baked.

SERVES 8

2 pounds (900 g) Yukon gold potatoes, peeled and sliced
⅛ inch (3 mm) thick

2 tablespoons plus 2 teaspoons extra virgin olive oil, divided use

2 tablespoons sliced garlic

1 tablespoon salt

1½ teaspoons freshly ground black pepper

2 tablespoons coarsely chopped flat-leaf parsley

2 tablespoons sliced chives

1. Preheat the oven to 475°F (245°C).

2. Mix the potatoes, 2 tablespoons of the oil, and the garlic, salt, and pepper in an 11- by 7- by 2-inch (28 by 18 by 5 cm) casserole dish or roasting pan. Cover with aluminum foil and bake for 35 minutes, or until fork tender. Remove the foil and roast the potatoes until they are golden, about 3 to 5 minutes.

3. Drizzle 2 teaspoons of oil over the roasted potatoes, sprinkle with the herbs, and serve.

Recipe by THE CULINARY INSTITUTE OF AMERICA

PIPERADA

A STANDARD BASQUE PREPARATION, piperada is made with the sweet peppers of the region, sometimes with a mixture of sweet and slightly hot peppers, tomatoes, garlic, and often onions. It's used as a sauce for fish or chicken, or as the base of a delicious egg dish that also includes Serrano ham, in which the eggs are added to the cooked peppers just before serving and stirred just until set. This simpler version of piperada may be eaten alone or piled onto slices of toasted bread.

SERVES 8

3 red bell peppers

¼ cup extra virgin olive oil

1¼ cups small-dice Spanish onions

3 tablespoons sliced garlic

2 cups finely chopped plum tomatoes, fresh or canned

Small pinch sweet pimentón

1 bay leaf

½ teaspoon sugar

1 tablespoon salt

1. Roast the whole peppers in a 375°F (190°C) oven until they are tender, about 30 minutes.

2. Place the peppers in a stainless steel bowl and cover with plastic wrap. Steam them for 2 to 3 minutes, then peel and seed them. Cut the pepper into ¼-inch (5 mm) strips. Strain the juices, then reserve the peppers in the juices.

3. Heat the oil in a large sauté pan over medium heat and cook the onions until translucent, about 4 minutes. Add the garlic and sauté until the vegetables are fully cooked and their juices rendered, about 2 minutes.

4. Stir in the tomatoes, pimentón, the peppers and their juices, the bay leaf, sugar, and salt. Bring to a boil over medium-high heat, then simmer over low heat. Simmer for 15 minutes, or until a thick and creamy consistency is reached.

Recipe by THE CULINARY INSTITUTE OF AMERICA

MINI-ESCALIVADA
WITH ROMESCO SAUCE

Escalivar means to cook in hot ashes. An *escalivada* can resemble a ratatouille, except the vegetables are first grilled before being simmered together; or it can be simply a feast of grilled vegetables, here served with a classic romesco sauce. If you can't find Ibérico lard, use Serrano lard or slab bacon instead.

SERVES 8 GENEROUSLY

2½ teaspoons salt, divided use

8 baby potatoes, halved (about 14 ounces or 400 g)

10 tablespoons extra virgin olive oil, divided use

8 baby artichokes, trimmed, cut in half, choke removed (about 1 pound or 450 g)

1 lemon, halved

8 baby zucchini, with flowers cut in half lengthwise (about 6 ounces or 170 g)

8 small onions, peeled, halved, and wrapped in foil (about 1 pound 13 ounces or 825 g)

8 baby eggplants (about 11 ounces or 310 g)

24 spring onions (about 2 pounds 12 ounces or 1.25 kg)

24 green or white asparagus stalks, trimmed (about 1 pound 4 ounces or 570 g)

8 miniature red peppers (about 6 ounces or 170 g)

8 miniature green peppers (about 6 ounces or 170 g)

40 green beans (about 10 ounces or 285 g)

32 wild mushrooms (about 12 ounces or 340 g)

1 teaspoon freshly ground black pepper

8 slices Ibérico or Serrano lard, or slab bacon

2½ cups Romesco (page 222)

1. Bring 2 quarts (2 liters) of water and ½ teaspoon of salt to a boil over high heat. Drop the potatoes into the boiling water and boil until a paring knife slips in and out of a potato easily, about 10 minutes. Drain, pat dry with paper towels, and brush with 2 tablespoons of oil.

2. Prepare the artichokes. Fill a bowl with 4 cups of water and squeeze the juice of the lemon into it. Cut the top ½ inch (about 1 cm) off each artichoke and remove the fibrous outer leaves until you reach the inner lighter leaves. Use a paring knife to peel the dark green skin from the base and stem of each artichoke. Slice each in half and drop into the lemon water until ready to cook.

3. Make the escalivada. Prepare a medium-hot grill. Drain the artichokes. Brush all the vegetables with ½ cup of olive oil and sprinkle with 2 teaspoons of salt and 1 teaspoon of pepper. Wrap the zucchini in foil to protect the flowers from the heat. Grill the vegetables (turning them regularly until charred and tender and removing them as they finish cooking), in the following order: the foil-wrapped onions for 20 minutes, the artichokes for 10 minutes, the eggplants, potatoes, and spring onions for 8 minutes, and the asparagus, zucchini, miniature red and green peppers, green beans, and mushrooms for 5 minutes.

4. Cook the lard slices in a medium-size skillet over medium heat until light golden brown, 4 to 5 minutes per side. Drain on paper towels; the slices will crisp as they cool. Serve the grilled vegetables with the lard on top and serve the romesco sauce over the top or on the side.

Adapted from a recipe by Nando Jubany

SEAWEED AND TUNA TORO
SALAD

CHEF JOAQUÍN FELÍPE of the Europa Decó restaurant at the Urban Hotel in Madrid garnishes his wonderful rendition of tuna carpaccio with a cooked ostrich egg. Since this might be a difficult ingredient for home chefs to find, it's optional here but we substituted four medium-boiled hen eggs instead. Tosaka seaweed was used as a bed for the salad in the original recipe, but you can use the more readily available kombu, dulse, or laver seaweeds instead.

SERVES 8

½ cup dried kombu, dulse, or laver seaweed

1¼ teaspoons salt, divided use

¾ cup green soybeans (edamame)

2 tablespoons extra virgin olive oil, divided use

2 pounds (900 g) Yukon gold potatoes, peeled and diced small

¼ teaspoon freshly ground black pepper, divided use

One 11.6–ounce (340 g) can white asparagus

1½ teaspoons wasabi paste

13 ounces (370 g) red tuna toro, belly cut or sushi-grade tuna

Extra virgin olive oil, as needed

2½ tablespoons high-quality caviar

4 medium-cooked egg yolks (optional)

1. Rehydrate the dried seaweed: Measure it into a nonreactive mixing bowl, then add 7 cups of water. Soak for 10 minutes, then drain well and dry on paper towels.

2. Bring 2 cups of water and ½ teaspoon of salt to a boil in a small saucepan over high heat and add the soybeans. Boil for 8 to 10 minutes, or until the beans are just tender, then transfer to a bowl of ice water. Shell the beans and set aside.

3. Heat 1 tablespoon of oil over medium heat in a large, wide heavy skillet and add the potatoes. Cook gently until tender and nicely browned, about 15 minutes. Remove from the heat with a slotted spoon and set aside. Season to taste with a pinch each of salt and pepper.

4. Purée the asparagus on medium-high speed with the wasabi paste and a tablespoon of oil in a blender until smooth, about 1 minute. Add ½ teaspoon of salt, or more or less to taste.

5. Place the toro in the freezer for 30 minutes to facilitate slicing. Thinly slice with a very sharp knife into about 24 slices. Season with ¼ teaspoon of salt and a pinch of pepper. Place on parchment paper, with a little oil between each slice.

6. Make 8 toro-potato "napoleons" by sandwiching 2 tablespoons of the potatoes between 3 layers of toro for each of 8 "napoleons." When all of the toro has been used up, toss any remaining potatoes with the seaweed and soybeans. Place 2 tablespoons of the seaweed/soybean mixture on each plate, place a toro-potato napoleon on top, and dress each with ¼ cup of the asparagus sauce. Top each with 1 teaspoon of caviar and 1 teaspoon of the crumbled egg yolk, if using.

Adapted from a recipe by JOAQUÍN FELÍPE

FISH TARTARE
WITH TOMATO AND CRUSHED POTATO

SPANISH COOKS, and especially those from Catalonia, love to combine products of the earth and sea. Nando Jubany, chef/owner of the Michelin-starred Can Jubany in Vic, Catalonia, specializes in preparing local ingredients in a contemporary Catalan way. This seafood appetizer, in which humble crushed potatoes, dressed simply with olive oil and coarse sea salt, are topped with a mustard vinaigrette-seasoned tartare of white-fleshed fish, is a perfect example.

SERVES 8

For the vinaigrette

2½ teaspoons Dijon mustard

½ teaspoon salt

Pinch ground white pepper, or as needed

5 teaspoons lemon juice

½ cup extra virgin olive oil

For the fish tartare

2 pounds 10 ounces (1.2 kg) sea bass, daurade (sea bream), or snapper, cleaned and scaled

5 teaspoons chopped chives, divided use

½ teaspoon salt, plus more as needed, divided use

Pinch ground white pepper, plus more as needed, divided use

7 medium Yukon gold potatoes, scrubbed (about 2 pounds 4 ounces or 1 kg)

3½ tablespoons extra virgin olive oil, divided use

Pinch coarse sea salt

3 medium ripe tomatoes

Pinch sugar

2 hard-cooked eggs, finely chopped

4 teaspoons caviar

½ cup Ñora-Infused Oil (page 232)

1. Place the mustard in a small bowl and add the salt, a pinch of white pepper, and the lemon juice, and slowly whisk in the oil. Reserve until needed.

2. Remove any bones from the fish carefully, using tweezers. Finely chop the fish and toss it with the vinaigrette and 1 teaspoon of chopped chives. Stir well to make sure that all of the fish is coated. Taste and adjust seasoning with salt and pepper, if desired. Refrigerate until needed.

3. Place the potatoes in a medium saucepan, cover with 6 cups of water, add ½ teaspoon of salt, and bring to a boil over medium-high heat. Cover partially, turn the heat to medium, and boil gently until tender, about 25 minutes. Drain and return to the pot. Cover and let stand for 5 minutes, then peel and crush with a fork until the largest pieces are about ½ inch (1 cm) in diameter, and the rest is crushed a bit more finely. Add 2 tablespoons of oil and a generous pinch of coarse sea salt and gently toss.

4. Cut each tomato in half crosswise and remove the seed sections. Place the cut side of each half against the coarsest section of a box grater, and grate the pulp while pressing with your palm to flatten the skin. Discard the skin. Season the tomatoes with a pinch each of salt, white pepper, and sugar, and add 1½ tablespoons of oil.

5. Assemble the dish: Place a 3-inch (7.5 cm) ring mold on a serving plate and layer ⅓ cup of crushed potatoes, 1 tablespoon of grated tomatoes, and ⅓ cup of the dressed fish tartare. Carefully remove the ring mold. Sprinkle with 1 tablespoon of the chopped hard-cooked eggs, ½ teaspoon of chives, ½ teaspoon of caviar, and 1 tablespoon of ñora-infused oil. Repeat with the remaining ingredients and serve immediately.

Adapted from a recipe by NANDO JUBANY

TUNA TARTARE

THE SPANISH LOVE TUNA, and cook it in many ways—or they don't cook it at all, as in this tuna tartare. Tuna tartare is a more recent arrival on the Spanish table, and although it's restaurant fare, it's surprisingly easy to make at home.

SERVES 8

For the tuna tartare

1 pound (about 3 cups or 450 g) small-dice sushi-grade tuna

2 tablespoons peeled and finely diced cucumbers

2 tablespoons peeled and finely diced carrots

2 tablespoons peeled and finely diced onions

2 tablespoons extra virgin olive oil

1 teaspoon chopped flat-leaf parsley

¼ teaspoon salt

¼ teaspoon freshly ground black pepper

For the vinaigrette

1½ tablespoons soy sauce

1½ tablespoons balsamic vinegar

1½ tablespoons lemon juice

½ cup avocado oil

Pinch plus ½ teaspoon salt

Pinch plus ½ teaspoon freshly ground black pepper

8 radishes, cut in half and very thinly sliced into half-moons

8 quail eggs

1 tablespoon white wine vinegar

8 edible flowers or 2½ tablespoons finely chopped chives

1. **Combine** the tuna, cucumbers, carrots, onions, oil, parsley, salt, and pepper in a small bowl. Set aside in the refrigerator until needed.

2. **Make** the vinaigrette. Stir together the soy sauce, balsamic vinegar, and lemon juice in a medium mixing bowl. Slowly drizzle in the avocado oil, stirring constantly with a whisk. Season with a pinch each of salt and pepper, or more or less as needed.

3. **Place** a 3-inch (7.5 cm) wide by 1-inch (2.5 cm) tall oiled ring mold in the center of a shallow bowl or plate. Fill with ⅓ cup of the tuna mixture and smooth the top. Slowly and carefully remove the ring to leave a perfect disk of tuna tartare. Garnish the sides of the tuna with the radish slices, slightly overlapping the pieces. Reserve the tartare in the refrigerator until needed.

4. **Poach** the quail eggs. Fill a medium skillet halfway with water, stir in ½ teaspoon of salt and 1 tablespoon of vinegar, and bring to a boil over medium-high heat. Reduce the heat to medium-low for a slow simmer. Crack each egg first into a tablespoon measure or small cup, then transfer gently into the water, cooking in batches of 3 or 4 eggs at a time. Poach for 45 seconds for loose yolks, or up to 2 minutes for firmer yolks. Lift the eggs from the water with a slotted spoon and drain over the skillet before transferring to the center of a disk of the tuna tartare. Repeat with the remaining eggs. Sprinkle each with a small pinch of black pepper.

5. **Place** a flower on the top of the tartare, or sprinkle a teaspoon of chopped chives over it. Drizzle 2 teaspoons of the dressing around the tartare and serve.

Adapted from a recipe by KIYOMI MIKUNI

ROCOTO AND PIQUILLO CAUSA
TOPPED WITH OCTOPUS IN OLIVE SAUCE

A CAUSA is a signature Peruvian dish that brings together Old and New World ingredients in the form of mashed potatoes, olives, and olive oil. In this variation there's a mix of Peruvian rocoto chiles and Spanish piquillos, as well as octopus and olives. You can find Peruvian rocoto chili paste at PeruCooking.com.

SERVES 8

For the causa

4 pounds (1.8 kg) yellow potatoes, preferably Peruvian, peeled

1 tablespoon plus 4 teaspoons salt, divided use

½ pound (225 g) octopus, sliced (about 1½ cups)

¼ cup vegetable or canola oil

6 tablespoons lime juice

¼ cup Peruvian rocoto chili paste

1 cup puréed canned piquillo peppers

4 plum tomatoes, cored and sliced ¼ inch (5 mm) thick

2 avocados, sliced ¼ inch (5 mm) thick

For the olive sauce

1¾ cups Mayonesa (page 225)

2 cups imported black olives, pitted

¼ teaspoon freshly ground black pepper, or as needed

6 tablespoons lime juice

¼ cup capers, drained and rinsed

1. Make the causa. Place the potatoes in a large saucepan and add enough water to cover (about 5 quarts or 5 liters). Add 2 teaspoons of salt and bring to a boil over medium-high heat. Reduce the heat to medium, cover partially and boil gently until tender, about 25 minutes. Drain and return to the pot. Cover tightly and let steam for 5 minutes.

2. Prepare the octopus while the potatoes cook. Bring 6 cups of water and 1 tablespoon of salt to a boil over high heat in a medium saucepan. Cut each octopus into two sections by slicing the tentacles off the body at the point where they are joined. Drop the tentacles into the boiling water and cook for 1 minute, then remove with a strainer and transfer to a bowl of ice water to stop the cooking; drain well when cool. Drop the head and body pieces into the boiling water and cook for 2 to 3 minutes, or until the interior of the thickest part of the bodies has just turned from translucent to completely opaque (you can slice them crosswise to check this). Transfer them to a bowl of ice water and drain well when cool. Dry the octopus with paper towels, then cut the heads and bodies into ⅛-inch (3 mm) thick slices, leaving the tails whole.

3. Use a food mill or ricer to purée the potatoes into a large mixing bowl. Add the oil, lime juice, rocoto chili paste, piquillo purée, and 2 teaspoons of salt. Use a wooden spoon to stir until well blended. The purée should be very smooth.

4. Oil a 9-inch (23 cm) springform pan and line with plastic. Lightly oil the plastic. Place 4 cups of the puréed potatoes into the mold. Arrange the tomato slices so they evenly cover the surface of the potato. Then layer the avocado slices over the tomato slices. Spoon the remaining potato mixture over the avocado slices, completely covering them. Cover and chill in the refrigerator until cold, about 3 hours.

5. Make the olive sauce. Use a food processor to blend the mayonnaise with the olives, processing it until almost smooth. Season with the pepper and add the lime juice. Refrigerate for at least 2 hours to allow the flavors to blend.

6. Unmold the causa onto a large plate. Top the causa with the sliced octopus and garnish with 2 tablespoons of the capers. To serve, slice into 8 wedges and top with about ⅓ cup of sauce and some of the remaining capers.

Adapted from a recipe by MARILÚ MADUEÑO

MURCIA

THE CUISINE OF MURCIA, the Mediterranean region between El Levante and Andalusia, is one of the best preserved and least well known in Spain. Its highlights are its many wonderful vegetable, rice, and seafood dishes. Murcia is the land of the *huerta*, the small irrigated vegetable plots that the Arabs developed over one thousand years ago in Spain, and that still exist today. Rice is important, as it is in El Levante to the north, but as you drive south from Valencia, rice paddies give way to orchards and vegetable farms, and this cornucopia of produce distinguishes the local cuisine.

◄◄ **Caldero**, a typical Murcian dish, partners rice, seafood (which is so abundant on the coast), and an intensely flavored broth.

◄ **Ñora peppers** are always used dry and add a distinctive earthy flavor to soups and stews.

► **Vegetables** and even fruit trees grow abundantly in well-tended huertas. These vegetable gardens rely on irrigation systems originally devised by the Arabs.

SOME TYPICAL MURCIAN DISHES

A Spanish dish with the suffix *a la Murciana* or simply *Murciano* can be a vegetable dish or a seafood dish. Just like the rest of the Mediterranean coastal regions, there are two cuisines here: the fish cuisine of the coast, and the meat and vegetable cuisine of the interior. *Menestra Murciana* is one of the most famous of the region's vegetable dishes, a huge vegetable stew made with a number of vegetables in season. Recipes vary, but a typical menestra will include onion, tomato, spinach, lettuce, green asparagus, artichokes, several kinds of beans, squash, eggplant, potatoes, and carrots. It might not include all of these vegetables, but there will be at least four or five different types. The vegetables are cooked in olive oil and white wine, along with some *jamón Serrano* for flavor, and local herbs. Other popular vegetable dishes include *tortilla Murciana*, a frittata filled with peppers, onions, and squash; and a vegetable ragout called *olla*

gitana Murciana, or Gypsy Cauldron, interesting because it includes pears in its mix of beans and vegetables.

Red and green peppers and tomatoes are much loved in Murcia, and the dishes they go into rival the famous pepper preparations from Navarra and La Rioja. The small round, intensely flavored dried ñora pepper is a key ingredient in many local dishes, such as *arroz rojo*, *champiñones a la Murciana*, and *arroz caldero del Mar Menor*, also known as *caldero Murciano* (Murcian cauldron). The Mar Menor is a large lagoon with a higher salt content than the Mediterranean. It is rich with seafood, many types of which are cooked to flavor the broth that is then used to cook the rice in the caldero. The rice and broth are eaten first, followed by the fish, which is accompanied by an allioli.

Murcia is also the birthplace of Spain's finest milk-producing goat breed, the Murciano-Granadina. The region has two Denomination of Origin (DO) cheeses, Queso Murcia and Queso de Murcia al Vino.

This latter variety of cheese is a creamy, elastic white on the inside with a purple rind. It is so called because during its maturation it is bathed twice in Jumilla, the local red wine, which gives the rind a purple color and floral aroma.

MURCIAN WINES

Jumilla and Yecla are at the center of Murcia's wine country, the western part of the region known as El Altiplano, and both areas produce DO wines. There is evidence that viticulture existed here even before the arrival of the Romans. Over 100,000 hectares are devoted to vineyards, with three Denomination of Origin wines being produced: Jumilla, Yecla, and Bullas. Jumilla was awarded its DO in the 1960s, Yecla in 1975, and Bullas, recently, in 1994. The region produces mainly red wines, with some wineries beginning to make whites and rosés.

The Monastrell grape is the secret to Murcian wines. Known as the Mourvedre in France, this is an intensely flavored, small, tightly bunched grape that has great color and body, strong tannins, and tremendous fruity flavor. The intense heat and dry climate of Murcia are ideal for the Monastrell.

In recent years there has been a concerted effort to improve the quality of Murcian wines. In the past they had a reputation for high alcoholic content and a tendency to oxidation. They were often sold abroad in bulk and mixed with other wines. But in the last two decades new techniques have been introduced to help create fruitier, fresher wines with less alcoholic content. The result is that Jumilla wines in particular are gaining acceptance abroad, with some doing well in international competitions and receiving high grades from wine critics such as Robert Parker. Sales tripled between 1998 and 2004, with a growing export market to the United States.

SEAFOOD

SEAFOOD
From the simple to the experimental

With over 3,000 miles of coastline bordering both the Atlantic Ocean and the Mediterranean Sea, Spain is a seafood lover's paradise. The Spanish certainly feel that theirs is the best seafood in the world, and they may be right. So important are the fruits of the sea that even landlocked Madrid boasts some of the best fish restaurants in the country.

In true Spanish style, the freshest halibut is simply grilled and served here with a traditional Catalan sauce.

SIMPLICITY IS KEY

Throughout Spain, seafood cookery tends to be simple, the fish utterly fresh. If the fish you desire did not come in on that day's boat, you won't find it on the menu. A perfect meal in the Mediterranean city of Malaga, for instance, will be at a beachside restaurant. The waiter tells you what the day's catch offers, and you watch as he takes the fresh fish out to a grill on the beach. Minutes later you have a platter in front of you, piled high with fresh grilled sardines and shrimp, or daurade, or sea bass. Nothing could be simpler. You might prefer your fish fried in olive oil, as the Andalusians do so well. No problem. Whichever way you take it, it is so fresh that it doesn't even beg for a squeeze of lemon.

In the regions of Valencia or Catalonia, fish is often served with a nutty, pungent romesco sauce, made with ground almonds and hazelnuts, peppers, tomatoes, sherry vinegar, and olive oil. The sauce will be stirred into a fisherman's stew called a *suquet*, or served as a condiment with grilled fish. In the cooler northern regions of Galicia and the Basque country, sauces are common. The signature dish of the País Vasco, and the measure of a cook, is hake—*merluza*—in a mild parsley sauce called *salsa verde* (green sauce).

SEASONS AND TRADITIONS

When you travel in Spain, you associate fish with a place. If you live there, you also associate it with a season. You look forward to the bream that is traditionally served on December 24, the fresh young anchovies that arrive in the spring, the sardines that you enjoy in August. Large bluefin tuna arrive in May and June, passing through the Strait of Gibraltar on their way to spawn in the Mediterranean, and into the nets of awaiting fishermen. Like the Sicilians, Spanish fishermen participate in the ritual known as the *Mattanza* in Sicily, the killing of the tuna. Fishermen haul hundreds of the fish onto their small boats; every part of the fish— the loin and belly, the eggs that the tuna have come to lay, the heart and liver, the prized cheeks—will be used. To the people of the coast, the tuna is the "pig of the sea."

The Spanish don't consider cost when it comes to their favorite shellfish and fish. Pricy *langostinos* (jumbo shrimp) from Sanlúcar de Barrameda near Cadiz, spiny lobsters from the north, prized goose barnacles and sea scallops from Galicia, hake cheeks from the Basque country, are regional treasures. They're enjoyed with abandon, simply prepared.

MAR Y MONTAÑA

Spanish seafood cookery has a rich tradition of bringing together products of the earth and the sea. They call this *mar y montaña*, sea and mountain, and it is most often defined by the presence of pork products in seafood

Humble salt cod, the quintessential Spanish fish, is elevated to modern restaurant fare and served with a coulis of potatoes and red peppers.

Contemporary chefs experiment by merging cuisines; here the classic sole meunière is prepared with a Japanese influence.

dishes, which is why you will find Serrano ham in several of the dishes in this chapter. Lenten dishes forgo the meat, and combine beans with seafood. One of the signature dishes of Asturias and Calabria, Fabes with Clams (page 133), is just such a dish.

Joan Roca, chef of the two-star Michelin Celler de Can Roca in Girona, serves a postmodern, minimalist expression of "*mar y montaña*" in a dish that he calls Treasure Island. Roca is interested in the complicity between aromas and flavor; he likes to explore the essence of a dish, to distill its primary components. He does this literally when he presents an oyster with a sauce made from distilled earth. He achieves his sauce by placing freshly dug earth from the base of an oak tree into a still and distilling a water that tastes of the earth. Using xanthan gum, he thickens the water to obtain a sauce, and this goes over the oyster.

NEW TAKES ON SEAFOOD

Roca is just one of many contemporary Spanish chefs who are inspired by seafood. They are cooking it in new ways, such as in vacuum packs, or submerged in olive oil that remains at a low temperature until the proteins in the fish break down; the fish tastes cooked and feels moist and velvety, yet it looks like sushi. In this chapter you'll find a mix of traditional and modern recipes, and see how chefs have been inspired to deconstruct familiar dishes, to merge cuisines, and to draw upon these new techniques to bring out the best in Spanish seafood.

SEA SCALLOPS
WITH GREEN RAISIN SALSA

THIS DISH has both Spanish and Latino overtones. In the salsa, the olive oil, raisins, almonds, garlic, and anchovies are distinctly Mediterranean, whereas the pumpkinseeds and chiles are New World ingredients.

SERVES 8

4 ripe but crisp Bosc pears

½ cup almond or walnut oil, divided use

2 teaspoons salt, divided use

¾ teaspoon freshly ground black pepper, divided use

24 sea scallops (about 2 pounds 10 ounces or 1.2 kg)

2 tablespoons extra virgin olive oil

1 cup Salsa de Pasitas Verdes (page 224)

4 cups watercress

3 limes, cut into 1-inch (2.5 cm) wedges

1. Core the pears and slice into ½-inch- (1 cm) thick wedge-shaped slices. Toss with ¼ cup of almond oil and season with ½ teaspoon of salt and ¼ teaspoon of pepper.

2. Clean the scallops and season with salt and pepper. Heat the oil over medium-high heat in a large nonstick or seasoned cast-iron skillet and sear for 1 to 2 minutes per side.

3. Arrange 5 of the pear slices and 3 of the sea scallops on each plate. Spoon a rounded teaspoon of salsa over each scallop. Arrange 3 or 4 watercress sprigs over the sea scallops. Season with a pinch of salt, then drizzle with 1½ teaspoons of almond oil, and garnish with 3 lime wedges.

Adapted from a recipe by ROBERT DEL GRANDE

ALASKAN SCALLOPS
ON SERRANO HAM AND LENTIL SALAD

SERVE THIS AS A STARTER or a light main course. It calls for piment d'Espelette, a spicy red pepper popular with the Basques of southwestern France. Look for it at Amazon.com, or substitute pimentón. Pebrella, the other exotic ingredient, is used in the region of Spain between Valencia and Alicante. Thyme can be substituted.

SERVES 8

For the scallops

¼ cup Spanish fino sherry

6 tablespoons extra virgin olive oil, divided use

4 teaspoons piment d'Espelette

½ cup orange juice

2 teaspoons pebrella

2 teaspoons ground cumin

2 teaspoons salt, divided use

40 Alaskan scallops (about 4 pounds 7 ounces or 2 kg)

¼ teaspoon freshly ground black pepper

For the lentils

2½ cups coarsely chopped yellow onions

6 garlic cloves, halved

6 flat-leaf parsley sprigs

2 bay leaves

2 cups black beluga lentils, rinsed

1 tablespoon extra virgin olive oil

1 pound (450 g) Spanish chorizo sausage, cut into small dice (about 3 cups)

For the vinaigrette

¼ cup sherry vinegar

2 tablespoons red wine vinegar

2 teaspoons honey

2 teaspoons pebrella

1 tablespoon minced garlic

Zest of ⅛ orange, finely minced

⅔ cup extra virgin olive oil

1 teaspoon salt

½ teaspoon freshly ground black pepper

4 pimentos, cut into large dice

¾ cup finely diced celery

¾ cup finely diced fennel

4 tablespoons extra virgin olive oil, divided use

1 cup Serrano ham, crumbled

8 teaspoons chopped flat-leaf parsley

1. Prepare the scallops. Whisk together the sherry, ¼ cup of the oil, the piment d'Espelette, orange juice, pebrella, cumin, and 1 teaspoon of salt. Wash and pat dry the scallops. Gently toss in the marinade, cover, and chill for 1 to 4 hours.

2. Make the lentils. Tie the onions, garlic, parsley, and bay leaves in cheesecloth and place in a medium saucepan. Add the lentils, cover with water by 1 inch (2.5 cm), and bring to a boil over medium heat. Reduce the heat to low, cover partially, and simmer until cooked through but still firm, 40 to 50 minutes. Drain and set aside.

3. Heat the oil in a large sauté pan over medium heat and sauté the chorizo, stirring frequently, until barely browned, 1 to 2 minutes. Transfer to a strainer set over a bowl to drain the grease, then drain briefly on paper towels. Add the chorizo to the lentils and set aside.

4. Make the vinaigrette. Whisk together the vinegars, honey, pebrella, garlic, orange zest, and ⅔ cup oil in a small bowl. Taste and adjust seasoning with the salt and pepper. Toss with the lentils and add the pimentos, celery, and fennel.

5. Heat 2 tablespoons of oil in a medium sauté pan over medium-high heat and cook the Serrano ham until crisp and browned, 6 to 8 minutes. Remove from the heat.

6. Cook the scallops. Heat 2 tablespoons of oil in a large heavy sauté pan over medium-high heat. Season the scallops with 1 teaspoon of salt and ¼ teaspoon of pepper. Sear for 4 minutes on one side, or until nicely browned and crisp. Turn and sear for 1 minute on the other side, or until browned.

7. Divide the lentil salad among 8 serving plates. Top with 5 scallops, crisp side up. Garnish with the crumbled Serrano ham and sprinkle with 1 teaspoon of parsley.

Adapted from a recipe by SUSAN WALTER

BROILED SCALLOPS

SCALLOPS ARE COMMON in Galicia. They are typically sold in the shell, and are often served in the shell too as in this recipe. In the United States, scallops in the shell are far less common, but you can buy just the shells at many cookware shops. If you can't find the shells for the presentation of this dish, use your favorite small flameproof ramekins.

SERVES 8

⅔ cup extra virgin olive oil

3½ cups finely chopped yellow onions

1½ teaspoons finely chopped garlic

2 tablespoons sweet pimentón or paprika

1 cup dry white wine

¼ cup Tomato Sauce (page 221)

1 teaspoon salt

1 teaspoon freshly ground black pepper

2 pounds (900 g) sea scallops, quartered, or whole bay scallops

¼ cup fine dry breadcrumbs

2 tablespoons chopped flat-leaf parsley

1. Heat the oil in a large sauté pan over medium heat. Add the onions and garlic and sauté, stirring occasionally, for 5 minutes, or until soft.

2. Decrease the heat to low, add the pimentón or paprika and cook for 1 minute, stirring to prevent it from burning.

3. Add the wine, raise the heat to medium high, and cook for about 10 minutes, stirring occasionally at first, then more frequently until the wine evaporates and the sauce has thickened. Add the tomato sauce, salt, and pepper and mix well with the rest of the ingredients. Cook for 2 minutes, or until heated through. Taste and adjust seasoning with salt and pepper.

4. Preheat the broiler. Have ready 16 sea scallop shells or at least 32 bay scallop shells, or use small ramekins.

5. Bring 6 cups of water to a boil in a medium saucepan over medium-high heat. Add the scallops, remove from the heat, and let the scallops sit in the hot water for 5 minutes, or until just opaque throughout. Drain well.

6. Arrange the shells or ramekins on a half-sheet pan. Spoon 5 or 6 of the cooked scallop quarters or whole bay scallops into each shell or ramekin, dividing all of them equally among the shells or ramekins. Spoon 1 tablespoon of the tomato mixture evenly over the scallops. Sprinkle each shell with a rounded ¼ teaspoon of the breadcrumbs and ½ teaspoon of the parsley. Slip under the broiler and broil for 2 to 3 minutes, or until the sauce is just beginning to bubble, the breadcrumbs are crispy, and the parsley is beginning to brown. Serve immediately.

Adapted from a recipe by TERESA BARRENECHEA

BATTER-FRIED HAKE
WITH GRILLED PEPPERS AND CREAM OF RICE SOUP

CHEF FRANCIS PANIEGO, of Echaurren in Ezcaray, Spain, likes this method of searing fish, then poaching it in oil. He accompanies this hake with a creamy rice "soup." Chef Paniego's recipe calls for "crystal"–type peppers, a very hot, citrusy Latin American variety that is also available in Spain. Look for them in Peruvian markets, and if you can't find them substitute other hot red or yellow chiles such as serranos.

SERVES 8

For the rice

6 tablespoons extra virgin olive oil

1¼ cups chopped onions

1½ teaspoons minced garlic

½ cup chopped carrots

1 cup medium-grain Spanish rice (7 ounces or 200 g)

6¼ cups chicken stock

2 teaspoons salt, or more as needed

For the fish

Eight 6-ounce (170 g) hake or cod fillets, cut into 1-inch- (2.5 cm) thick pieces

2 teaspoons salt

½ teaspoon freshly ground black pepper

2 large eggs, beaten

½ cup all-purpose flour, for dusting

8 medium hot yellow or red chile peppers, preferably aji crystal, roasted, peeled, and cut into strips

¼ teaspoon fine sea salt

2 cups extra virgin olive oil, divided use

½ teaspoon Maldon salt

1. Make the rice. Heat the oil in a small saucepan over medium heat and add the onions, garlic, and carrots. Cook gently, stirring often, until tender but not browned, about 5 minutes. Add the rice and cook, stirring frequently, for about 3 minutes, or until the rice is lightly toasted. Add 4 cups of chicken stock and the salt, and bring to a boil, then reduce the heat to low, and simmer for 25 minutes, or until the rice is tender. Remove from the heat and purée in a food processor fitted with the steel blade until fairly smooth, about 1 minute. Add up to 2¼ cups more chicken stock as needed to create a thick sauce consistency. Return the sauce to the pan, cover, and reserve warm.

2. Prepare the fish. Season the fish fillets with the salt and pepper, distributing it evenly on both sides. Dip them in the beaten eggs, then lightly flour, and transfer to a medium baking sheet.

3. Toss the peppers with the fine sea salt and reserve. Place all but 2 tablespoons of the oil in a large wide saucepan or skillet and insert a thermometer. Bring to 113°F (45°C) over very low heat.

4. Heat 1 tablespoon of the remaining oil in a separate large heavy sauté pan over medium-high heat and sear the fish in batches of four on both sides, about 2 minutes per side. Use paper towels to wipe out the skillet between batches. Transfer the first four fillets to the oil and allow to finish cooking for 4 or 5 more minutes, or until the fish is completely opaque throughout. Repeat with the remaining fillets, but remove the first batch from the warm oil and use a slotted spoon to transfer to plates before adding the second batch to the oil.

5. Spoon ¾ cup of the cream of rice soup onto each plate. Divide the peppers between the plates and place the fish fillets on top of them. Sprinkle with a pinch of Maldon salt and serve.

Adapted from a recipe by FRANCIS PANIEGO

ESCABECHE OF HALIBUT
WITH GOLDEN RAISIN SALSITA

THE SPANISH TRADITIONALLY preserve fish for a few days by cooking and marinating it in a vinegar-based mixture known as an *escabeche*. Here the fish is rubbed with a dry spice and sugar mixture, then cooked and chilled. The salsa that garnishes this escabeche has many of the Arab overtones that recur throughout the Spanish table. The almonds and raisins, the combination of sweet and savory, are among the many culinary legacies of the Moors.

SERVES 8

For the escabeche spice rub

2 tablespoons cumin seeds, toasted

2 tablespoons black peppercorns, toasted

1 tablespoon sugar

1½ tablespoons kosher salt

For the fish

1 pound 5 ounces (600 g) halibut fillets, each about 1½ inches (4 cm) thick

4 teaspoons extra virgin olive oil

8 paper-thin slices Serrano ham (about 6 ounces or 170 g)

2¼ cups Golden Raisin Salsita (page 225)

1. Pulverize the cumin and peppercorns in a spice mill until not quite finely ground, about 30 seconds. Transfer the mixture to a small bowl and mix in the sugar and salt.

2. Rub the fish with ¼ cup of the escabeche rub. Heat the oil in an extra-large sauté pan over high heat and sear the fish quickly on all sides, about 1 minute per side, or until a crispy, crunchy, toasted crust forms. Remove from the heat and set aside to cool to room termperature, then cover and refrigerate until cold.

3. Slice the fish into ¼-inch- (5 mm) thick slices and loosely wrap 2 to 3 pieces of fish together in a slice of ham. Spoon 2 to 3 tablespoons of the salsita either by the side of the fish or on top of it and serve.

Adapted from a recipe by NORMAN VAN AKEN

HALIBUT A LA PLANCHA
WITH JAMÓN SERRANO AND GARUM

GARUM IS A DISTINCTLY CATALAN CONDIMENT based on olives and anchovies that are pounded together with herbs, bread, and olive oil to make a pungent paste. The garum in this recipe is more like a sauce, and it makes a wonderful topping for grilled halibut.

SERVES 8

For the garum

1½ teaspoons chopped oregano

Leaves from 1 thyme sprig

2 tablespoons pitted, herb-marinated, imported black olives

1 tablespoon rinsed and coarsely chopped anchovies

2 tablespoons cubed day-old country-style bread

¾ cup extra virgin olive oil

For the sauce

½ cup (1 stick) unsalted butter

¼ cup minced onions

6 tablespoons Sofrito (page 222)

1 quart (1 liter) Fish Stock (page 65)

¾ cup heavy cream

For the fish

Eight 5-ounce (140 g) fresh halibut fillets

¼ cup extra virgin olive oil

½ teaspoon salt

8 slices Serrano ham, cut into thin slices, deep-fried until crisp

2 teaspoons extra virgin olive oil

1. Make the garum. Combine the oregano, thyme, olives, anchovies, and bread in a food processor and blend until the mixture forms a paste. Slowly drizzle in the oil until the ingredients are incorporated and the mixture is smooth. Set aside.

2. Make the sauce. Heat 2 tablespoons of the butter in a medium saucepan over medium heat and add the onions. Sauté, stirring frequently, until tender, 3 to 5 minutes, and add the sofrito. Stir together for a minute and whisk in the fish stock. Turn the heat to high and bring to a boil, then reduce the heat to medium high and continue to cook until the volume is reduced to about 1 cup, 18 to 20 minutes. Stir continuously during the last 5 to 10 minutes to ensure that the sofrito vegetables do not stick to the bottom of the pan. Reduce the heat to medium low and whisk in the cream and the remaining butter. Set aside and keep warm.

3. Preheat a griddle or a gas or charcoal grill to medium-high heat. If you are using a charcoal grill, build a fire with coals and let it burn down until the coals are glowing red with a thin coating of white ash. Spread the coals out in a single layer. Brush a grill grate with oil, place the grill grate on a regular grate and preheat for 5 minutes. Brush the halibut fillets with 2 tablespoons of oil, then sprinkle each with a pinch of salt. Place the fillets skin side down on the hot grill grate and grill for 3 minutes. Gently turn the fish with a spatula or tongs, and cook it for another 4 to 5 minutes on the other side, or until firm but not hard. If desired, check the inside of the thickest part of a fillet with a knife; the center should still be slightly translucent. Remove the skin from the fish, if desired, and transfer the fillets to a platter; they will continue to cook as they rest.

4. Spoon 2½ tablespoons of sauce over each plate. Set a fish fillet on top. Top the fish with about 1 tablespoon of the garum and a few strips of the crisp Serrano ham. Repeat with the remaining fish fillets. Drizzle ¼ teaspoon of oil around each plate.

Adapted from a recipe by DANIEL OLIVELLA

HAZELNUT-CRUSTED HALIBUT
WITH SPICY ROMESCO

THE CATALONIAN PEPPER that is used for romesco sauce is the ñora, which is available from LaTienda.com. American cooks often substitute ancho peppers, and these work well. This New World version of romesco heats it up a bit with some jalapeño. The kale contrasts well by adding a freshness of flavor.

SERVES 8

For the spicy romesco

1 ancho pepper

2 tablespoons extra virgin olive oil

½ small jalapeño, stemmed and seeded

2 small garlic cloves, peeled

2½ tablespoons hazelnuts, toasted and skinned

Leaves from 1 flat-leaf parsley sprig

2 small slices focaccia herb bread or 2 slices baguette, pan-fried in olive oil

1 medium plum tomato, roasted

½ teaspoon red wine vinegar

½ teaspoon kosher salt, or as needed

½ teaspoon freshly ground black pepper, or as needed

For the kale

1 generous bunch red kale, stemmed and washed

1 tablespoon salt, or as needed

Pinch freshly ground black pepper

For the fish

Four 6-ounce (170 g) halibut fillets (about 1 pound 8 ounces or 680 g)

1 teaspoon salt

Pinch white pepper

¼ cup Mayonesa or Soft Allioli (pages 225 and 226)

½ cup ground toasted hazelnuts

¼ cup extra virgin olive oil or clarified butter

1. Make the romesco. Cover the ancho in 4 cups of hot water and soak for 30 minutes. Drain the ancho, pat dry, and remove the seeds. Heat the oil in a small sauté pan over medium-high heat and sauté the ancho and jalapeño until lightly browned, about 3 minutes. Transfer to a food processor fitted with the steel blade. Add the garlic and process until the garlic and peppers adhere to the sides of the bowl, about 20 seconds. Scrape down the bowl and add the hazelnuts, parsley, and bread. Process to a paste, about another minute. Scrape down the bowl and add the tomato, vinegar, salt, and pepper. Process until smooth, about 1 minute. Taste and adjust seasoning with a pinch each of salt and pepper and ½ teaspoon of vinegar. Set aside.

2. Make the kale. Bring 6 quarts (6 liters) of water to a boil over high heat in a large saucepan, salt generously, and add the kale. Cook for 4 minutes, until wilted and tender to the bite. Transfer to a bowl of ice water, then drain and squeeze dry. Chop coarsely, season with a small pinch each of salt and pepper, and warm again in a small skillet before serving.

3. Prepare the fish. Preheat the oven to 400°F (205°C). Oil a baking dish large enough to accommodate all of the fish in a single layer. Season the halibut with the salt and a pinch of white pepper. Brush the tops with mayonesa or allioli and roll in the ground hazelnuts. Heat the oil or clarified butter in a large nonstick heavy sauté pan over medium-high heat. When it is hot, place the halibut crusted side down in the pan and immediately reduce the heat to medium low. Once the halibut crust is golden, after about 3 minutes, turn the fillets over and cook for another 2 minutes or until the fillets are crusty and light brown; transfer to the baking dish (or leave in the pan if they all fit) and place in the oven, crusted side up. Bake for 5 minutes, or until the fish is almost firm, opaque, and pulls apart when gently prodded with a fork.

4. Place ¼ cup of kale in the center of each plate with a piece of fish on top. Serve with 1½ to 2 tablespoons of the romesco around the fish and kale.

Adapted from a recipe by VICTOR SCARGLE

FABES WITH CLAMS

THIS CLASSIC from the Asturias and Cantabria regions evolved as a Lenten dish. It's one of the many ways that Spanish cooks bring together the land and the sea, and the combination is a wonderful one. You will need to soak the beans for 8 hours or overnight, and you can cook them a day ahead if you wish.

SERVES 8

For the beans

3⅔ cups fabes (beans from Asturias) (about 1 pound 4 ounces or 565 g) without hulls if possible, soaked in 10 cups water for 8 hours, then drained

2 quarts (2 liters) water

⅔ cup medium-dice carrots

½ cup medium-dice onions

¼ cup medium-dice leeks

6 tablespoons extra virgin olive oil

¼ teaspoon sweet paprika

2 teaspoons salt

1 cup Chicken Stock (page 64)

For the clams with salsa verde

2 tablespoons extra virgin olive oil

1 medium garlic clove, minced

1½ ñora peppers

2½ tablespoons flour

2 pounds 8 ounces (1.1 kg) littleneck clams, scrubbed and purged

¾ cup chopped flat-leaf parsley

2 cups hot water

1¼ teaspoons salt, divided use

¾ teaspoon freshly ground black pepper, divided use

2 teaspoons lemon juice

6 tablespoons Green Parsley Oil (page 232)

1. Cook the beans. Combine the beans in a large stockpot with the water and bring to a boil over medium-high heat. Just before it reaches a boil, skim off any foam that rises to the surface. Clean all impurities from the legumes. Gently stir in the vegetables, oil, and paprika, reduce the heat to low and cook, gently simmering and stirring as little as possible, for 1½ to 2 hours, or until the beans are tender. The beans are ready when they are still slightly firm but have a creamy and delicate interior texture. Season with the salt, using more or less to taste. Add small amounts of stock or water as needed to keep the liquid level high enough to just cover the beans.

2. Make the clams and salsa verde. Heat the oil over medium heat in a large sauté pan and fry the garlic with the ñora peppers, tilting and shaking the pan to help pool the oil under the garlic and pepper. Cook until the garlic is lightly browned and the peppers are blistering, about 3 minutes. Remove the garlic and peppers from the pan; discard the peppers. Mince the garlic and add it to the parsley oil.

3. Add the flour and cook, stirring constantly without burning or changing color for 30 seconds, or until the flour is smoothly incorporated and the mixture resembles wet sand.

4. Add the clams to the skillet with ¼ cup of the chopped parsley. Fry for 2½ to 3 minutes, or until the clams begin to open, using a whisk or shaking the skillet constantly to avoid burning the flour.

5. Turn the heat to high, add the 2 cups of hot water and the remaining parsley, and cook until the sauce has reduced by half and thickened, 3 to 4 minutes. The sauce may appear a bit thicker than desired at this point, but the clams will continue to give off their liquid. Season to taste with ¾ teaspoon of salt, ¼ teaspoon of pepper, and the lemon juice.

6. Remove the clams with a slotted spoon as they open, placing them in a covered bowl or pan in a warm place (a warm oven is fine).

7. Measure 1 cup of beans into a large soup bowl. Arrange 5 clams around the beans. Pour the sauce over the beans, then drizzle the clams and the beans with 2 teaspoons of parsley oil. Sprinkle each plate with a pinch each of salt and pepper. Serve immediately.

Adapted from a recipe by PEDRO MORÁN

PERUVIAN FISH ESCABECHE

AN ESCABECHE is a vinegar marinade that has long been used in Spain to prolong the viability of various foods. The method became popular in Latin America, as is reflected in this Peruvian recipe by Lima-based chef Marilú Madueño.

SERVES 8

Eight 4-ounce (115 g) sea bass fillets

1½ teaspoons salt, divided use

1 teaspoon freshly ground black pepper, divided use

1 cup all-purpose flour

6 tablespoons vegetable or canola oil

¼ cup extra virgin olive oil

2 medium red onions, sliced ⅛ inch (3 mm) thick

1¾ cups thinly sliced yellow Peruvian chiles

½ cup white wine vinegar

2 tablespoons dry chili paste

½ cup light or amber beer

1½ teaspoons dried oregano

2 cups Fish Stock (page 65)

4 sweet potatoes, boiled, peeled, and sliced ¼ inch (5 mm) thick

1. Season the fish with 1 teaspoon of the salt and ¼ teaspoon of the pepper. Combine the remaining salt and pepper with the flour, then dredge the fish lightly with the flour mixture. Heat the vegetable oil in a large nonstick skillet over medium-high heat and quickly fry until light golden on both sides, about 3 minutes each side. Remove from the heat, place in a 10- by 13-inch (25 by 33 cm) casserole or other nonreactive, shallow container, and set aside to cool. Cover and refrigerate once the fish has cooled to room temperature.

2. Clean and dry the skillet and heat the oil in it over medium heat. Add the onions and sliced yellow chiles and cook, stirring, until tender, 5 to 8 minutes. Add the vinegar, chili paste, and beer. Bring to a boil and cook for 5 to 10 minutes, or until the flavors blend and some of the alcohol evaporates. Add the oregano and fish stock, bring to a boil, then remove from the heat and allow to cool for 1 hour. Pour the cooled marinade over the fish, cover, refrigerate, and let stand for a few hours, or preferably overnight.

3. Divide the boiled sweet potatoes among the plates and carefully place a portion of fish on top. To serve, top each fish with ¼ cup of the onion-pepper mix, and drizzle with 2 tablespoons of the escabeche marinade.

Adapted from a recipe by MARILÚ MADUEÑO

PRAWN "CASSEROLES"

THE MORTAR MIX, a *picada* of flavorful ingredients like parsley, garlic, saffron, and ñora peppers, gives these shrimp and potato "casseroles" their Catalan personality.

SERVES 8

For the fish stock
2 tablespoons extra virgin olive oil
½ cup finely diced carrots
⅓ cup finely diced celery
⅓ cup finely diced leeks, white and light green parts only
¼ cup finely diced onions
¼ cup minced garlic
1¾ cups peeled, seeded, and chopped ripe plum tomatoes
2 pounds (900 g) rockfish or striped bass
4 pounds 13 ounces (2.2 kg) halibut bones
5 ounces (140 g) shrimp
9 ounces (250 g) crayfish
1 flat-leaf parsley sprig
¼ teaspoon salt, or more as needed

For the potatoes
2 large Yukon gold potatoes (1 pound 5 ounces or 600 g)
1 tablespoon salt, divided use
¼ teaspoon freshly ground black pepper
4 cups olive oil for frying, or as needed

For the mortar mix
5 toasted almonds
1 garlic clove, peeled
5 leaves parsley
1 pinch saffron threads
Generous pinch salt
Two ½-inch- (1 cm) thick slices baguette, fried in olive oil
3 ñora peppers, soaked and seeded
⅓ cup extra virgin olive oil
¼ teaspoon powdered saffron

For the shrimp
64 (3 pounds or 1.4 kg) (21 to 25 count) shrimp, heads on
½ teaspoon salt
2 tablespoons extra virgin olive oil
½ teaspoon Maldon sea salt

1. Make the fish stock. Heat the oil in a large stockpot or Dutch oven over medium heat and add the carrots, celery, leeks, and onions. Cook, stirring, until almost tender, about 5 minutes. Stir in the garlic and cook for 2 to 3 minutes, or until fragrant but not brown. Stir in the tomatoes and cook, stirring, for about 10 minutes. Add the whole rockfish, halibut bones, shrimp, crayfish, and parsley. Add enough water to cover by 2 inches (5 cm) and bring to a boil. Skim off any foam, then reduce the heat and simmer for 20 to 30 minutes, or until the meat is separating from the bones. Strain. Return the stock to the pot, bring to the boil, and reduce to 2½ cups, 45 to 60 minutes. Reduce the heat to medium low; adjust seasoning with the salt.

2. Peel the shrimp, leaving the shells on the tails. Remove the heads, setting half aside (about 32). Add the remaining heads to the reduced stock and simmer for 5 minutes. Strain; keep warm until ready to serve. Cook one of the potatoes in a medium pot in 1 quart (1 liter) of boiling water with 2 teaspoons of salt until tender, about 30 minutes. Drain and return to the pot. Cover and let steam for 5 minutes, then mash, using some of the fish broth to moisten. Season with ½ teaspoon of salt and the pepper. Keep warm.

3. Make the mortar mix. Place the almonds, garlic, parsley, saffron threads, and salt in a mortar and mash to a paste. Add the fried bread and ñora peppers and continue to mash. Drizzle in the oil, stirring, and add the powdered saffron. Set aside and allow the flavors to meld.

4. Cook the remaining half of the heads quickly with ½ teaspoon of salt and 1 tablespoon of oil on a griddle or in a hot skillet over medium-high heat until they are crisp and red, 3 to 4 minutes. Keep warm until ready to serve.

5. Heat the oil in a Dutch oven or deep skillet until 375°F (190°C). Meanwhile, slice the remaining potatoes into ¼-inch (5 mm) slices. Heat 2 tablespoons of oil in two large sauté pans over medium-high heat. Fry the potato slices in two batches in the Dutch oven, until golden brown and crisp. Season with ½ teaspoon of salt and drain on paper towels. While the second batch of potatoes is frying, cook the shrimp in the sauté pans just until pink, about 4 minutes.

6. Place about 2 tablespoons of mashed potatoes on each serving plate. Top with 3 shrimp heads and 6 tails per person. Place a crisp potato slice between each shrimp. Drizzle a line of the mortar mix over the shrimp (about 2 teaspoons per portion). Heat briefly under a broiler until the mortar mix is golden brown. Spoon a small ladle (¼ cup) of stock over the top and sprinkle with sea salt.

Adapted from a recipe by NANDO JUBANY

FISH AND SHELLFISH
CEVICHE

Ceviche is a Peruvian dish that is also popular in Mexico. In Peru the marinated fish is traditionally served with a garnish of sweet potatoes and corn. In this version of ceviche, the barely cooked fish is tossed with the lime juice and is served almost right away, rather than marinating and "cooking" in the lime juice for several hours. Peruvian aji chiles are sold in South American markets.

SERVES 8

3 medium sweet potatoes

2 medium ears of corn

8 ounces (225 g) (21 to 25 count) shrimp, peeled and deveined

8 ounces (225 g) colossal sea scallops, cut into thirds

2 pounds (900 g) (about 4) flounder or sole fillets, cut into 1-inch (2.5 cm) cubes

1½ cups lime juice

4 red aji chiles, finely chopped

2 cups diced red onions

Salt, as needed

3 tablespoons chopped cilantro

1. Bring the sweet potatoes (with skins on) and 3 quarts (3 liters) of cold water to a boil in a medium stockpot over high heat. Turn the heat to low. Simmer, covered, until tender, about 35 minutes. Set aside to cool to room temperature, then peel and slice into ¼-inch- (5 mm) thick slices.

2. Bring 2 quarts (2 liters) of water to a boil in a large pot. Add the corn and cook for 5 minutes. Transfer to an ice bath for 3 minutes, then drain and slice the corn off the cob, leaving some sections of the kernels intact.

3. Fill a large saucepan with 3 quarts (3 liters) of water and bring to a boil over high heat. Add the shrimp and scallops and boil for 60 seconds, or until whitened and curled. Remove from the water and transfer to a large mixing bowl.

4. Add the fish, lime juice, chiles, and onions to the bowl. Add salt to taste. Toss together. Let sit for 30 minutes, or until the fish starts to whiten and curl in on itself. Divide the sweet potatoes among plates, then top with the marinated seafood mixture. Garnish with a few of the corn pieces and about a teaspoon of cilantro.

Adapted from a recipe by Marilú Madueño

SALT COD

Some of the most beautiful stalls in La Boqueria, Barcelona's bustling central market, are devoted to salt cod. You might think of salt cod as a dry, salty preserved fish product that comes in wooden boxes, or you may have seen leathery sheets of it in Italian markets in the United States. But the best salt cod is fleshy and supple, moist and white, and almost satiny in texture. In some cases it can cost more than fresh fish.

THE QUINTESSENTIAL SPANISH FISH

No other country in the Mediterranean is as crazy about salt cod as Spain (and that's saying a lot). This is especially true in the Basque country and in Catalonia, where some of the most popular fish dishes are salt cod preparations. *Pil pil*, a salt cod and olive oil dish in which the salt cod is slowly cooked in olive oil until the proteins in the fish and the olive oil emulsify, resulting in a velvety sauce, is arguably the most famous Basque fish dish. Another well-known Basque specialty is *bacalao a la Vizcaína*, in which the salt cod is cooked with dried ñora peppers. Salt cod shops sell a range of cuts and grades of the preserved fish. The most prized cut is the thick, moist loin, while the tail end of the fish is cheaper and leaner. Salt cod trimmings, cheeks, and innards will also be available.

The medieval Basques perfected the method for curing salt cod, and ventured as far as the rich fishing grounds off the coast of Newfoundland to procure the fish. To preserve the vast quantities of cod that were fished from the Newfoundland banks, the fish was brined or salted, then brought back to Europe. The preserved fish was vital sustenance on the many fasting days decreed by the Catholic church, and trade in salt cod was a big business. The Scandinavians eventually became the biggest producers of salt cod, and remain so to this day.

REGIONAL APPROACHES TO SALT COD

Every region in Spain has at least one signature salt cod dish. In Catalonia it is often served with a ratatouille-like vegetable stew called *samfaina* (or *xamfaina*), or added to their signature dish of sautéed spinach with raisins and pine nuts. In Extremadura it goes into a chickpea and spinach stew, and in Navarra salt cod is cooked with peppers, tomatoes, potatoes, paprika, and garlic in a dish called *bacalao al ajo arriero*. *Croquetas* are another favorite salt cod preparation, served in tapas bars everywhere, but especially in Andalusia and Catalonia.

CONTEMPORARY DISHES

Spain's new wave chefs are as enthusiastic about salt cod as traditional chefs and home cooks. Inspired by the simple local dishes they grew up eating, their salt cod preparations are often modern reinterpretations. The Oil-Poached Salt Cod with Alboronía on pages 142–143 is a case in point. The bacalao is combined with traditional ingredients, but instead of poaching the salt cod in water, bacalao loins are poached at low temperatures in olive oil. Modern chefs also like to cook salt cod at low temperatures in vacuum packs.

DESALTING SALT COD

Well-prepared salt cod should not taste salty; it should taste cured, like good ham. Its texture should be satiny and moist. If it is dry and cottony, it's been overcooked. The first step in any salt cod recipe is properly desalting the fish. To desalt, place the cod in a large bowl and cover it by a couple of inches (about 5 cm) with cold water. Refrigerate for 24 hours, changing the water at least five times during this period. Taste a bit of the fish. If it still tastes salty, soak it for another 24 hours, changing the water five times.

COOKING SALT COD

When salt cod is properly cooked, it breaks up into large, slippery, silky flakes with the touch of a fork. To cook salt cod, drain the soaked cod and place it in a wide saucepan. Add water to cover the salt cod by 1 inch (2.5 cm). Over medium-low heat, bring the water to a simmer. It should never boil, or your salt cod will dry out. Once you see bubbles rising from the bottom of the pan and breaking on the surface, cover tightly, turn off the heat, and allow it to sit for 20 minutes. Drain. The cod should flake apart easily.

MAKING YOUR OWN

Here in the United States it may not be easy to obtain the high-quality thick, moist salt cod loins you find in Spain. You can, however, obtain good bacalao from LaTienda.com. And you can cure fresh cod yourself: Use ½ cup of coarse sea salt for every pound (450 g) of fresh cod fillets. Remove the pinbones from the fillets using tweezers. Sprinkle some of the salt over the bottom of a baking dish that is large enough to hold all of the fillets in a single layer. Lay the fillets on top and cover with the remaining salt. Cover and refrigerate for 12 hours. Pour off the water that has accumulated in the baking dish, and if the salt has dissolved, sprinkle on more. Cover and refrigerate for another 12 hours. To cook with it, desalt it as directed above. It will probably only take 12 hours. Use as directed in salt cod recipes.

SALT COD
WITH POTATO COULIS AND ROASTED RED PEPPERS

SALT COD WITH POTATOES is a classic Mediterranean dish, much loved in Spain. Chef Francis Paniego makes restaurant fare of this modest family dish by poaching the cod in oil, serving it over a luxurious purée of potatoes and garlic, and finishing it with strips of roasted red peppers. Note that the salt cod needs to be desalted beforehand, which takes 24 to 48 hours.

SERVES 8

Eight 3-ounce (85 g) salt cod fillets (see pages 138–139)

For the garlic and potato coulis

9 garlic cloves, peeled

3 potatoes, peeled (about 1 pound 6 ounces or 620 g)

2⅔ cups water

1 cup milk

2 teaspoons salt

1⅔ cups butter

For the salt cod

1⅓ cups extra virgin olive oil

2 cups grated unsweetened coconut

¾ cup (1½ sticks) butter

For the roasted peppers

8 sweet red peppers, roasted and cut into thin strips

1 teaspoon coarse sea salt, or as needed

2 tablespoons extra virgin olive oil, or as needed

1. Desalt the cod. Soak it in fresh cold water, refrigerated, for 24 to 48 hours, changing the water at least five times. Drain well.

2. Make the coulis. Bring 2 cups of water to a boil in a small saucepan over medium heat and add the garlic cloves. Blanch for 30 seconds and remove from the heat. Combine the cloves with the potatoes in a medium saucepan. Add the water, milk, and salt and bring to a boil over medium-high heat. Reduce the heat to medium and cook, uncovered, until the potatoes are tender and the liquid has reduced by half, about 30 minutes. Drain, retaining the cooking liquid, and purée the potatoes and garlic through a food mill into a mixing bowl. Add the butter and use a spoon to mix it into the potatoes until smooth, about 45 seconds. Thin out with only as much of the cooking liquid as needed to create a thin purée. Season to taste with additional salt, if desired. Cover and keep warm while you cook the fish; place in a warm oven if necessary.

3. Make the salt cod. Combine the oil, coconut, and butter in a large saucepan or skillet and insert a thermometer. Bring to 149°F (65°C) over low heat. Meanwhile, heat a separate large heavy nonstick skillet or a grill pan over medium-high heat and sear the salt cod on both sides until lightly browned, about 3 minutes on the presentation side and 1 minute on the other side, turning carefully to avoid breaking the cod pieces. Transfer to the heated oil mixture and cook for 5 minutes. Remove from the heat.

4. Season the roasted peppers with coarse sea salt and oil. Remove the salt cod from the oil, and slice into 1-inch- (2.5 cm) thick slices. Spoon ½ cup of the purée onto each plate, then arrange the cod fillet slices on top (approximately 1 fillet per serving). Garnish with 5 slices of the sliced roasted peppers and serve.

Adapted from a recipe by FRANCIS PANIEGO

OIL-POACHED SALT COD
WITH ALBORONÍA

ALBORONÍA IS A CLASSIC vegetable preparation from Andalucia that is much like ratatouille. It goes very nicely with salt cod. The Moors brought the dish to Spain, but it really came into its own after tomatoes and peppers arrived from the Americas. Some versions of the dish are seasoned with North African spices and herbs such as cumin and cilantro, others with pimentón or paprika. Kisko García's version includes quince jelly, which adds an interesting sweet/tart dimension to the dish. This sweet/savory combination is another Arab legacy. Note that the salt cod needs to be desalted beforehand, which takes 24 to 48 hours.

SERVES 8

2 pounds 8 ounces (1.1 kg) salt cod

For the alboronía

2⅔ cups peeled, medium-dice eggplant

2 teaspoons salt, divided use

¼ cup extra virgin olive oil, divided use

1¾ cups medium-dice onions

1 tablespoon garlic

1⅔ cups seeded, medium-dice green peppers

1⅔ cups seeded, medium-dice red peppers

3 cups medium-dice zucchini

2 cups peeled, medium-dice butternut squash

2 cups peeled and seeded medium-dice tomatoes

¾ cup quince jelly

1 teaspoon freshly ground black pepper

2 cups extra virgin olive oil

1. Desalt the salt cod. Soak it in fresh cold water, refrigerated, for 24 to 48 hours, changing the water at least five times. Drain well.

2. Make the alboronía. Place the eggplant in a colander, sprinkle generously with ½ teaspoon of salt and let sit for 30 minutes, or until the liquid seeps out. Rinse and pat dry with paper towels.

3. Heat 1 tablespoon of the oil in a medium Dutch oven over medium heat and add the onions. Cook, stirring frequently, until tender, 6 to 8 minutes, then add the garlic and the peppers along with ½ teaspoon of salt. Cook, stirring often, for 4 to 5 minutes, or until the peppers are just about tender, then add another tablespoon of oil and the eggplant. Cook, stirring often, until the eggplant begins to soften, 4 to 5 minutes. Add another tablespoon of oil and add the butternut squash. Cook, stirring often, for 6 to 7 minutes, until the squash is beginning to soften. Add 1 more tablespoon of oil and ½ teaspoon salt along with the zucchini. Cook, stirring often, for about 3 minutes, or until the zucchini begins to soften. Add the tomatoes with the quince jelly and ½ teaspoon of salt. Stir well and cover, turn the heat to low, then simmer for 5 minutes, or until the butternut squash is completely soft but still holding its shape. Taste and adjust seasoning with ½ teaspoon of pepper, or more or less to taste. Reduce the heat to very low, or transfer to a warm oven to keep warm until ready to serve.

4. Cut the salt cod into 2-inch (5 cm) pieces. Place the oil in a wide saucepan or skillet and heat over medium heat until it reaches 122°F (50°C). Add the salt cod and poach for 8 minutes. Remove from the oil. Divide the salt cod among the plates, and serve with about ¾ cup each of the stew.

Adapted from a recipe by KISKO GARCÍA

FLAMENCO STEW

THIS HEARTY DISH is based on a classic Spanish Lenten potage of chickpeas and spinach with flaked salt cod. In this version, the salt cod is made into dumplings that are simmered in the soup. Note that the salt cod needs to be desalted beforehand, which takes 24 to 48 hours.

SERVES 8

12 ounces (340 g) salt cod

2 cups dried chickpeas

For the stew

2 tablespoons extra virgin olive oil

2 cups chopped onions

2½ tablespoons minced garlic

2 teaspoons sweet paprika

Generous pinch saffron

1 bay leaf

2½ teaspoons salt

1½ pounds (680 g) waxy potatoes, cut into ½-inch (1 cm) cubes

1 pound (450 g) spinach, stemmed, washed, and coarsely chopped

½ teaspoon freshly ground black pepper

For the salt cod balls

2 eggs, beaten, or more as needed

2 tablespoons chopped flat-leaf parsley

2 teaspoons minced garlic

Shredded salt cod (from above)

4 cups breadcrumbs

2 teaspoons salt

¼ teaspoon freshly ground black pepper

1. Desalt the salt cod. Soak it in fresh cold water, refrigerated, for 24 to 48 hours, changing the water at least five times. Drain well. Soak the chickpeas in a bowl with enough water to cover by 2 inches (5 cm) overnight or for 6 hours. Drain.

2. Place the cod in a medium saucepan, cover with 10¾ cups water and bring to a simmer over high heat. As soon as the water begins to simmer, remove it from the heat and remove the cod from the water (retaining the water). Allow the fish to cool, then shred it. Discard any bones. Set aside.

3. Make the stew. Heat the oil in a large, heavy soup pot or Dutch oven over medium heat and add the onions. Cook and stir until tender, about 5 minutes, and add the garlic and paprika. Cook and stir until fragrant, about 1 minute, and add the chickpeas and the water from the salt cod. Bring to a boil, add the saffron and bay leaf, reduce to medium heat, cover, and simmer for 1 hour. Add the salt, then cover and continue to simmer for another 30 minutes to an hour, until the chickpeas are tender. Add the potatoes and simmer for another 30 minutes, until the potatoes are tender and the broth fragrant. Stir in the spinach and the pepper and remove from the heat. Let stand, covered, for 30 minutes to an hour while you make the salt cod balls.

4. Make the salt cod balls. Beat the eggs in a medium bowl and add the parsley, garlic, shredded salt cod, and breadcrumbs. Season to taste with the salt and pepper. Shape into 1½-inch (4 cm) balls and set aside on a 10- by 13-inch (25 by 33 cm) parchment-lined baking sheet.

5. Taste the stew and adjust seasoning with a pinch each of salt and pepper. Bring back to a simmer over low heat. Add the salt cod balls and poach gently for 5 minutes, or until cooked. Serve 1½ cups in a medium bowl.

Adapted from a recipe by KISKO GARCÍA

MARMITAKO
POTATO AND TUNA STEW

THIS TRADITIONAL BASQUE fisherman's stew takes its name from the stew pot in which it was cooked, the *marmita*. The original dish, made with stale bread, pork fat, water, and tuna, was greatly enhanced after peppers and potatoes made their way to Spain from the New World. Basque chefs insist that the potatoes should be broken into chunks rather than cut, so that more starch will be released as they cook, resulting in a thicker stew.

SERVES 8

¼ cup extra virgin olive oil

1¾ cups medium-dice Spanish onions

3 Anaheim peppers, seeded and cut into medium dice

¼ cup thinly sliced garlic

1 bay leaf

1 cup white wine

3 cups water

10 saffron threads

1 ancho pepper, soaked, seeded, and cut into ⅛-inch- (3 mm) thick slices

6 cups medium-dice Yukon gold potatoes

4½ teaspoons salt, divided use

⅛ teaspoon freshly ground black pepper

2 pounds (900 g) tuna, cut into 1-inch (2.5 cm) cubes

8 teaspoons coarsely chopped flat-leaf parsley

1. Heat the oil in a saucepan over medium heat. Sweat the onions and Anaheim peppers, stirring occasionally, for about 5 minutes, or until lightly browned. Add the garlic and bay leaf and sauté for 30 seconds, or until the garlic is aromatic.

2. Add the wine and reduce by half, about 2 minutes, then add the water, saffron, and ancho chiles, and bring to a boil for about 4 minutes. Add the potatoes, 1 tablespoon of salt, and ⅛ teaspoon of pepper and lower the heat to a simmer. Cover and cook until the potatoes are almost tender, about 12 minutes.

3. Season the tuna with 1½ teaspoons of salt and add it to the stew. Simmer the tuna with the rest of the vegetables for another 5 minutes, or until the tuna is cooked, stirring occasionally. Adjust seasoning if necessary.

4. Ladle 1½ cups of the stew into a bowl and finish with 1 teaspoon of the chopped parsley.

Recipe by THE CULINARY INSTITUTE OF AMERICA

PIQUILLO PEPPERS
STUFFED WITH DUNGENESS CRAB

PIQUILLO PEPPERS are becoming very popular with chefs in the United States, and they're getting easier to find. The small, pointy sweet red peppers are grown in the Navarra region of Spain. They're roasted in the fields right after they're harvested, then packed in jars or cans. You can find piquillo peppers at Whole Foods and through LaTienda.com.

SERVES 8

For the peppers and stuffing

2¼ cups roasted piquillo peppers

1 pound 5 ounces (570 g) fresh Dungeness crabmeat

⅔ cup dry breadcrumbs

3 eggs, beaten

3 tablespoons Dijon mustard

3 tablespoons honey

2 teaspoons pimentón

½ teaspoon salt, or as needed

¼ teaspoon freshly ground black pepper, or as needed

For the sauce

5½ tablespoons unsalted butter

⅔ cup diced yellow onions

¼ cup Sofrito (page 222)

½ cup heavy cream

2⅔ cups Fish Stock (page 65)

2 teaspoons pimentón

1 teaspoon salt, or as needed

1 cup chopped flat-leaf parsley or microgreens such as alfalfa sprouts, for garnish

1. Prepare the peppers. If the stems and seeds are intact, cut a lengthwise slit down the center of each pepper, gently remove the seeds, and discard. If the pepper stems and seeds have already been removed from the top and the peppers have not been sliced open, leave them intact. In a large bowl, mix together the crabmeat, breadcrumbs, eggs, mustard, honey, pimentón, and salt and pepper to taste. Stuff each pepper with about 2 tablespoons of the mixture.

2. Make the sauce. Melt the butter in a large skillet over medium heat and add the onions. Cook, stirring, until tender, about 5 minutes, then add the sofrito. Stir together, then add the cream and fish stock, and stir or whisk together evenly. Add the pimentón and salt to taste.

3. Add the peppers to the sauce, taking care to keep them intact. Cover, turn the heat to low, and cook gently until the filling feels firm, about 5 minutes. Stir the sauce occasionally, and turn the peppers over halfway through cooking.

4. Put 4 peppers on each plate. Bring the sauce to a boil over high heat and reduce by half, about 4 minutes. Spoon some of the sauce over the peppers and garnish with 2 tablespoons of coarsely chopped parsley or microgreens.

Adapted from a recipe by DANIEL OLIVELLA

SPIDER CRAB GRATIN

THERE ARE MANY LAYERS OF FLAVOR in this rich, comforting gratin. Shallots, onions, and leeks are cooked very slowly in butter until they melt down to a very tender marmalade, which is then mixed with a thick tomato sauce. All this makes a wonderful backdrop for the crabmeat, which is stirred in, then topped with butter and breadcrumbs and browned under the broiler. Chef Sotelino's original recipe called for spider crab, which should be used in place of the Dungeness crab when available. Prepare this in a large serving dish or as individual portions, and serve with bread and a salad.

SERVES 8

For the vegetables
½ cup (1 stick) butter
¼ cup extra virgin olive oil
½ cup small-dice shallots
3 cups small-dice sweet onions
2½ cups small-dice leeks, white parts only
¼ teaspoon salt
¼ teaspoon freshly ground black pepper

For the tomato confit
½ cup extra virgin olive oil
3 tablespoons small-dice shallots
2 teaspoons minced garlic
3½ cups peeled, seeded, and chopped plum tomatoes
  (about 4 pounds or 1.8 kg)
1 teaspoon salt
¼ teaspoon freshly ground black pepper

For the crab
1¼ pounds (565 g) (about 3½ cups) cooked and cleaned
  spider crab or Dungeness crabmeat
¼ teaspoon freshly ground black pepper
3 to 4 tablespoons Cognac
½ teaspoon salt
⅓ cup plus 1 tablespoon breadcrumbs
2 tablespoons (¼ stick) unsalted butter

1. Prepare the vegetables. Heat the butter and oil over low heat in a small saucepan. Stir in the shallots, onions, leeks, and salt and cook very slowly, stirring frequently at first, then occasionally, until the vegetables are very soft but not browned, 1 to 1½ hours. Season with salt and pepper and set aside.

2. Make the tomato confit. Heat the oil over medium-low heat in a small saucepot. Stir in the shallots and garlic and cook for 5 minutes, or until softened. Stir in the tomatoes and cook until they reach a thick sauce consistency, about 45 minutes. Season with the salt and pepper.

3. Chop the crabmeat coarsely into ½-inch (1 cm) pieces, season with the pepper, and reserve. Stir the tomato sauce into the vegetables, then fold in the crab. Add 3 to 4 tablespoons of Cognac, or to taste. Season to taste with the salt.

4. Preheat the broiler. Oil 8 single portion gratin dishes and divide the crab mixture among them. Alternatively, oil a 10- by 10-inch (25 by 25 cm) or 8- by 12-inch (20 by 30 cm) ovenproof dish and spread the crab mixture evenly in it. Top with the breadcrumbs and dot with the butter.

5. Cook under the broiler until the top is golden brown and bubbly, no more than 5 to 10 minutes. Watch carefully so that it does not burn, and serve immediately.

Adapted from a recipe by GABINO SOTELINO

CATALAN SALMON

THE CATALAN FLAVORS are in the sauce that goes over this grilled or baked salmon—olive oil, sherry vinegar, orange juice, capers, and anchovies give it a pleasant tartness. As a colorful New World twist, you can garnish the fish with avocado slices if you wish.

SERVES 8

1⅓ cups sliced almonds

1⅓ cups extra virgin olive oil, plus 2 tablespoons for brushing the fish

⅓ cup sherry vinegar

⅔ cup orange juice

¼ cup grated orange zest, or as needed

3 tablespoons capers, drained, rinsed, and finely chopped

¼ cup finely chopped or mashed anchovies

½ teaspoon salt

¼ teaspoon freshly ground black pepper, or as needed

Eight 6-ounce (170 g) salmon fillets, ¾ inch (2 cm) thick

3 avocados, halved and pitted (optional)

1. Preheat the oven to 350°F (175°C). Place the sliced almonds on a baking sheet and toast for 7 minutes, or until golden. Cool for a few minutes, then chop coarsely and set aside.

2. Whisk together 1⅓ cups of the oil and the vinegar, orange juice, zest, capers, and anchovies in a small bowl. Season with the salt and pepper. Set aside.

3. Preheat a gas or charcoal grill to medium-high heat. If you are using a charcoal grill, build a fire with coals and let it burn down until the coals are glowing red with a thin coating of white ash. Spread the coals out in a single layer. Brush a grill grate with oil, place the grill grate on the regular grate and preheat for 5 minutes. Brush the salmon fillets with 2 tablespoons of oil. Place the fillets skin side down on the hot grill grate and grill for 3 minutes. Gently turn the fish with a spatula or tongs, and cook for another 4 to 5 minutes on the other side, or until the fish is firm but not hard. To check if the fish is done, insert a knife into the thickest part of a fillet; the center should still be slightly translucent. Alternatively, brush the salmon fillets with 2 tablespoons of oil and bake at 400°F (205°C) for 10 to 12 minutes, or until it pulls apart when pierced with a fork. Remove the skin from the fish and transfer the fillets to serving plates; they will continue to cook as they rest.

4. Spoon ¼ to ⅓ cup of the sauce over each piece of the grilled (or baked) salmon.

5. Slice the avocados, if using, into thin slices to serve as a garnish. To serve warm and help prevent browning and loss of color, heat the avocado slices with a little oil in a large sauté pan over medium heat until warm, about 1 minute. Place the raw or warmed avocado slices around the salmon and drizzle the sauce over the platter. Finally, sprinkle the chopped almonds on top.

Adapted from a recipe by JOYCE GOLDSTEIN

JAPANESE SOLE MEUNIÈRE

TOKYO-BASED CHEF KIYOMI MIKUNI likes to explore the affinities between Japanese and Spanish cuisines, focusing on seafood, rice, and *umami* (the Japanese word for "savory"). He uses a mixture of olive oil and butter to sauté his fish, and gives this sole meunière a Japanese twist by using a reduction of soy sauce and mirin in the wine sauce that tops the buttery sole fillets.

SERVES 8

¾ cup (1½ sticks) plus 7 tablespoons unsalted butter, divided use

5¾ cups loosely packed shiitake mushrooms, stems removed

2 small yellow onions, cut into fine julienne

8 medium garlic cloves, finely chopped

1¾ cup dry white wine

⅔ cup mirin

6 tablespoons soy sauce, divided use

Eight 5-ounce (140 g) sole fillets

1 teaspoon salt

¼ teaspoon freshly ground black pepper, or as needed

½ cup flour, for dusting

½ cup extra virgin olive oil

3 tablespoons lemon juice

1 tablespoon sugar

3 tomatoes (1 pound 3 ounces or 460 g), peeled, seeded, and finely diced

¼ cup minced flat-leaf parsley

1. Heat 3 tablespoons of butter in a large sauté pan over medium heat and add the shiitakes, onions, and garlic. Sauté until the onions are tender, 5 to 8 minutes. Add the wine, mirin, and 3 tablespoons of the soy sauce. Bring to a boil, and reduce by three-quarters, about 10 minutes. Set aside and keep warm over very low heat.

2. Season the sole fillets with the salt and pepper, and dust lightly with flour. In a second large sauté pan (or ideally, in each of two large sauté pans), heat 4 tablespoons of oil and 4 tablespoons of butter over medium-high heat until the butter ceases to foam. Place the sole fillet skin side up and fry until golden brown and crispy, 2 to 3 minutes. Flip over and continue to cook until evenly done (1 to 3 minutes, depending on the thickness of the fillets), or until the fish is almost firm and has just turned completely opaque throughout. Remove from the pan and transfer to a baking sheet in a warm oven, or to 8 warm dinner plates. Deglaze the pan(s) with the lemon juice and 3 tablespoons of soy sauce. Set aside.

3. Heat the shiitake-wine reduction sauce until hot but not quite simmering. Cut the remaining ¾ cup of butter into small pieces and stir into the sauce along with the sugar. When the butter has melted, add the tomatos and parsley.

4. Drizzle 2 teaspoons of the soy-lemon pan-deglazing sauce over each of the fillets. Top each with ⅓ cup of the shiitake-wine sauce and season with pepper to finish.

Adapted from a recipe by KIYOMI MIKUNI

THE GALICIAN COAST

AT THE NORTHWEST EXTREMITY OF THE IBERIAN PENINSULA lies Galicia, a green,
misty, spectacularly beautiful region of Spain that may have more in common with Brittany
and Ireland than it does with central and especially southern Spain. This is Celtic Spain, where
blue-eyed, blond-haired bagpipers stand in for the dark-eyed flamenco dancers of the south.
Sometimes described as "Green Spain," it is famous for its temperate climate,
its rich and fertile land, and for the many beaches that line its coast.

◄◄ **Scallops** are bought in
their shells, simply cooked
in their shells, and often
served in them, too.

◄ **Hake** frequently turns
up in Spanish fishermens'
nets. Here it is seared, then
poached in oil and served
with grilled peppers and a
cream of rice soup.

► **A typical fish market**
in Galicia displays the
freshest langoustines and
shrimp—just some of the
shellfish for which this
region is famous.

SPECTACULAR SEAFOOD

The cooking of Galicia is dominated by seafood. The coast here
is spectacular, chiseled with fjord-like estuaries called *rías*, and
rocky coves and lagoons that are home to some of the best fish in
Spain. Galician shellfish is legendary, particularly its odd, prehistoric-
looking, succulent, and very expensive goose barnacles called *percebes*,
that are gathered at great risk from wave-battered rocks.

Coastal Galicia is the only region in Spain where scallops are
plentiful and, in fact, here they have a religious significance. The
scallop shell was the symbol of the crusaders of the Order of Saint
James (*Santiago* in Spanish, *St. Jacques* in French). Pilgrims to the
holy city of Santiago de Compostela pinned scallop shells to their
clothes when they returned home, as proof that they had made the
pilgrimage. Many of the buildings in Santiago are imprinted with
the scallop motif; the French call the bivalve *coquilles St. Jacques*
because of its identification with the town. The fan-shaped sea scallops
(*vieiras*), also known as the pilgrim's shell, harvested off the Galician

coast, are larger and tastier than scallops found elsewhere in Spain.
Galicians cook them simply, and serve them in their shells with a
splash of lemon or Albariña wine.

Other seafood that abounds along the Galician coast includes
spider crabs, langoustines, octopus, mussels, shrimp, razor clams
(*navajas*, which means pocket knives), medium-size clams (*almejas*,
which are cooked like mussels *à la marinara*), and Carril clams
(*berberechos de Carril*). Carril clams are cockles, tiny sweet clams about
the size of an olive, that are harvested from the mouths of Galician
rivers, where they flow into the ocean. One of those rivers feeds into
the little fishing village of Carril. The Galician company Los Peperetes
packs premium shellfish, including razor clams in olive oil, Carril
clams, mussels in vinegar sauce, baby squid in olive oil, and octopus in
olive oil, and sells their products on LaTienda.com.

The Galicians love grilled sardines with new potatoes, squid
cooked with its ink, and small, delicate baby squid (*chipirones*), usually
deep-fried in a fine flour batter and sprinkled with lemon juice. *Pulpo a*

feira—boiled octopus sprinkled with paprika, salt, and extra virgin olive oil, cut up with scissors and served on wooden boards—is a signature dish, sold at stalls in villages all along the coast. Hake, turbot, sole, cod, and sea bream are all part of the day's catch. Galicians cook their fish simply, grilled or griddled, poached or stewed, often with a light sauce.

Seafood empanadas are another specialty, the pride of Galician bakers. These are large, double-crusted pies filled with a sweet, soft mixture of onions and peppers cooked in olive oil, and fish or shellfish. Oysters, mussels, and clams; salt cod, sliced scallops, cooked chopped octopus, or squid; tuna, sardines, and hake, all of these find their way into Galician empanadas.

GALICIAN WINES

To wash down this marvelous seafood, in the past twenty years Galicia has begun producing some of the best white wines in Spain. The famous Albariño wines produced in the Rías Baixos are the best known. In the Denomination of Origin (DO) Ribeiro there are up-and-coming whites being produced with native varietals such as the Treixadura, Torrontés, and Loureira. And red wines made from the Mencía grape in the DO Riberia Sacra are also getting some notice.

RECOVERING FROM DISASTER

Unfortunately, all is not perfect in this picturesque corner of Spain. Galicia's bounty has been severely threatened in recent years. A terrible oil spill occurred in 2002, when an oil tanker named the *Prestige* sank off the Galician coast. More than 80 percent of the tanker's 77,000 tons of fuel oil has spilled off Galicia since the sinking, polluting the seabed and contaminating the coastline. In the immediate aftermath of the disaster, the Spanish government suspended offshore fishing for 6 months. Thousands of volunteers were organized in a massive cleanup of the affected coastline, and the campaign was a success. But it is still not known the extent to which marine life will suffer from the pollution caused by the *Prestige* spill; some predict that the effects will be felt for another ten years.

MEATS

MEATS
Spain's roasts, sausages, pies, and stews

Spain is a land of meat eaters, perhaps more so than any other Mediterranean country. This may strike you as odd, given that it is also a nation of seafood lovers and has an extraordinary market basket. But seafood and vegetables do not preclude meat, and the Spanish are capable of eating vast quantities of it, especially in the heartland of central Spain—the regions of Castile-León, Castile-La Mancha, Extremadura, and Aragon.

The Spanish love beef. Here New York steaks are served rare and juicy with a raisin sauce and asparagus salad.

THE SPANISH TASTE FOR MEAT
Spain's taste for meat is perhaps a function of the fact that for centuries this was a land of hungry peasants. In *Don Quixote*, Cervantes captures the Spanish preoccupation with hunger in Camacho's wedding scene, in which excessive amounts of food, particularly meat, are consumed. An entire steer, stuffed with two dozen suckling pigs, is spitted on an elm tree and roasted above a mountain of wood, and on the surrounding trees hang skinned hares, plucked chickens, and other game.

REGIONAL FAVORITES
Pork and lamb, roasted in wood-burning ovens or prepared in smoky stews, often in tandem with beans, dominate the cuisines of central Spain. The great roast houses (*asadores*) in Castile are renowned for their quartered suckling lambs and whole suckling pigs, served up to masses of people who think nothing of driving the three hours from Madrid for a filling Sunday lunch.

All over Spain, the pig and its many cured pork products is revered. Mountain hams hang in every bar; sausages, ham, and bacon bulk up and season stews. Extremadura is famous for its free-ranging acorn-eating Ibérico pigs, whose cured meats are the caviar of pork products. The cured pork products from Asturias—blood sausage, chorizo, and salt-cured ham—along with Asturian white beans (fabes) are what define that region's signature dish, *fabada Asturiana* (pages 176–177).

In the northern regions of Galicia, Asturias, Cantabria, and País Vasco (Basque country) you find steak houses and *asadores* serving up generous slabs of beef or grilled beef ribs and excellent veal. The pepper-producing regions of Navarra and La Rioja are also sheep-rearing regions and produce wonderful lamb stews and chilindrones, seasoned with lots of paprika and red peppers. Baby lamb chops are also a specialty here. The Catalans love to mix sweet and savory flavors in their meat dishes, a legacy of the Moors. Their meat stews, which are usually made with lamb but sometimes veal or shoulder of pork, will often include dried fruits, perhaps a stick of cinnamon, and in some cases a spoonful of honey.

Meat is also an important element in the rice dishes of Spain, from the humble *arroz con pollo* to some of the most elaborate paellas. The traditional Paella Valenciana is not a seafood and rice dish, but a country dish that combines rice with rabbit or chicken. The signature rice dish from the Alicante region calls for tiny meatballs, chicken, butifarra sausage, pork loin, and chickpeas; and a typical Catalan paella includes rabbit or chicken, pork ribs, butifarra sausage, and cured ham. One of the most famous paellas from the Valencia region is made with duck and turnips.

Pork is often added to flavor stews. Here it can be enjoyed in its own right. Succulent, bite-sized cubes of slab bacon are drizzled with a slightly sweet sugar syrup sauce.

Suckling pig's cheeks, a great delicacy in Spain, are served here with an Asian-inspired sauce and puréed potatoes.

Savory pies (*empanadas*) filled with meat or fish are a particular specialty of Galicia, whose most famous empanada is filled with a mixture of pork loin, veal, onions, and green peppers and seasoned with thyme, oregano, paprika, and a pinch of saffron. From neighboring Asturias comes a pork loin and chorizo empanada that also contains onions, pimientos, and hard-boiled eggs. The meat pies made in Murcia, called *pasteles*, are usually filled with a mixture of veal and chorizo, mixed with onions and green peppers, tomatoes, and hard-boiled eggs.

From Andalusia to Catalonia to Madrid, Spaniards are also crazy for meatballs. A delicious way to stretch meat with bread, they make them with beef and veal, with pork and chicken, and with lamb. They are large and robust in Madrid, a favorite tapa, served in a rich tomato sauce. In Andalusia, meatballs made with lamb and mint (pages 166–167) have a distinctly Arab cast.

CONTEMPORARY DISHES

Today's Spanish avant-garde chefs are doing wonderful things with meat. They've figured out how to get the effect of slow roasting by vacuum cooking it for hours, resulting in meltingly tender cuts with lots of juice to spare for sauces, which may be classic reductions or come in the form of foam or jellies. They re-create crispy skin using toasted bread or pistachios, season a leg of lamb with powdered coffee, and serve pig's cheeks in a sauce made with soy sauce, sake, and olive oil (pages 186–187). As always, modern chefs are deconstructing the classics, presenting meats in a futuristic way that speaks of tradition.

MOORISH LAMB ESPADAS
WITH RECADO ROJO AND LEMONY ALLIOLI

THIS IS A MEXICAN/SPANISH FUSION DISH. The Mexican part is the recado rojo, a Yucatecan sauce made with ground annatto seeds. Chef Norman Van Aken uses it to season lamb, which he grills on skewers, like shish kebab. The lamb, and the lemony mayonesa he serves it with, comprise the Spanish element of this dish. You can find sour oranges for the orange juice in specialty produce markets, or you can substitute a mixture of half orange juice/half lemon juice. You'll need to begin this a day ahead to marinate the meat.

SERVES 8

For the recado rojo
½ cup finely ground annatto seeds
1½ teaspoons dried, ground oregano
1½ teaspoons ground cumin
1½ teaspoons freshly ground black pepper
½ teaspoon ground allspice
½ teaspoon ground cloves
½ teaspoon ground cinnamon
1 tablespoon salt
1 tablespoon puréed roasted garlic
1 cup sour orange juice
1 cup extra virgin olive oil
1 cup canola oil
2 pounds (900 g) lamb loin, sliced ½ inch (1 cm) thick

For the lamb skewers
Eight (9- to 10-inch or 23- to 25-cm) skewers
1½ teaspoons kosher salt
¼ teaspoon freshly ground black pepper
1 cup Lemony Allioli (page 226)

1. Make the recado rojo. Whisk together all of the ingredients for the recado rojo. Toss with the lamb in a medium bowl and cover, or place in a zip-close plastic bag, and refrigerate overnight. If using bamboo or wooden skewers rather than metal ones, soak them in water overnight.

2. Make the lamb skewers. Drain the excess marinade from the lamb. Thread 5 pieces of the marinated lamb onto each of the skewers. Season to taste with salt and pepper. Preheat a charcoal grill to medium-high heat, or build a fire with coals and let it burn down until the coals are glowing red with a thin coating of white ash. Spread the coals out in a single layer.

3. Grill the skewers on both sides until dark and a char crust forms, 5 to 8 minutes. Serve each skewer with a generous tablespoon of the lemony allioli.

Adapted from a recipe by NORMAN VAN AKEN

BASQUE LAMB SAUSAGE
WITH WHITE BEANS

DRIED PEQUIN CHILES make this Basque country sausage very spicy indeed. Reduce the quantity of chiles to ¼ cup for a milder version of the sausage. Note that the meat needs to be refrigerated overnight so that it is very cold when you grind it to make the sausages. If you do not have a grinder, use the seasoning mix to season 4 pounds 8 ounces (2 kg) of ground lamb.

SERVES 8

For the lamb sausage

2 teaspoons cumin seeds

2 teaspoons fennel seeds

2 teaspoons caraway seeds

½ cup dried pequin chiles

1¼ teaspoons sweet smoked paprika (pimentón)

1 tablespoon plus ¼ teaspoon salt, divided use

1¼ teaspoons freshly ground black pepper

7 garlic cloves

1 tablespoon extra virgin olive oil

3 pounds 8 ounces (1.6 kg) boneless shoulder of lamb, trimmed and cut into 1-inch (2.5 cm) cubes

1 pound (450 g) pork belly, cut into 1-inch (2.5 cm) cubes

For the white beans

2 tablespoons extra virgin olive oil

⅔ cup small-dice Serrano ham

5 large garlic cloves, sliced

3 cups sliced yellow onions

1 bay leaf

3 tablespoons brandy

Two 15-ounce (425 g) cans cooked cannellini beans, drained

2 teaspoons thyme leaves

¼ cup coarsely chopped flat-leaf parsley

¼ teaspoon salt

½ teaspoon freshly ground black pepper, as needed

16 thyme sprigs, for garnish

1. Make the sausage. Toast the cumin and fennel seeds in a skillet over medium heat, stirring constantly for 3 to 5 minutes, or until they emit their fragrance. Combine the cumin, fennel, and caraway seeds, chiles, paprika, 1 tablspoon of salt, and the pepper in a spice grinder; pulse to a fine grind, 45 to 60 seconds.

2. Pound the garlic and ¼ teaspoon of salt to a paste in a mortar (or mince the garlic with the salt until it turns to a paste). Combine the garlic paste with the ground spices and oil in a small bowl and mix well. Toss the seasonings with the lamb and pork in a medium stainless steel bowl, cover, and refrigerate overnight.

3. Grind the meat through the medium plate of a meat grinder or stand mixer grinding attachment and into a large bowl or pan, passing the mixture through twice. Mix the ground meat well with your hands.

4. Portion the sausage into ¼-cup mounds (to make about 32) on two parchment-lined baking sheets. Shape portions into 4½- by 1-inch (12 by 2.5 cm) links. Alternatively, shape them into ½-inch- (1 cm) thick patties about 3 inches (8 cm) in diameter. Press a 1-inch- (2.5 cm) wide well in the center of each patty, flattening the meat in the well to about ⅓ inch (8 mm) thick, to help the centers cook more evenly as the meat shrinks. Refrigerate, covered, until ready to grill.

5. Make the white beans. Heat the oil in a large sauté pan over medium-high heat. Add the diced Serrano ham and sauté until crispy and dark brown, 6 to 8 minutes; remove from the pan and set aside. Add the garlic, onions, and bay leaf to the pan and turn the heat to medium. Cook the vegetables, stirring, until they begin to caramelize, about 12 minutes. Add the brandy and bring to a boil, stirring with a wooden spoon and scraping the bottom of the pan to deglaze. Remove the bay leaf and stir in the cannellini beans, thyme leaves, parsley, salt, and pepper. Cover and refrigerate for 4 to 6 hours to allow the flavors to blend. Bring the beans to room temperature before serving.

6. Grill the sausages over medium-high heat on a preheated gas or charcoal grill until medium or medium well done, 12 to 15 minutes for the links and 6 to 8 minutes for the patties. Don't prod the meat too much as it cooks. Grill in two batches if necessary, but for optimal flavor and texture, serve one batch immediately after cooking. Spoon ½ cup of the beans onto each plate and sprinkle with 1 tablespoon of the Serrano ham. Top with 4 of the grilled sausage links or patties and garnish with 2 thyme sprigs.

Adapted from a recipe by KEVIN MARQUET

LAMB
AND ROASTED PEPPER RAGOUT

THIS STEW is prepared *al chilindron*, which means that sweet paprika and sweet red peppers are combined in a rich sauce for the meat. A similar stew is prepared in Portugal, but there the peppers are ground into a paste with garlic and salt and rubbed on the meat before cooking. Note that the lamb needs to marinate overnight. This dish can be made the day before and reheated.

SERVES 8

For the lamb

4 pounds (1.8 kg) lamb shoulder, well trimmed of fat and sinew, cut into 1½- to 2-inch (4 to 5 cm) cubes

3 tablespoons Spanish sweet paprika

2½ teaspoons ground cumin

1 teaspoon finely crumbled bay leaf

⅔ cup extra virgin olive oil

1⅓ cup dry white wine, divided use

Zest of ⅓ large lemon, finely sliced

½ teaspoon salt

½ teaspoon freshly ground black pepper

1 tablespoon extra virgin olive oil, or as needed

For the ragout

¼ cup extra virgin olive oil

4 cups chopped onions

2½ tablespoons paprika

2½ teaspoons ground cumin

3 tablespoons finely minced garlic

2 teaspoons salt

1 teaspoon freshly ground black pepper

2 cups lamb or chicken stock

1 teaspoon lemon zest

2 tablespoons lemon juice, or more to taste

8 medium red peppers, roasted and cut into wide strips

8 teaspoons chopped flat-leaf parsley

1. Prepare the lamb. Place the lamb in a small nonaluminum container and toss well with the paprika, cumin, bay leaf, oil, ⅔ cup of wine, and the lemon zest. Cover the container and leave to marinate overnight in the refrigerator.

2. Transfer the lamb to a colander to drain well, and bring to room temperature. Season the lamb with the salt and pepper. Heat 1 tablespoon of the oil in a large sauté pan and brown one-third of the meat over medium-high heat for 3 to 4 minutes. Turn each piece to brown all sides evenly. Transfer with a slotted spoon to a 12-quart (12 liter) stew pot or Dutch oven. Pour off and discard all but 1 tablespoon of excess fat from the browning skillet, then repeat this process with the remaining meat, browning in 2 batches, draining off excess fat each time. Also pour off any excess fat that accumulates in the stew pot. Finally, deglaze the sauté pan with the remaining wine and add the pan juices to the stew pot. Clean the sauté pan before proceeding.

3. Make the ragout. Heat the oil in the sauté pan and cook the onions over medium heat, stirring occasionally, for about 10 minutes, or until translucent and tender. Add the paprika, cumin, and garlic and cook for a few minutes longer, or until the mixture begins to stick to the pan. Season the mixture with ½ teaspoon of salt and ½ teaspoon of pepper. Stir this mixture into the stew pot with the lamb.

4. Deglaze the sauté pan with ½ cup of the lamb or chicken stock, and add the pan juices to the lamb. Add the remaining stock, lemon zest, and lemon juice to the stew pot and bring to a boil over medium high heat. Reduce to low heat and cover the pan. Simmer gently for about an hour, or until the meat is nearly tender.

5. Add the roasted peppers to the stew pot with 1 teaspoon of salt. Bring back to a simmer and cook, stirring occasionally, for about 30 minutes longer, or until the largest pieces of lamb are tender. Adjust seasoning with ½ teaspoon of salt and ½ teaspoon of pepper (or more or less of each to taste). If you like, add 2 tablespoons to ¼ cup of lemon juice to taste. Garnish each serving of the stew with 1 teaspoon of chopped parsley.

Adapted from a recipe by JOYCE GOLDSTEIN

MINTED LAMB MEATBALLS
WITH ALMOND SHERRY SAUCE

ALMONDS AND MINT have long been used in North Africa to season lamb. This dish reflects these Moorish influences on Spanish cuisine. What is purely Spanish is the abundant sherry in both the meatballs and the sauce.

SERVES 8

For the meatballs

1 baguette, cut into ½-inch- (1 cm) thick cubes (about 2 cups)

⅓ cup dry sherry

3½ pounds (1.6 kg) ground lamb

3 eggs, beaten

3 tablespoons minced garlic

1 cup minced yellow onions

2½ tablespoons chopped mint

2 teaspoons salt

1 teaspoon freshly ground black pepper

½ cup all-purpose flour, or as needed

2 tablespoons extra virgin olive oil

For the almond sherry sauce

2 tablespoons minced garlic

2⅓ cups diced yellow onions

1⅓ cups dry sherry

1⅓ cups lamb stock

1⅓ cups toasted sliced almonds

1 tablespoon lemon zest

3 tablespoons lemon juice

⅓ cup extra virgin olive oil

⅓ cup chopped mint

6 tablespoons (¾ stick) butter, cut into chunks

1. Place the bread cubes on a baking sheet in a single layer and allow to dry at room temperature for 2 hours.

2. Soak the bread briefly in the sherry until the liquid is absorbed, then pulse in a food processor fitted with the steel blade for about 1 minute, or until the mixture is processed into fine crumbs. Transfer to a large bowl and combine with the lamb, eggs, garlic, onions, mint, salt, and pepper using a wooden spoon.

3. Form the lamb mixture into about 2½-tablespoon meatballs approximately 1½ inches (4 cm) in diameter. Dust with flour. Heat 1 tablespoon of the oil in a large skillet over medium-high heat. Add half of the meatballs and brown on all sides, about 5 minutes. Transfer to a medium baking dish or casserole. Repeat the process with 1 more tablespoon of oil and the remaining meatballs.

4. Make the sauce. Preheat the oven to 350°F (175°C). Combine the garlic, onions, sherry, and lamb stock in a medium saucepan or pot. Bring to a boil over high heat, then remove from the heat. Pour the sauce over the meatballs. Place in the oven and bake for 30 minutes, or until the meat registers 170°F (75°C) on a meat thermometer. Remove the meatballs with a slotted spoon and keep warm in a serving dish covered with foil.

5. Pour the sauce from the meatballs into a medium saucepan and set aside. Place the almonds, lemon zest, lemon juice, oil, and mint in a food processor fitted with the steel blade, and process to a paste, about 2 minutes. Whisk the paste into the reserved cooking juices. Heat through over medium-high heat for about 2 minutes. Add the butter a little at a time and whisk to finish the sauce. Pour the sauce over the meatballs and serve.

Adapted from a recipe by KEVIN MARQUET

GRILLED LAMB CHOPS
WITH SALSA DE PASITAS ROJAS AND FENNEL SALAD

HOUSTON-BASED CHEF ROBERT DEL GRANDE serves a salsa with grilled lamb chops that has Catalonian overtones, with almonds and raisins, black olives and chiles, garlic and olive oil. In Spain the chiles would most likely be ñoras; pasillas or anchos make a good substitute.

SERVES 8

For the salsa de pasitas rojas

1 cup (about 24) garlic cloves, peeled

½ cup sliced almonds

½ cup raisins

¼ cup imported black olives, pitted

2 pasilla or ancho chiles, seeded

¼ cup lemon zest

1 cup extra virgin olive oil

2 white anchovies

⅔ cup chicken broth

4 teaspoons balsamic vinegar

2 teaspoons salt

For the fennel salad and lamb chops

4 large fennel bulbs, green tops removed

½ cup black olives, pitted and slivered

½ cup plus 3 tablespoons extra virgin olive oil, divided use

4 teaspoons lemon juice

Salt, as needed

Freshly ground black pepper, as needed

Sixteen 1-inch- (2.5 cm) thick lamb loin chops (about 7 pounds 10 ounces or 3.5 kg)

1 teaspoon salt

¼ teaspoon freshly ground black pepper

1. Make the salsa. Combine the garlic cloves, almonds, raisins, olives, chiles, lemon zest, and oil in a large sauté pan. Heat over medium heat until the ingredients begin to fry lightly, 3 to 5 minutes. Cook until the garlic cloves are lightly browned and have softened and the raisins begin to puff, about 10 minutes. Add the white anchovies. Remove from the heat and allow the mixture to cool to room temperature.

2. Transfer the cooked mixture with the oil to a food processor. Process until nearly smooth, about 1 minute. With the food processor running, pour the chicken broth, vinegar, and salt into the ground mixture and process until nearly smooth, about 1 minute. Adjust seasoning and refrigerate. This should make 2 cups.

3. Preheat a charcoal grill to medium-high heat, or build a fire with coals and let it burn down until the coals are glowing red with a thin coating of white ash. Spread the coals out in a single layer.

4. Make the fennel salad while you wait for the grill or coals to heat up. Cut the fennel bulbs in quarters lengthwise. Slice the thick core off of each bulb. Remove any tough outer leaves. Slice the bulbs vertically into ¼-inch (5 mm) shards. In a medium bowl, mix the black olives, ¼ cup of the oil, and the lemon juice. Add a pinch each of salt and pepper. Add the fennel shards and toss to coat lightly.

5. Cook the lamb chops. Rub them with the remaining oil and season with the salt and pepper. Grill until medium rare, about 5 minutes per side. Arrange two grilled lamb chops on each dinner plate. Add ½ to ⅔ cup of fennel salad. Spoon 2 rounded teaspoons of salsa over each lamb chop, then drizzle 1 teaspoon of oil over each plate. Serve extra salsa in a bowl and place on the table for people to help themselves.

Adapted from a recipe by ROBERT DEL GRANDE

ROASTS AND STEWS

ON A SUNDAY IN SPRING, Madrileños do not hesitate to make the 3-hour drive to Segovia or to Campaspero for a long and hearty Sunday lunch at Cándido López Cuerdo's Mesón de Cándido, or Marco Antonio García's Mannix, two of Spain's most famous *asadores* (or roast houses). The Castilian heartland is meat country, home to famous rustic, country roast houses. This is where twenty-one-day-old suckling pigs and lambs are cooked over oak in earthenware casseroles in special wood-burning ovens.

TRADITIONAL ROASTING TECHNIQUES

When it comes to being roasted, a lamb and a pig have much in common, despite the lamb's more aristocratic standing. Both have been fed on nothing more than mother's milk and have been slaughtered at the age of twenty-one days. Castilian Churra lambs are quartered and placed skin side down in large earthenware casseroles. The casseroles are placed in clay ovens and roasted over oak for 2½ hours at 400°F (205°C). Then they're turned and roasted for another 15 minutes, until the skin is crisp and golden. Suckling pigs are roasted whole, sometimes in earthenware casseroles, sometimes on wooden slats set in roasting pans. They too are placed skin side down; they're brushed with a little fat and sprinkled with coarse salt, and roasted at about 350°F (175°C) for 2½ hours. Then they're turned and roasted for another hour, or until the skin is crisp. When properly cooked, they are so tender that they can be quartered with a plate, and that is exactly how it is done in the asadores.

CONTEMPORARY ROASTS AND STEWS

Spain's new chefs have no less reverence for these meat traditions. They explore the relationship between the old and the new with their innovative dishes, never straying from their commitment to bringing out the essence of the basic ingredient. Joan Roca of El Cellar de Can Roca, for example, riffs off the traditional roast suckling pig when he makes his Iberian suckling pig and caramelized shallots with orange and cloves. His Iberian suckling pig has been cut into six pieces, and each piece vacuum-cooked on the bone for 18 hours at 70°F (20°C). This yields cooked pork that is tender and succulent like the slow-roasted pork from Segovia. He takes the pork off the bone, and crisps the skin by cooking the pieces skin side down in olive oil. Meanwhile, he makes a sauce with caramel, vinegar, orange juice, cloves, roasted shallots, and the juice from the vacuum-packed pork, the sweet and sour flavors influenced by Chef Roca's Catalan traditions. The tender piece of pork, elegantly squared off, goes on top of the sauce, its utterly crunchy skin up, garnished with the caramelized shallots and a drizzle of thick, reduced orange juice.

Spain is just as enthusiastic about meat stews. Every region in the country has its version of *cocido*, a hearty boiled dinner that usually includes beans such as chickpeas, limas, white beans, or broad beans and cured pork products, meats, and vegetables, all of which are simmered slowly for hours. The fragrant broth is served as a first course before the meat, beans, and vegetables.

The new chefs of Spain deconstruct traditional stews, as is their penchant. They might vacuum-cook the meats for hours at a low temperature until they are juicy and tender, and transform the beans into a foam. The elements of the stew might be presented layered on a plate and topped with something surprising, like pan-fried *espardeñas* (sea cucumbers) and their crunchy crisp-fried skins.

SOME OF SPAIN'S FAVORITE STEWS

Cocido Madrileño (pages 172–173): This consists of chickpeas, meats, sausage products, and vegetables (potatoes, onions, carrots, cabbage). In central Spain cocidos include meatballs. In Catalonia other beans called *escudellas* accompany the chickpeas, and chorizo is replaced by butifarra, a white Catalan sausage. Cocidos of Andalusia are made with chickpeas and chorizo; those from the Canary Islands can include squash, pears, and corncobs.

Caldo Gallego: A specialty of Galicia, this is made with white beans, salt pork, cured ham and beef, turnips, potatoes, and greens. The fresh turnip greens (*grelos*) and the new potatoes make this unique.

Fabada Asturiana: One of the most famous cocidos, this is made with Asturias white beans (fabes), blood sausage (morcilla), chorizo, ham hocks or smoked pork, slab bacon, paprika, and olive oil.

Judías con chorizo: From central Spain, this is made with large, dried white beans (judías), chorizo, onions, pig's foot, garlic, paprika, scallions, vinegar, and red peppers.

Judiones de el Barco de Ávila: From Segovia, Ávila, and La Rioja, this broad bean stew contains giant white beans or lima beans, garlic, pig's foot, Serrano ham, chorizo, black sausage, onions, sweet paprika, chile pepper, pimiento, and potatoes.

Sopa de albóndigas (page 82): This meatball soup contains meatballs made with veal, chicken, ham, breadcrumbs, and parsley.

CHICKPEA, MEAT, AND VEGETABLE
COCIDO

THE COCIDO HAS ITS ORIGIN in the much older *olla podrida*, a stew containing legumes, meats, and sausages that was cooked for long hours over low heat. *Adafina*, the equivalent Sephardic dish popular in every Jewish quarter in Spain, is cooked at the lowest heat all Friday night until dawn on Saturday, so the dish is ready for the Sabbath.

Though undeniably humble in origin, cocidos gained respectability during the years the Hapsburgs ruled Spain, when aristocrats and peasants alike were drawn to these bountiful dishes. Today, Madrid offers a long list of prominent establishments that prepare excellent cocidos. Some Madrileños add a *pelota*, a large dumpling made of ground pork or beef, or breadcrumbs, garlic, parsley, and egg, to their cocidos. It is slipped into the pot toward the end of cooking. Cocidos are traditionally served in three courses, usually with the broth first, followed by the chickpeas and vegetables, and then finally the meats. You can, of course, alter the order if you like and serve all three courses together.

SERVES 8 GENEROUSLY

- 1 pound 5 ounces (600 g) boneless beef shank, round, or chuck, cut into 1-inch (2.5 cm) pieces
- 1 small chicken or stewing hen (about 2 pounds 14 ounces or 1.3 kg), quartered
- 11 ounces (310 g) fatback or bacon, preferably in 1 piece
- 3 small soup bones, preferably marrow bones
- 1 small ham bone (optional)
- 2¾ cups dried chickpeas, washed, picked over, and soaked for 8 hours or overnight in water to cover by 3 inches (8 cm)
- Four 3-ounce (85 g) Spanish chorizo sausages
- Three 4-ounce (115 g) morcilla sausages

- 3 tablespoons salt plus 1 teaspoon, or more as needed, divided use
- 4 large carrots, peeled and halved crosswise
- 4 russet potatoes, peeled and halved crosswise
- 1 medium head green cabbage, coarsely chopped
- ½ cup extra virgin olive oil
- 1 tablespoon thinly sliced garlic cloves
- ½ teaspoon freshly ground black pepper
- 2⅔ cups Tomato Sauce (page 221)
- 1⅓ cups angel hair pasta, broken into 3-inch (8 cm) pieces (optional)
- 1 loaf country-style bread or baguette, sliced and toasted (if using marrow bones)

1. Combine the beef, chicken, fatback, soup bones, and ham bone, if using, in a large stockpot. Add 12 cups of water, or enough to cover the meats by 3 inches (8 cm). Bring to a boil over high heat and boil for 10 minutes. Skim any foam from the surface as it rises. Turn the heat down to medium.

2. Drain the chickpeas and wrap them in a cheesecloth pouch tied with kitchen string (to make it easier to retrieve them for serving later). Add the chickpea pouch to the stockpot holding the meats.

3. Cover the pot, decrease the heat to medium low, and simmer for about 1½ hours. Skim the foam from the surface every 30 minutes; add more water if necessary to keep the ingredients covered at all times.

4. Add the sausages and 2 tablespoons of salt, decrease the heat to low, and simmer for 30 minutes longer, or until the sausages are fork tender. At that point, the chickpeas and the meats will be fork tender. When the meats and chickpeas are ready, retrieve the cheesecloth pouch of chickpeas and place in an ovenproof bowl; cover with foil and hold in a warm oven. Lift out the beef, chicken, fatback, soup bones, ham bone, if using, and sausages; place in a medium casserole or baking pan, cover with foil, and hold in a warm oven. Pour the broth through a fine-mesh sieve placed over a clean medium saucepan.

5. Bring 2 quarts (2 liters) of water and 2 teaspoons of salt to a boil over high heat in a separate large stockpot or saucepan. Do this about 15 minutes before the meat and beans are done. Add the carrots,

potatoes, and cabbage, decrease the heat to medium, and cook for 30 minutes, or until the carrots and potatoes are fork tender. When the vegetables are ready, drain them into a sieve or colander. Place the carrots and potatoes on a large warmed platter (which will also hold the cabbage and chickpeas), cover with foil, and hold in a warm oven. Transfer the cabbage to a colander and press thoroughly to eliminate any excess liquid.

6. Heat the oil over medium heat in a large sauté pan. Add the garlic and sauté for 2 to 3 minutes, or until golden. Add the cabbage with 2 teaspoons of salt and the pepper, and turn several times in the oil and garlic to heat through and blend the flavors, about 5 minutes. Transfer the cabbage to the platter holding the carrots and potatoes, and keep warm.

7. Heat the tomato sauce in a small saucepan over medium heat until hot, about 5 minutes. Remove from the heat, cover to keep warm, and leave in the saucepan until ready to serve.

8. Bring the broth to a boil over high heat and add the pasta, if using. Boil for 3 to 5 minutes, or until the pasta is almost tender. Remove from the heat and keep warm.

9. Cut all the meats and sausages into 1- to 1½-inch (2.5 to 4 cm) pieces and arrange on a warmed serving platter. If the soup bones contain marrow, remove the marrow, spread it on the toasted bread, sprinkle with salt, and keep warm; otherwise, discard the bones. If you have used the ham bone, cut the meat from the bone and add it to the platter.

10. Remove the chickpeas from the cheesecloth pouch and add them to the vegetable platter.

11. Serve ¾ cup of the broth with pasta in a small or medium bowl as the first course, reheating it if it has cooled. Serve ½ to ¾ cup of the chickpeas, ⅔ cup of cabbage, ½ potato, and ½ carrot with ⅓ cup of the tomato sauce. (This can also be served on the side, if preferred.) Serve ¾ to 1 cup of the meats and sausages, along with the marrow-topped toast, if using marrow bones, as the third course. Alternatively, serve this meal family style. Provide plates and bowls, and allow guests to serve themselves. The broth is delicious as is with the pasta, and it also nicely complements the meats and vegetables.

Adapted from a recipe by TERESA BARRENECHEA

LENTIL STEW
WITH CÈPES, PUMPKIN, AND QUAIL

THIS LENTIL AND PUMPKIN (or squash) stew is garnished with mushrooms and quail legs, both of which are submerged in olive oil and cooked very slowly, like confit.

SERVES 8

For the quail legs

16 quail legs

1 teaspoon salt

¼ teaspoon freshly ground black pepper

1 teaspoon chopped garlic

3 tablespoons chopped flat-leaf parsley

4 cups extra virgin olive oil

3 thyme sprigs

For the lentils

¼ cup extra virgin olive oil

½ cup small-dice tightly packed Serrano ham

1¼ cups small-dice leeks

1 cup small-dice onions

1 tablespoon slivered garlic cloves

2¾ cups peeled, medium-dice pumpkin or other winter squash (such as butternut)

1½ cups dried brown lentils, rinsed and soaked for 30 minutes in water to cover

1 small bay leaf

3 thyme sprigs

1¼ teaspoons salt

½ teaspoon freshly ground black pepper

4 teaspoons sherry vinegar

For the mushrooms

½ cup small-dice onions

1 teaspoon finely chopped garlic

5 cups extra virgin olive oil, divided use

12 ounces (340 g) creminis, cleaned and caps separated from stems

1½ ounces (45 g) dried porcini mushrooms, soaked in hot water for 30 minutes, then drained

4 tablespoons chopped flat-leaf parsley, divided use

1. Prepare the quail legs. Remove the thigh bone, if desired, and chop off the tip of the leg bone closest to the foot. Season with the salt and pepper, garlic, and parsley. If you removed the thigh bone, fold the thigh over the tip of the leg bone, piercing it to secure it. Place in a medium sauté pan or saucepan and cover with the oil. Add the thyme. Warm the oil to 156°F (68°C) and confit the quail legs for 2 hours, or until tender. Reserve in the oil.

2. Cook the lentils while the quail legs confit. Heat the oil in a large saucepan over medium-low heat and add the Serrano ham. Cook for 3 minutes, until some of the ham fat has been rendered, then add the leeks, onions, and garlic. Cook gently for 5 minutes, stirring often, until they are tender and the garlic begins to brown. Stir in the pumpkin, lentils, bay leaf, and thyme and cover with 5 cups of water. Increase the heat and bring to a boil, then reduce the heat and simmer, partially covered, for 40 to 50 minutes, or until the lentils are tender. Add the salt and pepper and remove from the heat. Remove the bay leaf and thyme; set the stew aside or refrigerate for up to 4 days.

3. Prepare the mushrooms. Preheat the oven to 350°F (175°C). Place the onions and garlic in an ovenproof casserole or baking dish large enough to accommodate the mushrooms. Toss the onions and garlic with ¼ cup of oil and warm in the oven for 10 minutes, or until hot. Add the cremini mushroom caps and porcinis and enough oil to cover (about 1½ cups). Place the stems in another similar size baking dish and add enough oil to cover (about 1½ cups). Place both baking dishes in the oven and bake the caps for 25 minutes and the stems for 45 minutes, or until tender and lightly browned. Add 1 tablespoon of chopped parsley and toss together. Remove from the oven and let cool in the oil in the pan.

4. Drain the mushroom caps and stems in a large colander, then cut them into medium dice and reserve in the oil. Warm the lentils over medium heat, about 10 minutes, stirring occasionally. Season with 4 teaspoons of sherry vinegar, or more or less to taste. Warm the mushrooms in a large sauté pan. Remove them from the olive oil with a strainer. Remove the quail legs from the oil and gently fry in a medium sauté pan over medium-high heat until the skin is crisp, 5 to 8 minutes. Spoon 1 cup of the lentils into each bowl and top with ⅓ cup of the mushrooms and 2 quail legs. Drizzle 1 tablespoon of the mushroom confit oil over the mushrooms and lentils. Top with 1 teaspoon of chopped parsley and serve.

Adapted from a recipe by GABINO SOTELINO

PRENDES-STYLE
ASTURIAN BEAN STEW

THIS TRADITIONAL FABADA ASTURIANA is the one that Pedro Morán makes at his one-star restaurant, Casa Gerardo, in Prendes, Spain. In addition to chorizo, this fabada contains blood sausage (morcilla). Note that the beans need to be soaked overnight beforehand.

SERVES 8

2 pounds (900 g) large white beans, preferably from Asturias (fabes)

1 ham hock, soaked in water for 2 hours

3 cups chicken stock

8 ounces (225 g) pancetta, bacon, or salt pork, soaked in water for several hours and drained

¾ cup extra virgin olive oil

4 blood sausages (morcilla) (about 1 pound or 450 g)

8 Spanish chorizo sausages (about 14 ounces or 400 g)

1⅓ cups chopped onions

1½ teaspoons Spanish sweet paprika

¼ teaspoon saffron threads diluted in 1 tablespoon water

1 to 2 teaspoons salt

1. Sort through the beans to remove any rocks or debris. Soak overnight in 3 quarts (3 liters) of water. Drain well in a colander.

2. Bring the ham hock and chicken stock to a boil over medium-high heat in a small saucepan; reduce the heat to low and simmer until the ham is tender and falls away from the bone, about 2 hours. Remove from the chicken stock and when cool enough to handle, shred the meat and set aside or refrigerate until ready to serve.

3. Make the beans while the ham hock is cooking. Combine the pancetta, bacon, or salt pork and ½ cup of the oil in a large flameproof casserole or Dutch oven and cook over medium-high heat for 10 minutes, or until some of the fat has been rendered.

4. Add the beans and the sausages and 10 cups of water, then slowly bring to a boil over medium-high heat. Skim away the foam that comes to the top before the beans reach a boil. Reduce the heat to low and simmer, partially covered, for 1½ to 2 hours, or until the beans are just tender. Add small amounts of water or stock as needed to keep the liquid level ½ inch (1 cm) above the beans.

5. Heat the remaining oil in a medium sauté pan over medium heat and add the onions. Cook, stirring, until the onions are tender, about 5 minutes, and add the sweet paprika. Continue to cook, stirring, for another 5 minutes, until fragrant and very tender. Stir into the beans, along with the saffron. Cover tightly, remove from the heat, and let sit for 1 hour. Taste and adjust seasoning, adding salt as desired.

6. Turn on the heat again and bring the beans back to a simmer over medium heat. Add more liquid if necessary. Do not boil, but cook gently until the beans are tender and creamy, 30 minutes to an hour.

7. Remove the meats and cut into ½-inch (1 cm) pieces. Serve 1¼ cups of the beans, half a blood sausage, and 1 chorizo in a large soup bowl, and garnish with 1 tablespoon of the meat from the ham hock.

Adapted from a recipe by PEDRO MORÁN

BRAISED
VANILLA PORK BELLY

WHEN CHEF NORMAN VAN AKEN makes this dish, which is really a fusion Asian/Spanish rendition of braised pork belly, he injects the belly with vanilla paste. Since most home cooks will not have the means to do this, in this recipe you score the belly and rub it with the vanilla paste.

SERVES 8

One 5-pound (2.25 kg) pork belly, skinned and boned

½ cup vanilla paste

3 tablespoons kosher salt

2½ tablespoons dark brown sugar

1½ tablespoons Asian five-spice powder

1 tablespoon freshly ground black pepper

3 tablespoons extra virgin olive oil

1 cup chopped onions

½ cup chopped carrots

½ cup chopped celery

2 lemongrass stalks, cut into 2-inch (5 cm) lengths and quartered

3 tablespoons chopped ginger

1 tablespoon thinly sliced kaffir lime leaves

1 cup Asian black vinegar

3 cups plum wine

3 cups Tempranillo red wine

2 cups sake

2 quarts (2 liters) veal stock

1 quart (1 liter) Chicken Stock (page 64)

1. Score both sides of the pork belly with the tip of a sharp knife in a ½-inch (1 cm) crosshatch pattern and rub with the vanilla paste. Combine the salt, brown sugar, five-spice powder, and black pepper in a small bowl and rub both sides of the belly with the mixture. Place the meat in a large, wide non-reactive container. Cover with plastic and refrigerate overnight.

2. Preheat the oven to 325°F (165°C).

3. Heat the oil in a large, wide casserole or saucepan over medium heat and add the onions, carrots, and celery. Cook the mixture, stirring occasionally, until lightly browned, 8 to 10 minutes. Add the lemongrass, ginger, and kaffir lime leaves and continue to cook for 2 more minutes, or until aromatic.

4. Add the black vinegar and bring to a boil over high heat, stirring and scraping the bottom of the pan to deglaze. Cook until the liquid has evaporated, 5 to 8 minutes.

5. Add the plum wine, red wine, and sake and bring to a boil. Reduce by half, 20 to 30 minutes. Add the veal stock and chicken stock and bring to a boil.

6. Grill the pork belly on both sides over medium heat until nicely browned, about 10 minutes per side. Place in the pot with the broth and the vegetables. Cover with aluminum foil, and place in the oven. Cook until the meat is fork tender, 1½ to 2 hours.

7. Lift the pork belly out of its cooking broth and transfer it to a cutting board (keep the broth hot until ready to serve). Slice the belly into 6- or 7-inch- (15 to 17 cm) long by ¼-inch- (5 mm) wide strips, and place 4 in each of 8 bowls. Taste the broth; if it's too salty or concentrated for use as a dipping sauce, add water to thin it a little. Pour ¼ cup of hot broth into each bowl and serve immediately.

Adapted from a recipe by NORMAN VAN AKEN

SLAB BACON
IN PANCA PEPPER/BROWN LOAF SUGAR SYRUP

PANCA PEPPERS are South American peppers that resemble sweet chipotles. Maricel Presilla uses them in a marinade for slab bacon at her New Jersey pan-Latin restaurant, Cucharamamma. The dish brings together Old World Spanish ingredients such as olive oil and sherry vinegar with New World chiles. She suggests serving this dish with fresh corn tamales and toasted Andean corn. Note that the meat needs to marinate for a minimum of 6 hours.

SERVES 8

4 pounds (1.8 kg) skinned and boned pork belly or slab bacon, in 1 piece

18 dried panca peppers, stemmed and seeded

2 tablespoons extra virgin olive oil

⅔ cup garlic cloves

2 teaspoons ground cumin

1 teaspoon Spanish sweet paprika

¼ cup Spanish aged sherry vinegar

½ cup orange juice

1 tablespoon honey, preferably Catalan wild oak honey, or 2 teaspoons Peruvian sirope de algarrobina

1 cup Oloroso Brown Loaf Sugar Syrup (page 230), divided use

2 teaspoons salt, or more as needed

1. Rinse the pork belly or bacon and pat dry. Cut a grid pattern on the meat side, being careful not to cut through.

2. Heat a large heavy skillet or griddle over medium heat. Add the dried peppers, in batches, and toast lightly until they puff slightly and emit their fragrance, 3 to 4 seconds on each side. Place in a medium bowl and cover with 3 cups of warm water for 30 minutes to soften. When the peppers are soft, drain them and place in a blender with the oil, garlic, cumin, paprika, sherry vinegar, orange juice, honey or sirope de algarrobina, and ½ cup of the brown loaf sugar syrup. Process to a smooth paste, about 2½ minutes. Stir in the salt, or more or less to taste.

3. Place the pork belly or bacon meat side up in a large casserole roasting pan that can fit the meat in an even layer. Pour the marinade over the meat and rub thoroughly all over. Cover with plastic wrap and allow to marinate in the refrigerator for 6 hours or overnight.

4. Preheat the oven to 350°F (175°C), with the rack adjusted to the middle. Uncover the meat and bake until fork tender, 3 to 4 hours. The paste will turn very dark brown in color and it may be necessary to cover the meat halfway through the cooking process.

5. Transfer the meat to a large cutting board and cut into bite-sized cubes. Drizzle each serving of meat with 1 tablespoon of the brown loaf sugar syrup, or serve 2 to 3 tablespoons on the side in a small bowl or ramekin.

Adapted from a recipe by MARICEL E. PRESILLA

THE SPANISH PIG

OF ALL THE MEATS IN SPAIN, pork is the most highly revered. This reverence has its roots in Christianity. After the Spanish Christians defeated the Moors and expelled them from Spain in 1492, along with any Jews who refused to convert to Christianity, there was an intense period of ethnic cleansing (the infamous Inquisition). Since the dietary laws of both Muslims and Jews forbid eating pork, this became a symbol of being Spanish, a way of affirming one's Christianity.

PORK REPLACES BEEF AND LAMB

Once the Moors were expelled from Spain, cured pork products began to be used instead of beef and lamb in *cocidos* (pages 172–173), the long-cooking stews that the Jews had cooked for Sabbath meals for centuries; in their new incarnations they became signature dishes throughout Spain. Lard became the favored cooking fat in the interior regions (though olive oil continued to be the fat of choice in the Mediterranean), and pork products were soon established as staples in the Spanish kitchen.

Even today, a rural family can live on one pig for an entire year, and the slaughter of the family pig has long been a fall ritual in rural Spain. Every part of the animal is turned into a cured product— hams and salt-cured hocks, cured loins and bacon, sausages, blood puddings, lard and crispy skin, all have an exulted place on the Spanish table.

THE ICONIC SPANISH HAM

Cured Spanish ham is the most iconic of the country's pork products. You would be hard-pressed to find a tapas bar that doesn't have a ham hanging from its rafters; there are even *jamón* museums in many Spanish cities. Most of the cured mountain ham—*jamón Serrano*—comes from the Sierras of Andalusia. Serrano ham is to Spanish cuisine what *prosciutto di Parma* is to Italian—a lean, dry yet supple ham with great depth of flavor. The higher quality Serrano hams are eaten on their own, often with melon, or with bread. Lesser quality *jamón Serrano* is used in cooking, a key flavoring ingredient in many Spanish dishes.

The caviar of Spanish hams is *jamón Ibérico* from Jabugo, made from free-ranging acorn-fattened *pata negra* (black-footed) pigs in southwestern Spain. One hundred percent *jamón Ibérico de bellota* is fattened during the last three to five months of its life on acorns and grasses exclusively (75 percent *jamón Ibérico* is fattened on a mixture of acorns, cereals, and legumes). After the pigs are slaughtered, the hams are covered with sea salt for one day per 2 pounds (1 kg), then they are washed and air-cured in a climate controlled room, where the temperature is very gradually increased. Seventy-five percent

jamón Iberico is cured for two years, 100 percent for three. The high percentage of nutty-tasting fat in their muscle mass makes them the most exquisite hams—and the most expensive—in the world. The acorn-fed pigs are also used for prized chorizo, salchichón, and lomo that is processed in the same highly controlled way.

A GLOSSARY OF SPANISH PORK PRODUCTS

Asturiana: Blood sausage from the Asturias region.

Bisbe: A large blood sausage from Catalonia.

Butifarra or **botifarra**: Popular Catalan white pork sausage spiced with cinnamon, fennel seeds, and black pepper. Also popular in Asturias. Butifarra negra is made with pig's blood.

Camaiot: A butifarra-like pork sausage from the Balearic Islands.

Chorizo: Pork sausage made from lean pork, garlic, paprika, red bell peppers, and red pepper flakes; different from Mexican chorizo.

Extremeña: Blood sausage made with chopped meat, potatoes, and pumpkin from high plains.

Jabuguito: A small chorizo sausage, eaten raw or deep-fried.

Jamón Serrano: Although this cured mountain ham comes from Andalusia, it is used in regional cooking everywhere.

Jamón Ibérico de Jabugo (also known simply as *Jamón Jabugo, Jamón Ibérico*, and *Jamón Ibérico de bellota*): The most prized Serrano ham in Spain, this is made from free-range *pata negra* pigs fattened on acorns, and cured in strict temperature-controlled rooms over three years.

Lomo: Cured pork loin.

Llonganissa, longaniza: Pork sausage seasoned with paprika, cinnamon, aniseed, garlic, and vinegar.

Malagueña: A spicy Andalusian sausage.

Morcilla: Blood sausage stuffed with rice, paprika, onions, garlic, and spices; most commonly used in the Asturias region.

Salchichón: Smoked sausage made from chopped lean pork and pork fat, salt, and black pepper. It is known as *llonganissa* in Catalonia and the Balearic Islands. Salchichón can also be made from acorn-fed pigs, in which case it is known as *salchichón Ibérico*.

Sobrasada, sobrassada: This Majorcan pork sausage is very soft in texture and is flavored with garlic and paprika.

PIG'S TROTTERS
STUFFED WITH VEAL AND WILD MUSHROOMS

CATALAN CHEF NANDO JUBANY uses stewed veal snout in his stuffing for these off-the-bone pig's trotters. Veal snout is quite gelatinous, which makes it good for stuffing. Since it's difficult to get, you can substitute veal stewing meat in this recipe. The forests in Catalonia are rich sources of the wild mushrooms that are used in the sauce. Be very careful when handling the pig's trotters or they will fall apart. Chef Jubany serves this with potato purée, or with a traditional garnish of boiled and sautéed cabbage and potatoes.

SERVES 8

8 pig's trotters

2 tablespoons salt

1 teaspoon freshly ground black pepper

For the veal

10 plum tomatoes

¼ cup extra virgin olive oil

1 teaspoon cayenne pepper

½ cup finely diced green peppers

½ cup finely diced red peppers

2 cups finely diced sweet red onions

8 ounces (225 g) veal snout, washed, blanched, and minced, or veal stewing meat, minced (about 1 cup)

1 teaspoon salt

Pinch freshly ground black pepper

Pinch red pepper

For the pig's trotters

1½ cups vegetable oil

½ cup all-purpose flour, for dusting

1⅓ cups minced onions

¼ cup minced carrots

3 cups peeled, seeded, and finely chopped plum tomatoes

Bouquet garni made with a celery stalk, a halved leek, a few thyme sprigs, and a bay leaf

1 small ham bone

½ teaspoon crushed red pepper

⅔ cup verjus

13½ ounces (385 g) wild mushrooms, such as chanterelles, morels, oyster, or porcinis

2 tablespoons extra virgin olive oil

4 garlic cloves, minced

½ teaspoon salt, or more as needed

Pinch freshly ground black pepper, or more as needed

1 pound 6 ounces (620 g) pork caul, cut into 8 pieces, each about 12 by 12 inches (30 by 30 cm) square

1. Split open the pig's trotters. Season with the salt and pepper and refrigerate, covered, in a baking pan or large casserole overnight.

2. Cook the veal. First cut each tomato in half crosswise and remove the seed sections. Place the cut side of each half against the coarsest section of a box grater, and grate the pulp while pressing with your palm to flatten the skin. Discard the skin. Heat the oil in a large nonstick skillet over medium heat and add the cayenne pepper, the diced peppers, and the onions. Cook, stirring constantly, until tender, 5 to 8 minutes. Add the grated tomatoes and stir together. Cook, stirring often, for about 5 minutes, until the tomatoes have cooked down a little and the mixture is fragrant. Season the veal with the salt, black pepper, and red pepper. Add the veal to the mixture and cook, stirring often, until the meat is cooked through and the mixture is fragrant, about 15 minutes. Taste and adjust seasoning if needed, and refrigerate until ready to assemble.

3. Prepare the pig's trotters. Heat about ¼ inch (5 mm) of vegetable oil in a large cast-iron Dutch oven over medium-high heat. Dust the pig's trotters lightly with flour and brown in the hot oil on both sides, about 4 minutes each side, working in two batches of 4 each. Remove from the heat and transfer them to a clean sheet pan. Pour off all but 2 tablespoons of the oil remaining in the Dutch oven and heat over medium heat. Add the onions and carrots and cook, stirring, until tender, 5 to 8 minutes. Add the tomatoes, bouquet garni, ham bone, and red pepper and stir together. Add the pig's trotters and verjus and enough water to cover the pig's feet (about 5 quarts or 5 liters) and bring to a simmer over medium heat. Cover partially and simmer

for 2 hours, until the trotters are very tender. Carefully remove the trotters from the pot and set aside to cool on a sheet pan or cutting board.

4. Clean the wild mushrooms while the trotters are cooking. Heat 2 tablespoons of oil in a large sauté pan over medium-high heat, and when hot, add the mushrooms and garlic. Sauté, stirring or shaking the pan, until lightly colored and tender, 4 to 5 minutes. Season with the salt and a pinch of pepper and set aside to cool.

5. Preheat the oven to 425°F (220°C). Lightly oil a baking dish large enough to fit the 8 reassembled pig's trotters in a single layer (10- by 15- by 3-inches deep) (25- by 38- by 7.5-cm deep). While the trotters are still hot, work quickly to remove the skin from the bones, slipping it off and separating each trotter into two halves, leaving the tips of the hooves intact. Stuff each half of the boned foot with a scant ¼ cup of the veal mixture, then place the halves together to make a whole foot. Transfer to the center of a sheet of caul, wrap each trotter up like a big cannelloni, and place in the baking dish. Bake for about 8 minutes, so that they shed excess fat. Use a spoon to remove the fat.

6. Add the bones back to the pan with the juices and bring to a boil over medium-high heat. Boil for a couple of minutes, then strain the mixture through a fine-meshed sieve into a bowl, then return to the pan. Add the sautéed wild mushrooms, season to taste with salt and pepper if needed, and bring to a simmer over medium heat. Pour the sauce over the trotters in the baking pan. Serve family style, or serve each trotter whole in a shallow bowl. Top with about ⅓ cup of mushrooms and ½ cup of tomato sauce.

Adapted from a recipe by NANDO JUBANY

SUCKLING PIG'S CHEEKS
WITH SOY SAUCE AND POTATO CREAM

In Spain no part of the pig goes to waste, and the cheeks are considered a great delicacy. You can find pig cheeks in Chinese markets; indeed, this recipe is infused with Asian flavors as well as the familiar Mediterranean ingredients.

SERVES 8

For the pig's cheeks

2 pounds (900 g) suckling pig's cheeks (2 cheeks per serving)

1 teaspoon salt

5 tablespoons extra virgin olive oil, divided use

1 ham bone (about 1 pound or 450 g), preferably Serrano ham

⅔ cup chopped onions

1 teaspoon chopped garlic

½ cup soy sauce

½ cup sake

For the potato purée

9 ounces (250 g) starchy potatoes, such as Russets, peeled

1 teaspoon salt, divided use

1 cup plus 2 tablespoons (2¼ sticks) unsalted butter

1½ teaspoons chopped rosemary or flat-leaf parsley

1. Make the pig's cheeks. Place the pig's cheeks in a large saucepan, add 4 quarts (4 liters) of water to cover, the salt, 1 tablespoon of oil, and the ham bone and bring to a boil over high heat. Reduce the heat to medium low, cover partially, and simmer for 1½ hours, or until the skin and meat is very tender.

2. Drain the cheeks and allow them to cool until they can be handled. Slice them into ¼-inch- (5 mm) thick slices and set aside.

3. Heat the remaining oil in a large skillet over medium heat and add the onions. Cook, stirring, until tender, about 3 minutes, then add the garlic. Cook, stirring, for a minute, until fragrant, and add the sliced suckling pig cheeks, the soy sauce, and sake. Bring to a boil over medium-high heat and reduce for 10 minutes, or until the oil and liquids have reduced to a little over ½ cup. Reserve warm.

4. Make the potato purée. Place the peeled potatoes in a medium saucepan with enough water to cover by an inch (2.5 cm) (about 8 cups). Add ½ teaspoon of salt and bring to a boil over medium heat. Cover partially and boil until tender, about 25 minutes. Drain and return to the warm pot. Cover tightly and let sit for 5 minutes.

5. Mash the potatoes through a food mill or potato ricer or by hand in a mixing bowl. Gradually add the butter, using a whisk to stir until you have a fine potato cream, 2 to 3 minutes. Season to taste with ½ teaspoon of salt.

6. Place 2 spoonfuls (about 3 tablespoons) of potato cream in the middle of each plate. Top the potato with 4 slices of pig's cheeks and drizzle over 1 tablespoon of the jus. Sprinkle with rosemary or parsley and serve.

Adapted from a recipe by Cándido López Cuerdo

NEW YORK STEAKS
WITH GOLDEN RAISIN SAUCE AND ASPARAGUS SALAD

YOU WON'T FIND THICK NEW YORK STEAKS in Spain, but you will find the garlicky sauces that combine sweet and vinegary flavors, like the one Robert Del Grande serves with his New York steaks.

SERVES 8

For the raisin sauce

1 cup garlic cloves, peeled

½ cup chopped white onions

⅔ cup golden raisins

½ cup chopped fennel bulb

4 dried chiles de arbol, seeds and stems removed

½ cup grapeseed oil

½ cup extra virgin olive oil

4 white anchovies

4 egg yolks

1 cup buttermilk

¼ cup heavy cream

1 tablespoon champagne vinegar or cider vinegar

2 teaspoons salt, or as needed

¼ teaspoon freshly ground black pepper, or as needed

For the asparagus salad

32 spears jumbo asparagus, woody ends trimmed (2 pounds 3 ounces or 1 kg)

2 tablespoons extra virgin olive oil

½ teaspoon salt

¼ teaspoon freshly ground black pepper

For the steaks

Four 16-ounce (450 g) New York strip steaks (or beef strip loin)

2 tablespoons extra virgin olive oil

2 teaspoons salt

1 teaspoon freshly ground black pepper

1. Make the raisin sauce. Combine the garlic cloves, onions, golden raisins, fennel, chiles de arbol, grapeseed oil, and olive oil in a medium saucepan over medium heat. Lightly fry the ingredients until the garlic is lightly golden and soft and the raisins begin to puff, about 5 minutes. Add the anchovies, remove from the heat, and let cool to room temperature.

2. Transfer the cooled ingredients with the oil to a food processor fitted with a steel blade. Blend until fairly smooth, about 1 minute. Remove from the food processor and set aside in a medium bowl.

3. Add the egg yolks, buttermilk, and cream to the purée and whisk until thoroughly combined. Add the vinegar, salt, and pepper. Adjust seasoning to taste. Refrigerate (you should have approximately 3 cups).

4. Prepare the asparagus salad. Peel the lower half of each spear with a vegetable peeler while you bring a large pot of lightly salted water to a boil. Blanch the asparagus in salted boiling water for 1 to 2 minutes so that the asparagus is just barely cooked at the center. Remove with a slotted spoon and chill in ice water. Cut the asparagus into halves or quarters, depending on the size. Toss the asparagus in the oil. Lightly season with salt and pepper.

5. Preheat a charcoal grill to medium-high heat, or build a fire with coals and let it burn down until the coals are glowing red with a thin coating of white ash. Spread the coals out in a single layer.

6. Prepare the steaks while the grill or coals heat up. Lightly rub the steaks with the oil and season with the salt and pepper. Grill the steaks to medium rare (145°F or 65°C), turning occasionally, about 25 minutes. Allow to rest for 5 to 10 minutes.

7. Carve the steaks into ¼-inch- (5 mm) thick slices. Divide the slices among 8 dinner plates (about 6 slices per plate). Spoon ⅓ cup of the raisin steak sauce over the slices. Finally, divide the asparagus salad among the plates and serve.

Adapted from a recipe by ROBERT DEL GRANDE

ASTURIAS

EAST OF GALICIA ON THE NORTHERN COAST OF SPAIN LIES ASTURIAS, another misty green region with a dramatic coastline and scenic mountains. Historically, Asturias stands out because it was never occupied by the Arabs. The Kingdom of Asturias defeated the Moors in the 8th century at the Battle of Covadonga, slowing the Arab advance into northern Spain and France. Gastronomically, Asturias is well known for its seafood like its neighbors to the east and west, but the real treasures of this region are the large white haricot beans called *fabes* and its blue-veined Cabrales cheese.

◄◄ **Fabes** from Asturias have Denomination of Origin status. Look for this seal of authenticity when you buy them.

◄ **Asturian bean stew** is just one of the hearty dishes containing fabes for which this region is so famous.

► **Cabrales** is produced in small quantities and aged in cold, humid conditions in special caves, where its characteristic blue veins develop.

THE FAMOUS FABES

Fabes de la granja (the very large, oblong white beans are called *fabes* in the center of the region, *fabas* in the west, and *jabas* in the east) were a New World food that came to northern Spain via Valencia. With its temperate, rainy summers, the region was ideal for these beans. Grown on vertical poles, they're planted in May and harvested in September and October. Most of the crop is dried, but some is sold fresh. Whether fresh or dried, fabes are eaten within a year of being harvested. They received Denomination of Origin (DO) protection in 1990; all fabes grown in Asturias are so labeled.

Fabes are at the heart of the most famous dish from Asturias, *fabada*, arguably the masterpiece of all Spanish cocidos. The beans are cooked with local chorizo and blood sausage, and sometimes pancetta, bacon, and/or lacon, a pink, salt-cured ham. The meats are first blanched to rid them of some of their fat, and the beans are

cooked slowly, at a simmer but never at a boil, so that they maintain their integrity. The meats in a fabada are referred to as the *campagno*, or complement—a clear sign that the beans get top billing here. The beans are often served as a first course, followed by the *campagno*.

Another famous Asturian bean dish is *fabes con almejas*, beans with clams. The Spanish love dishes that bring together *mar y montaña*, sea and mountain, and no dish does it better than this one.

ASTURIAN SEAFOOD

Tuna, hake, and monkfish are particularly popular here, as are spider crabs. Some of the local dishes include *atún a la Asturiana*—tuna steaks cooked with onion, garlic, vinegar, and paprika; and *merluza a la sidra*, hake served with clams and potatoes in a hard cider sauce. There is also abundant freshwater fish such as trout and salmon in the streams that run through the mountainous region of Asturias.

RICE PUDDING

Interestingly, Asturias is famous for its rice pudding, a dessert that is popular throughout Spain but particularly in Asturias. Here it is made without cream or eggs; rice is simmered in a large quantity of milk for 3 hours (and stirred often during this time), until the mixture has the consistency of custard. Sugar is then stirred in and the pudding is simmered for another 15 minutes, then chilled or cooled to room temperature. Sometimes, particularly in restaurants, sugar is sprinkled over the top and caramelized to form a sweet and crunchy crust—a lovely contrast to the creaminess of the pudding.

ASTURIAN CHEESES

Over twenty varieties of cheese are produced in Asturias, and three have obtained DO status—Cabrales, Gamonéu, and Afuega'l Pitu. Of these Cabrales in the most famous. It's a crumbly, sharp blue cheese with a flavor that is distinctly spicy (locally it is called *picón* or *picañón*, which means spicy). Made from a mixture of cow's, sheep's, and goat's milk, Cabrales matures in caves for at least three months and develops its own natural blue veins.

ASTURIAN CIDER

Asturias is not a wine-producing region. Here the drink of choice is cider, made from three types of apples and protected by a Denomination of Origin, *Sidra de Asturias*. They are dry ciders that go well with Asturian food. There are three types of DO ciders: natural, new expression, and sparkling. Natural cider is the traditional cider, sold in characteristic bottles and poured into glasses from high above. New expression cider is a blended, elegant cider, meant to accompany food. Sparkling cider is the champagne of ciders, with delicate bubbles and a light hue.

RICE

RICE

From the traditional to the truly inventive

Spain, particularly the Eastern Mediterranean regions, has been a country of rice lovers for over one thousand years. Paella is the iconic Spanish rice dish, and it comes in many forms. But as you cook your way through the recipes in this chapter, you'll see that paella is just one tradition. There are creamy rice dishes (*arroces melosos*), such as the Valencian Seafood Rice on pages 200–201, soupy rices, and cutting-edge contemporary rice dishes.

The classic Paella Valenciana is cooked in the traditional paella pan, which then makes a dramatic serving dish when brought to the table.

PAELLA TRADITIONS

Paella is the most familiar Spanish rice dish. It's also the most festive, traditionally cooked in the open air in wide, flat pans of the same name over wood fires made with vine cuttings. The iconic Paella Valenciana (pages 196–197) is made with rabbit and land snails, and sometimes chicken and/or duck, a country dish that also contains flat green beans and fresh lima beans, sometimes artichokes, a sofrito made with tomatoes and lots of garlic and paprika and, of course, saffron. If snails are not available, a sprig of rosemary is substituted, perhaps to give it the earthy essence that the snails contribute. It's a dish that came about because agricultural workers had to eat when they were toiling in the fields; they gathered wood cuttings, made fires, and used ingredients that were available to them. Paella evolved into a ritual, enjoyed outside on Sunday afternoons by families all over Valencia.

Authentic paellas are cooked over an open flame in large wide metal pans called *paellas* (the actual name of the dish is *arróz à la paella*). However, you can still achieve a perfect paella over a hot grill at home. Other *arroces* (as paellas are often called), such as the Valencian Seafood Rice on pages 200–201, are cooked in earthenware or cast-iron casseroles (*cazuelas*), on top of the stove or in the oven.

Caldero, the rice and seafood stew on pages 202–203, was traditionally cooked on board fishing boats. The fish was cooked in seawater in an earthenware casserole, then the rice was cooked in the resulting broth. The rice was eaten separately as a first course, followed by the fish.

One of the most dramatic paellas is black paella, made with squid and squid ink, a signature dish that is savored all along Spain's eastern coast. So much of the ink is used that the rice really is jet black, with an incredibly rich seafood flavor.

PAELLA FROM THE ALBUFERA

One of the best places in Spain to experience authentic paellas is the village of El Palmar, near the city of Valencia. The drive from Valencia takes you through the Albufera, the beautiful lagoon that surrounds the city. On both sides of the road you will see bright green fields of rice stretching for miles, for it is here that the best rice in Spain is grown.

El Palmar is filled with paella restaurants, all serving regional specialties, particularly *arroz a banda* (made with a very aromatic fish broth), *arroz alli e pebre* (with eels), and *arroz amb fesols i naps*, a brothy paella made with local duck, white beans, turnips, and blood sausage. You have to order *arroz amb fesols i naps* a day ahead, because the duck is

Sushi rice is cooked in red wine, formed into a round, and garnished with Serrano ham and vegetables in this playful Red Wine Sushi Rice.

This rich, risotto-like rice dish is an innovation of Chef Jesús Ramiro and is slightly more soupy in texture than a traditional paella.

wild from the Albufera, and it must be hung and prepared ahead of time. Be warned that if you go on a Monday you won't have much of a choice, because none of the seafood specialties will be available: fishermen do not work on Sundays. However, if you visit on any other day of the week you'll find tables filled for many hours with people eating many different rice dishes.

EXPERIMENTAL PAELLA

Contemporary chefs both in Spain and abroad are playing with Spanish rice concepts and ingredients. Japanese chef Kiyomo Mikuni, chef/owner of the Hôtel de Mikuni in Tokyo, calls his exquisite saffron-hued sushi rice tapa, which consists of small nori-framed squares of cooked Japanese rice garnished with shellfish, Sushi Paella (pages 212–213); he garnishes his rounds of Red Wine Sushi Rice (pages 214–215) with Serrano ham. Michelin-starred chef Raúl Alexaindre, of Ca'Sento in Valencia, makes a deconstructed paella with crispy puffed rice. Javier Andrés, at La Sucursal restaurant inside the Instituto Valenciano de Arte Moderno, makes an inventive, creamy paella, seasoned with ginger and garnished with baby clams and octopus shavings. In the pages that follow, you'll find examples of both the comforting traditional dishes and the edgy contemporary ones; and one or two, like Chef Jesús Ramiro's Rich Rice with Pig's Ears and Chorizo (pages 206–207), which are somewhere in between.

PAELLA VALENCIANA

THIS IS THE CLASSIC COUNTRY PAELLA of Valencia, made with chicken and rabbit, and in snail season, cooked snails called *vaquetas*. Authentic paella should be made over firewood. Twigs from olive or orange trees are used for hot flames, and thicker logs are used for a slower fire. The trick is to have both at the same time, so that the meat and vegetables can be browned slowly, then the rice brought to the boil over the hottest part of the fire, then set over a lower flame. If you can't build a wood fire, a charcoal one will do. Valencian *bachoqueta de herradura* and Valencian *garrofón* (special green and flat green beans, respectively, from the region) were called for in the original recipe, but other green beans can be substituted, and cooked dried beans or lima beans can be substituted for the flat green beans. You can also have your butcher cut up the rabbit for you, if desired.

SERVES 8 GENEROUSLY

- 1¾ cups dried lima beans (broad beans), soaked overnight in 10 cups water and drained
- 6½ teaspoons salt, divided use
- 1 rabbit (about 2 pounds or 900 g)
- ½ cup extra virgin olive oil
- 1 large chicken (about 4 pounds 8 ounces or 2 kg), cut into 8 pieces
- 2 teaspoons freshly ground black pepper
- 4 ripe tomatoes, peeled and puréed
- 1¾ cups chopped onions
- 2½ teaspoons minced garlic
- 2¾ cups green beans (preferably flat romano beans)
- 2½ to 3 quarts (2½ to 3 liters) water, plus more as needed
- 1 rosemary sprig
- 2 generous pinches saffron
- 4 cups Bomba rice

1. Bring 10 cups of water to a boil over medium-high heat and add the dried beans. Reduce the heat to a simmer and cook until just tender, 1 to 1½ hours. Stir in 2 teaspoons of salt and let rest in their liquid for about 30 minutes before draining.

2. Cut up the rabbit: Cut off the hind legs, using a sharp boning knife to slice between each leg and the hip joint. Cut each hind leg into two pieces, slicing at the joint between the thigh and leg. Cut off the front legs, slicing between each leg and the shoulder joint. Cut the body into three sections: ribs, loin, and bottom, using a heavy meat cleaver. Cut the loin in half, then cut the ribs in half through the breast and backbone, then cut each half in half.

3. Prepare a wood (or charcoal) fire and heat the oil in a large paella pan set over the hottest part of the fire. Season the chicken and rabbit with 2 teaspoons each of salt and pepper. When the oil is hot, add the chicken and rabbit and fry over medium-high heat, turning the meat to brown all sides evenly, 8 to 10 minutes.

4. Add the tomatoes, onions, garlic, and green beans and continue to cook over medium heat until the beans are nearly tender, about 15 minutes. Add 10 cups of water and the rosemary sprig and move to the hottest part of the grill, or rearrange or add coals to raise the heat to high. Cover the pan with a grill lid.

5. Remove the lid when the water comes to a boil. Stir in 2½ teaspoons of salt and the saffron, then sprinkle the rice evenly around the pan directly into the liquid, avoiding the meat.

6. Add the broad beans. Stir gently one time only to evenly distribute the rice (do not stir again). Remove the rosemary.

7. Cook, uncovered, turning the pan one-quarter turn every 5 minutes to help ensure even heat distribution. Cook the rice over high heat for 10 minutes, or until the water is almost absorbed, then move to a cooler part of the grill and cook at a gentle simmer over low heat for another 10 minutes, or until the rice has absorbed all of the liquid. The rice should be al dente when it is done; if it is too firm when the liquid is absorbed, add additional water 1 cup at a time, continuing cooking until the rice is done. During this period, keep the heat at a level that allows the liquid to simmer gently.

8. Remove the paella from the heat, and cover and allow to sit for 5 to 10 minutes before serving. Serve about 2 cups of the rice and vegetables and 1 piece each of the rabbit and chicken for each of 8 servings in large heated soup bowls. Or place the warm paella pan on the table and allow guests to serve themselves.

Adapted from a recipe by RAFAEL VIDAL

PAELLA WITH VEGETABLES

ALTHOUGH MOST PAELLAS contain a few types of vegetables—onions, tomatoes, one or two types of beans—until recently it was rare to find a vegetable paella that didn't also include seafood or meat on a menu. However, with more vegetarians visiting paella restaurants, this has changed as demand has grown. It's a demand that's not a challenge to meet, given the abundance and variety of fresh produce in Spain.

SERVES 8

For the sofrito

2 tablespoons extra virgin olive oil

2½ cups small-dice onions

1½ cups thinly sliced leeks, white parts only

Generous pinch salt

4¼ cups chopped plum tomatoes, canned or fresh if in season

For the paella

3 tablespoons extra virgin olive oil

6 artichoke hearts, cut into eighths (about 4½ cups)

1 head cauliflower, cut into florets (about 5 cups)

1 cup plus 2 tablespoons Calasparra rice

1 tablespoon minced garlic

Sofrito (from above)

3¼ to 3½ cups vegetable stock

1⅓ cups fresh or frozen peas

1 teaspoon salt, divided use

1 teaspoon freshly ground black pepper, divided use

3 red peppers, roasted, peeled, and cut into strips

1 tablespoon coarsely chopped flat-leaf parsley

1. Make the sofrito. Heat the oil in a large sauté pan or skillet over low heat. Sauté the onions and leeks with the salt, stirring frequently for 8 minutes, or until the vegetables are soft. Add the tomatoes, raise the heat to medium low, and cook, stirring occasionally, for 30 minutes, or until the vegetables are tender and their liquid has almost completely evaporated. Remove and reserve.

2. Make the paella. Heat the oil over medium-high heat in a large paella pan, add the artichoke hearts, and sauté until golden, about 6 minutes. Add the cauliflower and cook until slightly colored, another 3 minutes.

3. Add the rice and garlic and stir continuously to toast the rice and lightly brown the garlic, 2 to 3 minutes. Stir in the sofrito.

4. Add 2 cups of vegetable stock, or just enough to cover the rice, and if using fresh peas, add them now. Add ½ teaspoon of salt and ½ teaspoon of pepper; bring to a boil, then reduce the heat to medium low and simmer, uncovered, until the rice has absorbed most of the stock, about 15 minutes.

5. Add 2 more cups of vegetable stock and cook until the rice has absorbed all of the liquid, about 12 minutes. If using frozen peas, add them during the last 6 minutes of cooking. The rice should be al dente when it is done; if it is too firm when the liquid is absorbed, add additional water ½ cup at a time, continuing cooking until the rice is done. During this period, keep the heat at a level that allows the liquid to simmer gently. Taste and adjust seasoning with the remaining salt and pepper. When the rice is finished cooking, garnish the top with the roasted red pepper strips and chopped parsley.

Recipe by THE CULINARY INSTITUTE OF AMERICA

VALENCIAN
SEAFOOD RICE

THIS CREAMY CAZUELA is a typical Valencian seafood rice dish that María Muria Lloret makes at Ca'Sento in Valencia. This small Michelin-starred restaurant specializes in seafood, the best in Valencia, serving traditional Valencian dishes prepared by María along with more contemporary dishes prepared by her son, Chef Raúl Aleixandre.

SERVES 8

For the fumet

¼ cup extra virgin olive oil

5 ounces (140 g) shrimp (21 to 25 count)

5 ounces (140 g) crab

2 pounds (900 g) rockfish or sea bass

1¼ cups chopped onions

1 tablespoon minced garlic

1½ cups chopped leeks, white parts only

3 cups chopped tomatoes

4 quarts (4 liters) water

2 tablespoons salt

For the rice

½ cup extra virgin olive oil

10 ounces (285 g) baby squid or sliced squid

1 pound 8 ounces (680 g) shrimp (21–25 count), peeled

5 tablespoons minced garlic

2½ cups Tomato Sauce (page 221)

4 teaspoons sweet paprika

3½ quarts (3½ liters) Fumet (from above)

3¼ cups Bomba rice

1. Make the fumet. Heat the oil in a large soup pot or Dutch oven over medium heat and cook the shrimp, crab, and rockfish for 2 to 3 minutes, or until they begin to turn pink. Add the onions, garlic, and leeks and cook, stirring, until lightly colored, about 10 minutes. Add the tomatoes and cook for another 10 minutes, then add the water and bring to a boil. Reduce the heat to medium low, cover partially, and simmer for 45 minutes, then strain through a cheesecloth-lined strainer. Season generously with the salt.

2. Make the rice. Heat the oil in a large Dutch oven over medium-high heat. When the oil is hot, lightly fry the baby squid and the shrimp until they lose their translucency, about 5 minutes, and remove from the pan. Turn down the heat slightly, add the garlic, and then the tomato sauce. Cook for about 3 minutes, until bubbling, and add the paprika. Add enough fumet to cover (about 14 cups), bring to a boil, and add the squid, shrimp, and rice. Cook for approximately 16 minutes, or until the rice is al dente. Remove from the heat and allow to rest for 10 minutes, then serve 2 cups of rice in each of 8 bowls.

Adapted from a recipe by MARÍA MURIA LLORET

CALDERO

THIS MURCIAN FISHERMAN'S STEW with rice was traditionally eaten on fishing boats. The creamy (*meloso*) rice was eaten as a first course, followed by the fish. Murcian chef Juan Antonio Pellicer dresses up his caldero. He vacuum-cooks small pimentón-seasoned squares of daurade with olive oil, and places the fish over the rice. Then he reduces his fish stock, seasons it with garlic and ñora powder, and serves it in a glass, for guests to pour over their fish and rice. In this recipe the fish is cooked in parchment, which yields juicy, tender fillets. You can stir the juice into the rice just before serving.

SERVES 8

For the fish stock

1 pound 8 ounces (680 g) white-fleshed fish fillets or steaks, such as monkfish, daurade, sea bass, or mullet, or the equivalent in fish heads and bones

3 to 4 ñora peppers, seeded and crumbled or ground in a spice mill or blender

16 shrimp (26–30 count), with shells and heads if possible

¾ head garlic

6 quarts (6 liters) water

1½ tablespoons salt, or more to taste

Freshly ground black pepper to taste

For the caldero

9 tablespoons extra virgin olive oil, divided use

Sixteen 2-ounce (60 g) daurade pieces

Salt, as needed

Freshly ground black pepper, as needed

2¼ teaspoons Spanish sweet paprika

2 tablespoons finely chopped parsley

¾ head garlic, cloves peeled and minced

3 to 4 ñora peppers, seeded and ground in a spice mill or blender

3 medium tomatoes, grated or peeled, seeded, and finely chopped

3 cups Spanish short-grain rice (not Bomba)

Generous pinch crumbled saffron threads

1. Make the fish stock. Combine the fish (or heads and bones), peppers, shrimp, garlic, water, salt, and pepper to taste in a soup pot and bring to a boil. Reduce the heat, cover partially and simmer very gently for 30 minutes. Strain through a cheesecloth-lined strainer. Set aside 7 cups. Reduce the remaining stock to 1½ cups.

2. Make the caldero. Cut 8 double pieces of aluminum foil and oil the foil with olive oil. Season the fish fillets generously with the salt, pepper, and paprika. Place 3 pieces of fish on a foil square and drizzle on 2 teaspoons of oil. Sprinkle with chopped parsley and about ½ teaspoon of minced garlic. Fold up the edges of the foil and seal tightly to make a packet. Repeat with the remaining fish. Place the packets on a baking sheet. Set aside.

3. Preheat the oven to 425°F (220°C).

4. Heat 2 tablespoons of the oil in a large, heavy saucepan or casserole over medium heat, add a tablespoon of the garlic and half of the ground ñoras. Stir together for a minute, and remove the pan from the heat. Scrape into the cup of reduced fish stock that you set aside earlier.

5. Heat the remaining oil in the saucepan over medium heat and add the remaining garlic. Cook, stirring, for about 30 seconds, until fragrant. Stir in the tomatoes and cook, stirring often, until the tomatoes have cooked down and the mixture is very fragrant, about 8 minutes. Add the rice and stir together, then add the remaining ground ñoras. Stir together and add the 7 cups fish stock and the saffron. Season generously. Bring to a boil and cook for 10 minutes, stirring the bottom of the pot from time to time to make sure the rice doesn't stick, then reduce the heat to medium low and continue to simmer until the rice is cooked al dente and the mixture is creamy like risotto, about 15 minutes. Stir occasionally.

6. Roast the fish in the packets while the rice cooks. Place the baking sheet with the fish papillotes in the preheated oven and bake for 10 minutes, or until the fish is just tender. Keep hot in the foil packets.

7. Divide the rice among soup plates, dinner plates, or bowls. Open the foil packets one by one by cutting across the top with scissors, and tip the liquid in the packet over the rice. Place the fish fillets on top of the rice. Heat the stock that you set aside and divide among 8 small glasses or pitchers. Serve a glass or pitcher with each portion for guests to pour over their fish and rice.

Adapted from a recipe by JUAN ANTONIO PELLICER

DRY RICE WITH ESPARDEÑAS

THIS IS A SIMPLE PAELLA-STYLE rice dish made with a flavorful fish broth and baby sea cucumbers, or *espardeñas*. Use a paella pan if possible or a wide nonstick skillet. The original recipe called for *espardeñas*, but you can substitute calamari or octopus, if desired.

SERVES 8

For the broth

1 tablespoon extra virgin olive oil

1 tablespoon minced garlic

½ cup chopped onions

⅓ cup chopped leeks

3 tablespoons chopped celery

1 to 2 parsley sprigs

½ cup peeled, seeded, and diced tomatoes (about 1½ large)

1 pound 5 ounces (600 g) small shrimp or small fish for broth

2 quarts (2 liters) water

1 tablespoon tomato paste

2½ teaspoons salt

For the mortar mix

4 tablespoons extra virgin olive oil

Two ½-inch- (1 cm) thick baguette slices, cut into ½-inch (1 cm) cubes

1½ garlic cloves

½ teaspoon salt

¼ cup flat-leaf parsley leaves, loosely packed

¼ teaspoon saffron threads

1¼ dried ñora peppers

2 slices country-style bread

For the rice

¼ cup extra virgin olive oil

3 sea cucumbers, or 1 pound 8 ounces (680 g) calamari or octopus

4 teaspoons nigella seeds

½ cup Mortar Mix (from above)

3 cups Carnaroli or Arborio rice

1. Make the broth. Heat the oil in a medium soup pot or Dutch oven over medium heat and add the garlic. Cook, stirring, until golden, 2 to 3 minutes, and add the onions, leeks, celery, and parsley. Turn the heat to medium-high and cook, stirring, for 2 to 3 minutes, or until the garlic begins to brown. Stir in the tomatoes and shrimp or fish, then add the water and tomato paste, stirring until the paste is dissolved. Bring to a boil and skim off any foam that rises to the surface. Reduce the heat to medium low and simmer for 20 to 25 minutes, skimming off the foam from time to time. Strain through a cheesecloth-lined strainer and season generously with the salt.

2. Make the mortar mix. Heat the oil in a small skillet. Sauté the bread cubes until lightly browned and crisp, 8 to 10 minutes.

3. Combine all the ingredients for the mortar mix, including the sautéed bread cubes, in a food processor fitted with the steel blade and pulse to a pastelike consistency. Set aside.

4. Make the rice. Bring the broth to a simmer in a large saucepan over medium-high heat. Preheat the oven to 500°F (260°C). Heat a large flat paella pan or ovenproof skillet over medium heat and add the oil, sea cucumbers, calamari, or octopus, nigella seeds, and the mortar mix. Cook, stirring, for 3 minutes, then add the rice. Cook, stirring constantly, until the rice begins to color and crackle, 8 to 10 minutes. Add enough of the broth to cover the rice by about ½ inch (1 cm) (about 3 cups). Boil for 5 minutes on high heat. Add 2 cups of stock, then place in the oven for another 5 minutes, or until the rice has absorbed all the water. It may begin to stick to the pan in some areas, creating a dark brown, crusty layer of rice, which is very delicious if not burned. Remove from the heat, stir once lightly, and allow to settle for a few minutes before serving. Remove the sea cucumbers, calamari, or octopus. Depending on what you are using, slice the sea cucumbers into ¼-inch (5 mm) half-moons and the calamari heads into rings. If using octopus tentacles, cut them in half, if desired. Arrange these over the rice as a garnish, or stir them into the dish before serving. Allow about 2 tablespoons of sliced sea cucumbers, calamari, or octopus per serving.

Adapted from a recipe by NANDO JUBANY

RICH RICE
WITH PIG'S EARS AND CHORIZO

Chef Jesús Ramiro calls this rich country rice dish "Rice in Movement, Zamorano Style" after the famous soccer player Iván Zamorano. The rice never stops "moving" because liquid is added to it at different intervals: first wine, then stock made with ham bones, then butter and cream.

SERVES 8

¾ cup extra virgin olive oil

6 cups chopped onions

2 tablespoons sliced garlic

3 cups short-grain Spanish rice (about 1 pound 8 ounces or 680 g)

2¼ cups dry white wine

9 ounces (250 g) pig's ears, cooked in boiling water for 30 minutes and diced

1⅔ cups chopped cured chorizo sausages (preferably Ibérico), (about 9 ounces or 250 g)

6 cups Brown Pork Stock (page 66)

1½ teaspoons salt

½ teaspoon freshly ground black pepper, or more as needed

1½ cups (3 sticks) butter

1½ cups heavy cream

2 tablespoons chopped oregano

3 tablespoons toasted, chopped almonds

1. Heat the oil in a medium Dutch oven over medium-low heat and add the onions and garlic. Cook slowly, stirring often, for 20 minutes, or until the onions are very soft.

2. Add the rice and stir together for 5 minutes, then stir in the wine, pig's ears, and chorizo. Cook slowly until the wine has evaporated, 8 to 10 minutes, then add the pork stock, salt, and pepper. Bring to a boil over medium-high heat, reduce the heat to medium low, and simmer for 10 minutes, or until the rice has absorbed the stock. Add the butter, cream, and oregano and cook, stirring, for about 5 minutes, or until the oregano has released its flavor and the rice is very creamy. Stir in the almonds.

3. Serve in large, shallow soup bowls or on plates, topping each serving with freshly ground black pepper and 5 to 7 very thin shavings of tuna scales, if using.

Adapted from a recipe by Jesús Ramiro

SPANISH RICE

Arroz, the Spanish word for rice, comes from the Arabic word, *al-ruzz*. The Moors brought rice to Spain in the 8th century. They planted it in the flat eastern Mediterranean region, El Levante ("where the sun rises"), where they had established a sophisticated system of irrigation canals to channel water from the inland mountains and rivers so that it wouldn't be lost into the Mediterranean. As a result, vast, fertile rice fields as well as *huertas* (see page 97) were cultivated throughout the region, especially around the large Albufera lagoon south of the city of Valencia. Valencia has been rice country ever since, and home of the great rice dishes of Spain.

TRADITIONAL SPANISH RICE DISHES

The most famous Spanish rice dish is, of course, paella. Valencians feel very proprietary about Paella Valenciana (pages 196–197), and they are purists about what can and cannot go into it. But there are literally hundreds of other paellas: seafood paellas of all kinds at the coast, including black paellas made with squid and its ink, and *arroz a banda*, in which the seafood and the rice, cooked in a rich seafood broth, are eaten separately. Paellas are made with vegetables from the *huertas* (fertile gardens) and different kinds of sausages, with potatoes and meatballs, with pork and vegetables. What they all have in common is the type of rice used, a short- or medium-grain rice that absorbs the flavors of the ingredients it's cooked with while still remaining chewy. They are "dry" rice dishes, or *seco*, meaning that the rice absorbs all of the tasty liquid in which it's cooked. The layer of rice is thin, with a crusty layer on the bottom of the pan—the *socarrat*—that is scraped off at the end and passed around to all of the diners, the prize of a properly executed paella. Most are seasoned with saffron, which gives the paella its characteristic golden color and contributes to its complex, rich flavor. Some paellas, particularly those with seafood, are served with *allioli*, or garlic mayonnaise.

Spain's rice dishes don't stop with paellas. *Cazuelas* are made in earthenware or cast-iron casseroles (*cazuelas*). They can be cooked on top of the stove, or in the oven, in which case the dish might be called *arròz al horno*. Rice dishes are also defined by their consistency. While paellas are *secos*, or dry, other rice dishes are *melosos*, or slightly creamy, like a risotto. Then there are *arroces caldosos*, which are brothy like a thick rice soup. One of Valencia's most famous soupy rice dishes is *arròs amb fesols i naps*, rice with white beans, turnips, wild Albuferra duck, pork, and black sausage. People will order this a day ahead and drive out to one of the many rice restaurants in El Palmar, in the Albufera, to eat it. Another famous Valencian *arròz* is *arròz all i pebre*, a rich, soupy *cazuela* made with eels, peppers, and garlic.

The Levante extends south from Valencia into the regions of Murcia and Alicante, also rice country. Murcia's famous rice dish is a fisherman's *caldero*, or cauldron, called *caldero Murciano* (pages 202–203). *Caldero* is eaten in two courses—first the rice, which has been cooked in a flavorful fish broth, then the fish. The rice is sometimes served with *allioli*, and the fish with a garlic and pepper sauce.

PAELLA DECONSTRUCTED

Rice traditions have not eluded Spain's avant-garde chefs. At the Michelin-starred Ca'Sento in Valencia, renowned for its exquisite seafood, Chef Raúl Aleixandre deconstructs paella while his mother, María Muria Lloret, offers up traditional Valencian dishes, such as *arroz marinero*, a *meloso* mixture of chiparones, shrimp, garlic, tomatoes, and Senia rice cooked in a rich, saffrony fumet in a cast-iron pot. While Chef Aleixandre lets his pristine seafood speak for itself in many of his dishes, he is a bit more iconoclastic with his paella; he serves a puffed fried rice with cuttlefish on the side and a cauliflower foam, all united in a cuttlefish broth. Chef Carles Gaig, of the Michelin-starred Gaig restaurant in Barcelona, riffs on a rice and squid paella, and also on the very Catalan tradition of *mar y montaña*—combining earthy mountain food with seafood in a dish—in his rice with lacquered squid. The squid, lacquered with a reduction of a pork broth, is served over the rice, along with *espardeñas* (a sea anemone sometimes called a "sea cucumber") and with *trompetas de la muerte* mushrooms, all the elements brought together with a sauce made from the pork broth.

VARIETIES OF RICE

Three types of Valencian rice are used by cooks and chefs; Senia is the most popular, followed by Bahía and Bomba. Bomba rice absorbs the most liquid, and will expand, like an accordion, to three times its size. It can be more expensive than other rices, but cooks like it because the grains do not stick together when cooked. Another popular Spanish rice is Calasparra, the oldest strain of rice grown in Spain. Calasparra rice, which arrived with the Moors, has exceptionally hard kernels that absorb a great deal of liquid—and the tastier the liquid, the tastier the rice dish. Bahía rice is a quick-cooking short-grain paella rice that is also grown in the Calasparra region.

RICE WITH DUCK

THIS IS A GOOD EXAMPLE of the exciting fusion that is going on between European and Latin American chefs. Lima-based, French-trained chef Marilú Madueño has created a sort of Peruvian risotto using duck confit and duck breast, Peruvian yellow chili paste, and Arborio rice. You can find yellow chili paste online at several sites, including Amigofoods.com (see Sources, page 263). A chef's tip is to start cooking the duck breasts about halfway through the risotto-making process so that they both are finished at the same time.

SERVES 8

For the cilantro paste

2 garlic cloves

¼ teaspoon salt

¼ cup extra virgin olive oil

2 medium bunches cilantro, leaves only (about 4 cups, lightly packed)

For the risotto

2 quarts (2 liters) Chicken Stock (page 64)

¾ teaspoon salt

¼ teaspoon freshly ground black pepper

3 tablespoons extra virgin olive oil

1 cup small-dice red bell peppers

½ cup finely chopped red onions

⅓ cup Cilantro Paste (from above)

2 tablespoons yellow chili paste

1 cup dark beer or Guinness

2⅓ cups Arborio rice (about 2 pounds or 900 g)

1 cup shredded duck confit

½ cup cooked fresh or thawed frozen peas

½ cup grated Parmesan, plus a little extra to garnish

4 duck breasts

1. Make the cilantro paste. Pulse the garlic, salt, and 2 teaspoons of the oil to a paste in a food processor fitted with a steel blade. Add the cilantro and process until finely chopped, about 30 seconds. Then add the remaining oil and continue to process, scraping down the sides occasionally until you have a smooth mixture, about 3 minutes. Set the paste aside.

2. Bring the stock to a simmer in a large saucepan over medium-high heat. Make sure it is well seasoned with the salt and pepper. Meanwhile, heat 1 tablespoon of the oil in a large saucepan or nonstick frying pan over medium heat and add the red peppers. Cook, stirring often, until lightly browned and tender, 10 to 15 minutes. Remove from the pan and set aside.

3. Make the risotto. Return the skillet to medium heat and add the remaining oil. Add the onions and cook, stirring frequently, until caramelized, 10 to 15 minutes. Stir in the cilantro paste, chili paste, and beer. Stir together and add the rice. Transfer to a large saucepan with a wide mouth. Cook, stirring constantly, for 5 minutes, or until the beer has just about evaporated. Add a ladleful, or about ½ cup, of the chicken stock. Cook, stirring, until most of the stock has evaporated, about 5 minutes, and add another 2 to 3 ladles of stock. Continue to cook the rice gradually, stirring and adding more stock as it evaporates, until the rice is cooked al dente, 30 to 35 minutes.

4. Stir in the duck confit, the cooked red peppers, the peas, another ladleful of stock, and the Parmesan. Remove from the heat.

5. Score the skin of the duck breast with a sharp knife to help render and crisp the skin.

6. Heat a large cast-iron skillet over medium heat and cook the duck breasts until crisp on the outside and rare on the inside, 6 to 8 minutes on the skin side and 5 minutes on the other. Remove from the heat.

7. Distribute the rice among 8 plates and sprinkle with a little grated Parmesan. Slice the duck breasts into ¼-inch- (5 mm) thick slices and serve immediately with the risotto.

Adapted from a recipe by MARILÚ MADUEÑO

SUSHI PAELLA

CHEF KIYOMI MIKUNI'S interest in Spanish food is reflected in this conceptual saffron-hued sushi rice. It's a fusion dish that brings together elements of sushi, risotto, and paella with a splash of classic creamy French sauce thrown into the mix. The vinegared rice is combined with Parmesan and olive oil after cooking, then artistically "framed" with sheets of nori seaweed. It's sauced with a classic saffrony white wine sauce as well as an Asian soy sauce vinaigrette, and it's garnished with various types of shellfish that you might find in a paella.

SERVES 8

For the rice

4 cups fish stock

½ cup sugar

2 teaspoons salt

¼ cup Japanese rice vinegar

¼ teaspoon saffron powder or threads

2¾ cups Japanese white sushi rice (about 1 pound or 450 g)

⅔ cup grated Parmesan

3 tablespoons extra virgin olive oil

2 tablespoons (¼ stick) butter

Three 8-inch- (20 cm) square nori sheets

For the saffron white wine sauce

¼ cup sliced shallots

1 cup dry white wine

1 tablespoon white wine vinegar

1½ cups heavy cream

¼ teaspoon saffron powder

¼ teaspoon salt

Generous pinch white pepper

For the garnish

25 baby mussels, cleaned (about 1 pound 4 ounces or 565 g)

2 tablespoons vegetable oil, for frying

4 scallops, quartered (about 6 ounces or 170 g)

9 medium black tiger or pink shrimp, cut into 3 or 4 pieces (about 11 ounces or 310 g)

1 teaspoon salt

3 tablespoons soy sauce

½ cup extra virgin olive oil

2 ounces (60 g) salmon roe

25 pink peppercorns

1. Make the saffron rice. Bring the fish stock to a boil in a medium saucepan over medium-high heat and add the sugar, salt, rice vinegar, saffron, and rice. Bring back to a boil, reduce the heat to low, cover and simmer for 10 to 15 minutes, or until all of the liquid has been absorbed. Remove from the heat and let sit, covered, for 10 minutes, then stir in the Parmesan, oil, and butter.

2. Toast the nori sheets. Holding the nori sheets 4 to 5 inches (10 to 13 cm) above low heat using metal tongs, move the nori back and forth slowly and continuously until the entire sheet changes color from dark green to lighter green, and it crisps slightly. Cool to room temperature and cut the nori sheets into 1¼- by 2-inch (3 by 5 cm) rectangles.

3. Make the sushi squares. Press 3½ cups of the rice mixture firmly and evenly into the bottom of a plastic wrap-lined 6-inch- (15 cm) square baking pan, adjusting the pressure until the rice is about 1¼ inches (3 cm) thick throughout the pan. Place a small cutting board over the baking pan. Turn the pan and board over and tap the pan gently to release the rice, then remove the pan. Use a hot, wet knife to score the surface of the formed rice in three 2-inch- (5 cm) wide rows in each direction, creating a grid of 9 squares of equal size. Using the grid, cut the formed rice into squares, cleaning and wetting the knife before each slice. Separate the rice squares and flatten any rough sides. Adhere one nori strip to each side of each rice square. Reserve until needed.

4. Make the sauce. Combine the shallots, white wine, and white wine vinegar in a small saucepan and bring to a boil over medium-high heat. Boil until the liquid is reduced to 2 tablespoons, about 15 minutes. Add the cream and bring to a boil over high heat. Reduce the heat to medium high and continue to cook uncovered for 7 to 8 minutes, or until the sauce is reduced to about 1½ cups. Add the saffron powder and remove the sauce from the heat. Season to taste with the salt and white pepper.

5. Prepare the topping. Shuck the mussels. Fry them quickly in a large sauté pan with 2 tablespoons of vegetable oil over medium-high heat until they change color and begin to firm up, about 1 minute. Set aside.

6. Blanch the scallops and shrimp. Bring 2 quarts (2 liters) of water and the salt to a boil over medium-high heat in a medium saucepan. Add the scallops and cook for 2 minutes, or until they lose their translucency and turn opaque. Drain and set aside, return the cooking liquid to the pan, and return to a boil. Add the shrimp and cook for 30 seconds, or until they turn pink but just before they begin to curl.

7. Whisk together the soy sauce and olive oil in a small bowl.

8. Drizzle 2½ tablespoons of the saffron sauce and 1 tablespoon of the vinaigrette around each plate. Place a sushi square in the center of the plate and garnish with 2 pieces of the scallops, 3 of the mussels, 3 to 4 pieces of the shrimp, 1 teaspoon of the salmon roe, and ¼ teaspoon of the pink peppercorns.

Adapted from a recipe by KIYOMI MIKUNI

RED WINE SUSHI RICE
WITH SERRANO HAM

IN THIS Japanese/Italian/Spanish/French fusion recipe from Chef Kiyomi Mikuni, the rice is cooked in red wine so the risotto is a beautiful purple color. It's garnished with Ibérico or Serrano ham and vegetables, and served with a rich red wine butter sauce. If you can't find kinome (a Japanese herb), shiso leaves, watercress, or wild spring cress can all be substituted.

SERVES 8

For the risotto

2¾ cups red wine (such as Tempranillo)

½ cup sugar

1¾ teaspoons salt

¼ cup Japanese rice vinegar

2¾ cups Japanese white sushi rice (about 1 pound or 450g)

⅔ cup grated Parmesan

¼ cup extra virgin olive oil

2 tablespoons (¼ stick) butter

For the red wine sauce

3½ cups red wine

½ cup sugar

½ cup veal or chicken stock

½ cup (1 stick) butter

For the garnish

2 cups medium-dice Yukon gold potatoes

2 teaspoons salt

¼ cup extra virgin olive oil

4 green asparagus stalks, peeled and woody ends trimmed

4 thin slices Serrano ham (4 ounces or 115 g)

8 kinome sprigs or watercress leaves

Freshly ground black pepper, as needed

For the vinaigrette

¼ cup soy sauce

¼ cup extra virgin olive oil

1. Make the red wine risotto. Bring the wine to a boil in a medium saucepan over high heat and reduce to a little over 2 cups, 10 to 15 minutes. Add the sugar, salt, and vinegar, bring back to a boil, and add the rice. Cover and simmer for 15 minutes. Turn off the heat and let sit, undisturbed, for 10 minutes. Toss with the Parmesan, oil, and butter.

2. Make the red wine sauce. In a medium saucepan, bring the wine to a boil over medium-high heat and reduce to ¾ cup, about 25 minutes. Add the sugar and stock and reduce to ¼ cup, another 30 minutes. Add in the butter 1 tablespoon at a time to produce a thick syrup consistency.

3. Prepare the garnish. Place the potatoes, 4 quarts (4 liters) of cold water, and the salt in a large saucepan. Bring to a boil over high heat, reduce the heat to medium low, and simmer until the potatoes are just tender, 8 to 10 minutes. Drain well. Heat the olive oil over medium heat in a large nonstick skillet; sauté the potatoes until browned and crisp, stirring occasionally, 10 to 15 minutes. Remove from the heat and drain.

4. Blanch the asparagus in salted boiling water so that it is just barely cooked in the center, about 1 to 2 minutes, then remove it with a slotted spoon. Cut the asparagus into ½-inch (1 cm) slices.

5. Mold the risotto into circles using a 3- by ¾-inch (7.5 by 2 cm) ring mold. Place ⅓ cup of the risotto into each mold and smooth over the top.

6. Prepare the ham. Slice the ham into 3- by ½-inch (7.5 by 1 cm) strips, then carefully fold, twist, and/or roll the strips to form ½-inch (1 cm) "balls."

7. Whisk together the soy sauce and oil in a small bowl. Drizzle 4½ teaspoons of the red wine sauce and 1½ teaspoons of the soy sauce/oil mixture around the edge of a plate. Place a risotto circle in the middle and place 5 balls of the Serrano ham, 1 tablespoon of the green asparagus, and 3 tablespoons of the sautéed potatoes around the plate. Place a kinome sprig or a watercress leaf on top. Sprinkle with pepper and repeat with the remaining ingredients.

Adapted from a recipe by KIYOMI MIKUNI

SAUCES
AND CONDIMENTS

SAUCES AND CONDIMENTS

From subtle to robust

Spanish sauces run the gamut from brothy and subtle to thick and robust. They often define a dish; for example, if the name of a dish includes the words *al ajillo*, the food (shrimp, mushrooms, potatoes) will be served with a garlic sauce, the garlic having been cooked with the food. A squid dish described *en su tinta* will have a squid ink sauce. Some sauces are associated with regions: a fish dish that is prepared *a la Vasca* will be served with a green parsley and wine sauce.

During the seasonal Calçotada in Catalonia, spring onions are grilled, steamed in newspaper, and finally dipped in romesco sauce and eaten in great quantities.

SOME TRADITIONAL SAUCES

Many traditional Spanish sauces are robust, substantial enough to stand alone as condiments with a number of different types of food. Spanish chef José Andrés once said that he thought that the main function of the wonderful Catalan grilled spring onion feast called the Calçotada was to give people an excuse to eat romesco sauce, a thick, pungent, nutty sauce made with ground ñora peppers, almonds and/or hazelnuts, tomatoes, olive oil, sherry vinegar, and garlic. Romesco (page 222) is one of the defining condiments in the cooking of Mediterranean Spain. It is served with fish and with vegetables, stirred into fish stews and beans. There are as many variations as there are cooks, but they differ from one another mainly in their consistency. Another such condiment/ sauce is *samfaina* (or *xamfaina*), a much-loved vegetable ragout that is one of the building blocks of Catalan cuisine. The ratatouille-like medley is cooked down to an almost jamlike consistency, and is often served as a sauce with roast chicken, fish, and salt cod.

Spain is a country that loves garlic, and the pungent garlic mayonnaise known here as *allioli* (and across the border in France as *aïoli*) (pages 226–227) accompanies a variety of foods, from grilled or boiled vegetables and beans to fish, paella, grilled meats, and chicken. The wonderful tapa favorite, *patatas bravas*, sautéed potatoes topped with a layer of spicy tomato sauce, are at their best when the tomato sauce is in turn topped with *allioli*, and other tapas, such as *croquetas* and steamed mussels, follow suit. Traditionally, the garlic and oil emulsion was made without eggs and required a strong arm. Today most chefs and home cooks include egg yolks in the mixture, mounting it like a traditional mayonnaise, with the pungent garlic stirred in. Sometimes, to make hers less pungent, Alicante-based chef Mari Carmen Vélez blanches her garlic first. Others roast theirs, or fry it in olive oil. Chefs are experimenting with other flavors in their *alliolis*. Chef Mari Carmen Vélez makes some ultra-modern *alliolis* flavored with unheard of ingredients as disparate as passion fruit and seaweed, raspberries, coffee, and chocolate.

Mayonnaise (or *Mayonesa*, page 225) isn't always spiced up with garlic. On its own, it is ubiquitous on the Spanish table, and is essential for one of Spain's most beloved tapa salads, Ensaladilla Rusa (pages 94–95), a mixture of diced cooked vegetables, tuna, and mayonnaise.

SAUCES AS BUILDING BLOCKS

There are other preparations in Spain that could be considered sauces, but are really more like building blocks. Their purpose is

A smooth Lemony Allioli makes the perfect dipping accompaniment to skewers of lightly spiced Lamb Espadas.

This spicy Mango, Scotch Bonnet, and Sesame Mojo, which resembles a blended salsa, is fantastic with chicken or fish.

to give depth of flavor to a dish. Many Spanish dishes are begun by cooking onions and/or garlic and tomatoes in olive oil, until the mixture is cooked down to a deeply rich-tasting mixture that will season the dish as it simmers or stews. This is called the *sofrito* or, in Catalan, *soffregit*. Similarly, many dishes are finished with a *picada*, a pungent mixture of pounded garlic, parsley, almonds, and dried bread. The *picada* is the final flavor-intensifying step of the cooking process, added during the last 5 minutes of cooking.

In the Canary Islands, condiments take the form of spicy, uncooked, pounded mixtures called *mojos*. They're made with olive oil, vinegar, garlic, peppers, often a generous amount of cilantro, and spices such as cumin and paprika.

CONTEMPORARY SAUCES

The new wave chefs in Spain are taking sauces to a stratospheric level. They transform their taste memories into airy foams that float over and around the foods they garnish. Chefs have figured out how to thicken liquids without heating them (they use xanthan gum and agar agar), retaining the integrity of the food from which they're made. They paint them onto plates in a broad swath, or make droplets with an eye dropper or the tip of a brush. Emerald green herbal oils are drizzled over grilled meat and seafood, or onto the surface of a soup. Traditional soups, too, like *ajo blanco* and Salmorejo (page 221), are beginning to show up as sauces for seafood. Like Spanish cooking everywhere, sauces today are a work in progress.

QUINCE SAUCE

THIS TANGY SAUCE goes beautifully with the Manchego Croquettes on page 34. It makes perfect sense, as quince paste (*membrillo*) is traditionally served with Manchego. It also makes a great accompaniment to pork.

MAKES ⅔ CUP

6 tablespoons quince paste (*membrillo*)
2 teaspoons sherry vinegar
⅓ cup hot water

Combine all of the ingredients in a blender and blend on low speed until smooth, 5 to 10 seconds. Serve at room temperature or slightly warmed. This will keep in the refrigerator for up to 1 week.

Adapted from a recipe by JANET MENDEL

TOMATO, ANCHO, AND XERES JAM

THIS SWEET, SPICY JAM is a bit like a chutney. It goes well with pork and chicken, and with egg dishes and bocadillas.

MAKES 2 CUPS

4 pounds (1.8 kg) plum tomatoes, peeled, seeded, and chopped (about 4 cups)
½ cup honey
1 cup sugar
¼ cup minced ginger
Two 3-inch (8 cm) cinnamon sticks
2 star anise pods
2 large garlic cloves, minced
¼ teaspoon ground toasted cumin
2 medium ancho peppers, toasted and seeded (½ cup)
1 cup plus 2 tablespoons sherry vinegar
Kosher salt, as needed

Combine all of the ingredients in a medium saucepan and bring to a simmer over medium heat. Cook, stirring often, until the liquid has evaporated and the tomatoes have cooked down to a jamlike consistency, 1 hour 15 minutes. Serve at room temperature. This will keep in the refrigerator for up to 1 week.

Adapted from a recipe by NORMAN VAN AKEN

SALMOREJO

SALMOREJO IS A FIRST COUSIN of gazpacho, and it can double as a soup. The pungent combination of tomatoes, sherry vinegar, and olive oil makes this versatile mixture almost like a thick tomato vinaigrette. Some versions of salmorejo also include garlic and roasted peppers. The sauce goes well with poultry, fish, rice, or vegetables.

MAKES ABOUT 3¾ CUPS

2 pounds (900 g) whole plum tomatoes

1 cup Arbequina olive oil or extra virgin olive oil

3 tablespoons sherry vinegar

2 teaspoons salt

¼ teaspoon freshly ground black pepper, or as needed

Pureé the tomatoes with the oil and vinegar in a blender until smooth, about 1½ minutes. Season with salt and pepper. Pass through a fine mesh strainer and serve immediately, or store in the refrigerator for 3 to 4 days.

Adapted from a recipe by JOAQUÍN FELÍPE

TOMATO SAUCE

KEEP A CONTAINER of this sweet tomato sauce on hand and you can create a meal in no time. In Spain, this versatile sauce might be served with mussels or pasta, or with fried eggs.

MAKES 3 CUPS

1 cup extra virgin olive oil

3 cups finely chopped yellow onions

Two 28-ounce (795 g) cans whole tomatoes, with juice (about 7 cups)

2½ cups water

1 tablespoon salt, or more as needed

3 tablespoons sugar

1. Heat the oil over medium heat in a large sauté pan. Add the onions and sauté, stirring often, for about 15 minutes, or until they are golden.

2. Add the tomatoes with their juice, and the water, salt, and sugar and bring to a boil. Decrease the heat to low and simmer uncovered, stirring occasionally, for about 1½ hours, or until the sauce has reduced to a purée.

3. Remove from the heat and set aside to cool slightly. Pass the sauce through a food mill fitted with the medium plate or sieve held over a medium bowl. Taste and adjust seasoning with salt, if needed. Use immediately, or allow to cool, cover, and store in the refrigerator for up to 1 week.

Adapted from a recipe by TERESA BARRENECHEA

ROMESCO

THE CLASSIC SAUCE calls for a fleshy dried sweet red pepper called a ñora (also known as a choricero). Ñora peppers are available from LaTienda.com.

MAKES 2½ CUPS

1 dried ñora pepper (choricero)
1 pound 4 ounces (565 g) ripe tomatoes
4 garlic cloves, peeled and roasted until golden
½ cup extra virgin olive oil, divided use
1 slice day-old country-style bread
1 garlic clove, peeled
⅔ cup hazelnuts, roasted and skinned
2 tablespoons sherry vinegar
½ teaspoon salt
¼ teaspoon freshly ground black pepper
1 tablespoon chopped flat-leaf parsley

1. Cut open the pepper, remove the seeds, and place it in a bowl. Cover with ½ cup of hot water and soak for 30 minutes, or until soft.

2. Preheat the broiler. Place the tomatoes on a foil-covered baking sheet, and place under the broiler about 1 inch (2.5 cm) beneath the flame (or roast the tomatoes over coals). Broil for 2 to 3 minutes, until the skins blacken. Turn the tomatoes over and repeat on the other side. Remove from the heat and put through the fine blade of a food mill, along with the roasted garlic.

3. Heat ¼ cup of the oil in a small sauté pan over medium heat and fry the bread until crisp, about 2 minutes per side. Be careful not to burn the bread. Remove from the heat.

4. Scrape the pulp from the soaked ñora with a sharp knife.

5. Turn on a food processor fitted with the steel blade and drop in the raw garlic clove. Blend until it adheres to the sides of the bowl, about 15 seconds, then stop the machine and scrape down the sides of the bowl. Add the hazelnuts and fried bread with its oil, and process to a paste (this can also be done in a mortar and pestle), about 2 minutes. Add the tomatoes and ñora pulp, and turn on the machine. With the machine running, drizzle in the remaining oil and the vinegar and process to a smooth paste, about 2 minutes. Season to taste with the salt, pepper, and chopped parsley. Serve immediately, or refrigerate for up to 1 week.

Adapted from a recipe by NANDO JUBANY

SOFRITO

THIS FLAVOR BASE, made by cooking down onions, tomatoes, and garlic (in Catalonia the garlic is often omitted) until very soft and fragrant, can be made in a large batch and kept in the refrigerator under a thin layer of olive oil, then used as recipes call for it. Sofrito, or *sofregit* (as it is called in Catalonia), is such an important base for Spanish and Catalan cooking that a recipe for it must be included in this collection.

MAKES 1 CUP

2 tablespoons extra virgin olive oil
2½ cups minced onions
1 large red bell pepper, cored, seeded, and minced
2 medium ripe plum tomatoes, peeled, seeded, and chopped

1. Heat the oil over medium-high heat in a large skillet, and add the onions and pepper. Reduce the heat to medium low and cook, stirring frequently, for 40 to 45 minutes, or until the onions are golden brown and almost caramelized. If necessary, add small amounts of water toward the end of the cooking to keep the mixture from burning.

2. Add the tomatoes and continue to cook over low heat until the juices have evaporated, 10 to 15 minutes. Remove from the heat and serve immediately, or allow to cool, then cover, and store in the refrigerator for up to 1 week.

Adapted from a recipe by DANIEL OLIVELLA

MANGO, SCOTCH BONNET, AND SESAME MOJO

Miami-based chef Norman Van Aken likes to fuse flavors from the Caribbean, Spain, and Asia. This spicy salsa is a perfect example. Serve it with fish, chicken, or rice.

MAKES 2 CUPS

2 ripe mangoes, peeled and pitted

½ cup white wine, such as Chardonnay

½ cup freshly squeezed orange juice

1 tablespoon rayu (hot sesame oil)

2 teaspoons Scotch bonnet, habanero, or other hot chile, stemmed, seeded, and minced

¼ cup black sesame seeds, toasted

1 teaspoon kosher salt

Combine the mangoes, white wine, orange juice, and rayu in a blender and purée until smooth, about 30 seconds. Add the chile and sesame seeds and blend together until smooth, about 5 minutes. Season to taste with salt. Serve within an hour of preparation or refrigerate for up to 1 week.

Adapted from a recipe by Norman Van Aken

TOMATILLO, POBLANO, AND CILANTRO MOJO

Mojos originally came from the Canary Islands, but this one, with its tomatillos and poblano peppers, is a fusion recipe that reflects today's exchange between Latin America and Spain.

MAKES 2½ CUPS

1½ heads garlic, halved horizontally

½ cup plus 3 tablespoons extra virgin olive oil, divided use

2 poblano peppers

6 tomatillos, husks removed and cored

2 tablespoons canola oil

1 tablespoon sherry vinegar

2 tablespoons lime juice

1 cup cilantro leaves, loosely packed

2 tablespoons sour orange juice

½ teaspoon salt

2 teaspoons ground toasted cumin seeds

½ teaspoon freshly ground black pepper

1. Preheat the oven to 350°F (175°C). Place the garlic heads cut side down in a small pan and pour over 3 tablespoons of olive oil. Cover with foil and bake for 45 minutes, or until the garlic is soft. Remove the cloves from their husks and mash with a fork; reserve until needed.

2. Rub the poblanos and tomatillos with the canola oil. Place on a baking sheet and roast the tomatillos for 20 minutes, or until very tender, and the poblanos for 40 minutes, or until very tender.

3. Set the tomatillos aside to cool. Put the poblanos in a bowl, cover with plastic wrap, and let stand for about 15 minutes in order to steam the skins loose. Peel the poblanos and remove the stems and seeds.

4. Combine the garlic, tomatillos, and poblanos with the remaining ingredients in a food processor and purée until fairly smooth. Refrigerate for up to 1 week.

Recipe by The Culinary Institute of America

SALSA DE PASITAS VERDES

This spicy green sauce is a fusion of Mexican and Spanish foodways. Serve it with fish or chicken. It's especially good with tacos or quesadillas. Chef Robert Del Grande serves this sauce with scallops (pages 122–123).

MAKES 3 CUPS

⅓ cup pumpkinseeds

⅓ cup blanched almonds

⅓ cup tightly packed golden raisins

⅓ cup garlic cloves, peeled

1 cup extra virgin olive oil

½ teaspoon lemon zest

1 medium poblano chile, charred, peeled, and seeded

2 serrano chiles, charred and peeled

4 white anchovies (about 1 tablespoon)

1 cup Fish Stock or Chicken Stock (pages 65 and 64)

3⅔ cups tightly packed flat-leaf parsley leaves (about 1 large bunch)

2 tablespoons coarsely chopped tarragon leaves

1 tablespoon lemon juice

2 teaspoons salt

1. Combine the pumpkin seeds, almonds, raisins, garlic, oil, and lemon zest in a small saucepan. Cook over medium heat until the garlic cloves are light brown and have softened and the raisins begin to puff, about 5 minutes. Add the poblano and serrano chiles and the anchovies. Remove from the heat and let cool to room temperature.

2. Transfer the cooked mixture with the oil to a food processor fitted with the steel blade. Process until smooth, about 1 minute.

3. Combine the stock, parsley, and tarragon in a blender and purée until well blended, about 30 seconds.

4. Turn the food processor on and pour the blended stock, lemon juice, and salt into the ground mixture. Process until nearly smooth, about 2 minutes. Adjust seasoning and serve at room temperature, or refrigerate for up to 3 days.

Adapted from a recipe by Robert Del Grande

GOLDEN RAISIN SALSITA

Miami-based chef Norman Van Aken is known for his Latin-inflected fusion cooking. He serves this sweet and pungent, nutty salsita with a Spanish-influenced halibut escabeche, which he serves wrapped in slices of Serrano ham (pages 128–129).

MAKES 3 CUPS

½ cup golden raisins
⅔ cup Chardonnay
¾ cup toasted Marcona almonds
⅔ cup flat-leaf parsley leaves
1⅓ cups extra virgin olive oil
4 teaspoons capers, rinsed
4 teaspoons sherry vinegar, or as needed
1 cured anchovy fillet, rinsed
1 teaspoon kosher salt, or as needed

1. Soak the raisins in the Chardonnay for 30 minutes, or until plump. Strain the raisins and discard the wine. Place all of the salsita ingredients, except for half the parsley, in a high speed blender and purée, until smooth, about 30 seconds. Add the remaining parsley and pulse until the parsley is roughly chopped.

2. Taste and adjust seasoning with salt and sherry vinegar. Serve at room temperature, or refrigerate for up to 4 days.

Adapted from a recipe by NORMAN VAN AKEN

MAYONESA

An important condiment in the Spanish repertoire, mayonesa is served with seafood, used on bocadillos, and eaten with many other tapas. Add crushed garlic to it and you have the signature Catalan sauce *allioli* (or *aïoli*, as it is known in France). You can make this very easily in a food processor or, with a little more effort, in a mortar and pestle.

MAKES 2¼ CUPS

1 egg
2 tablespoons water
1 tablespoon lemon juice
¾ teaspoon salt
2 cups extra virgin olive oil
¼ teaspoon salt
Small pinch ground white pepper
Water, as needed

1. Combine the egg, water, lemon juice, and salt in a food processor fitted with the steel blade. Turn the processor on and slowly drizzle in the oil in a thin, steady stream. The mixture will thicken as the oil is added. Alternatively, combine the egg, water, lemon juice, and salt in a mortar and stir rapidly as you drizzle in the oil.

2. Taste and adjust seasoning with salt and pepper. Thin out as desired with water. Serve immediately, or refrigerate for up to 1 week.

Adapted from a recipe by JOSÉ ANDRÉS

SOFT ALLIOLI

THIS IS A THIN, SLIGHTLY RUNNY, garlic mayonnaise. If you prefer a stiffer consistency, reduce the quantities of oil and water or substitute only egg yolks for the eggs.

MAKES 4 CUPS

5 large garlic cloves

1 teaspoon kosher salt

2 eggs

2 teaspoons lemon juice

2 cups extra virgin olive oil

2 cups sunflower oil

⅓ cup water, or as needed

1. Chop the garlic coarsely. Combine it with the salt in a mortar and mash it to a paste. Add the eggs and lemon juice and stir vigorously until well combined. Alternatively, place the mashed garlic in a food processor, add the eggs and lemon juice, and blend for 30 seconds.

2. Combine the oils in a medium bowl or 4-cup measuring pitcher and, stirring rapidly, or with the machine running, very slowly drizzle it into the egg mixture, until you have a medium thick mayonnaise. This should take 1 to 2 minutes in a food processor, a little longer if working by hand. Thin out as desired with water. Serve immediately, or refrigerate for up to 1 week.

Adapted from a recipe by MARI CARMEN VÉLEZ

LEMONY ALLIOLI

INSTEAD OF GARLIC, this *allioli* uses fresh lemon juice and zest to heighten the flavor of this standard emulsion. Serve this as a dressing for vegetable dishes, a dip for Lamb Espadas (pages 160–161), or simply spread it on bread to give it a light lemony flavor.

MAKES 2 CUPS

4 egg yolks

3 tablespoons lemon juice, divided use

1½ cups canola oil

½ cup extra virgin olive oil

Kosher salt, as needed

⅓ cup lemon zest

1. Place the egg yolks and 1 teaspoon of the lemon juice in a medium mixing bowl, a mortar, or a food processor.

2. Whisk or work in the oils gradually until smooth and creamy, beginning with the canola oil.

3. Adjust seasoning with the lemon juice, adding it slowly so the allioli does not separate, and add salt to taste. Fold in the lemon zest. Serve immediately, or refrigerate for up to 1 week.

Adapted from a recipe by NORMAN VAN AKEN

SAFFRON TOMATO ALLIOLI

SAFFRON AND TOMATO are combined here to form an exciting variation of the traditional garlic mayonnaise known as *allioli*. This recipe produces a smooth spread with hints of olive, garlic, tomato, and saffron. Here you will find a great way to add color and extra flavor to recipes that call for mayonnaise.

MAKES 2 CUPS

⅛ teaspoon saffron threads

2 tablespoons warm water

1 tablespoon tomato paste

6 tablespoons egg yolks

4 teaspoons sherry vinegar

1½ teaspoons minced garlic, mashed to a paste

1 teaspoon lemon juice, or more as needed

2 cups extra virgin olive oil

1 teaspoon salt

Pinch cayenne pepper

1. Infuse the saffron threads in the warm water for 10 minutes in a medium bowl, then stir in the tomato paste. Whisk in the egg yolks, vinegar, garlic, and lemon juice until the mixture is slightly foamy. Alternatively, blend these ingredients in a food processor until foamy.

2. Add the oil gradually in a thin stream, whipping until all of it has been incorporated and the mayonnaise is thick. Alternatively, add the oil to the mixture in a food processor and blend until thick.

3. Season with salt, cayenne pepper, and lemon juice, as needed. Serve immediately, or refrigerate for up to 1 week.

Recipe by THE CULINARY INSTITUTE OF AMERICA

THE SPANISH OLIVE

THIRTY PERCENT OF THE WORLD'S OLIVE OIL COMES FROM SPAIN. Drive through the country, especially through Andalusia, and vast olive groves will be forever etched in your memory. There are over 5 million acres of olive groves—over 300 million trees. Eighty percent of these are in Andalusia, in particular the province of Jaén, which makes Andalusia the largest olive-growing region on the planet.

A BRIEF HISTORY OF THE SPANISH OLIVE

The olive came to Spain with the Phoenicians, over 3,000 years ago. The Greeks brought it again between 600–700 BC, but it was the Romans who established an olive oil industry in Iberia that took on a major importance throughout the empire. Olive oil amphorae from Spain have been unearthed in every Roman province, most of them in Rome itself. The emperor Hadrian even created a coin that had the insignia of an olive branch and the inscription "Hispania."

The production of olives and olive oil did not decline with the fall of the Roman Empire. In fact, in time it increased, because the Arabs brought the olive with them when they arrived in the 7th century. They introduced new varieties and production techniques, and also the word that is the root of the Spanish word for olive, *aceituna*.

The use of olive oil did decline, however, during the period of Catholic fundamentalism that followed the expulsion of the Moors and Jews in the 15th century. At this time, pork fat supplanted olive oil as the cooking fat of choice, because pork consumption was a good way to prove one's Christianity.

In the 1960s, the olive entered another difficult period when Franco's Spanish State began to export olive oil to the United States in exchange for cheap American soybean oil. Many Spaniards were persuaded to use soybean and sunflower oils instead of olive oil. They began to rip up their venerable olive groves and replace them with soybeans and sunflowers, which required more water to cultivate, and produced oil that did not have the health benefits of olive oil.

Luckily, by the late 1970s the Spanish olive industry was beginning to recover, with a growing worldwide awareness of the olive's health benefits and gastronomic virtues. During the difficult years, the Italian olive oil industry had surged ahead of Spain's and won a large foreign market; but it couldn't meet the demand, and to this day Spain exports tons of olive oil to Italy, where it is bottled and labeled.

SPANISH OLIVE OILS

Ninety-two percent of Spain's olive groves are dedicated to olive oil production. Most is of a very high quality, as during the last few decades production techniques have improved, and the best olive growing regions are now protected by the *Denominación de Origen* (DO) system. Several types of olives are produced.

The extra virgin olive oils produced in Andalusia are full-bodied with a strong flavor that can stand up to frying and to foods with strong flavors, such as anchovies. The *Picual* produces more oil than any other olive in the world and is grown mainly in the province of Jaén. Other DO olives cultivated in Andalusia are the *Verdala*, *Real*, and *Manzanilla de Jaén*. In the provinces of Seville and Córdoba, the DO varieties include *Picuda* (also known as *Carrasqueña de Córdoba*), *Picual*, *Lechín*, *Chorrío*, *Pajarero*, and *Hojiblanco*.

The oils produced in Catalonia tend to be lighter, fruitier, and more elegant than the Andalusian oils. They're less suitable for frying, better for dressing salads and vegetables. The main production areas in Catalonia are les Garrigues, in the province of Lleida, and nearby Siurana, in the province of Tarragona. Here the main olive is one of Spain's most prized, the *Arbequina*. Other DO varieties include *Real* (royal), *Verdiel*, and *Morrut* olives.

Other popular Spanish olives used for oil are the *Cornicabra*, found mainly in Castille-La Mancha; and the *Empeltre*, grown mainly in the south of Aragon and the south of Catalonia. Like the Arbequina of Catalonia, these are elegant olives used for fine, light, and fruity extra virgin olive oils.

HARVESTING OLIVES

Olives for olive oil are harvested between November and the end of March, when the olive is black or changing from green to black. Once picked, they go immediately to the mill where they must be pressed within 24 hours of harvesting or the oil will be too acidic. They are then milled to form a paste. If extra virgin olive oil is being produced, all the liquid is extracted from the paste and this juice is then placed in vats, where the oil and water separate. If the oil is not going to be classified as extra virgin, the liquid can be extracted from the paste and the oil and water can be separated in a centrifuge.

Olives that are destined for curing and eating are harvested while they're still green. *Arbequinas* are tiny, round, light brown olives with a nutty flavor. *Gordals*, also known as Queens, are large, fat green olives whose texture is firm and meaty. They are often stuffed, with garlic, almonds, anchovies, or piquillo peppers. Manzanillas are perhaps the best known Spanish olive. These cracked brownish-green olives are smaller, crisper, and nuttier than *Gordals*.

SQUID STOCK WITH CITRUS FRUITS

CHEF JOAQUÍN FELÍPE recommends serving this lime-perfumed squid and vegetable reduction with white-fleshed fish.

MAKES 2¾ CUPS

2 tablespoons extra virgin olive oil

2 pounds (900 g) squid, washed and drained

1 cup chopped onions

¾ cup chopped carrots

1 cup chopped leeks, white and light green parts only

1 cup chopped celery

3 quarts (3 liters) water

⅓ cup lemon juice

10 tablespoons orange juice

½ teaspoon salt

Pinch white pepper

Grated zest of 3 limes

1 teaspoon lemon zest

1 teaspoon orange zest

1. Heat the oil in a medium stockpot over medium-high heat and add the squid. Stir for 5 minutes, or until lightly browned. Add the onions, carrots, leeks, and celery and continue to cook, stirring frequently, until the vegetables are lightly browned, about 10 minutes.

2. Add the water, lemon juice, and orange juice and bring to a boil over medium-high heat. Reduce to 2¾ cups, about 55 minutes.

3. Remove from the heat and strain through a fine wire mesh sieve or a large strainer lined with cheesecloth. Season to taste with the salt and pepper, and stir in the grated lime, lemon, and orange zests.

Adapted from a recipe by JOAQUÍN FELÍPE

OLOROSO BROWN LOAF SUGAR SYRUP

UNREFINED DARK BROWN SUGAR is shaped into solid cones and squares in Latin America. In Mexico it's called *pilloncillo*. It has a rich molasses flavor. Chef Maricel Presilla uses it for both sweet and savory dishes at her pan-Latin restaurant Cucharamamma in Hoboken, New Jersey.

MAKES 1½ CUPS

1 pound (450 g) brown loaf sugar (*pilloncillo*, available in Mexican markets), dark Muscovado sugar, or dark brown sugar

2½ cups water

Two 3-inch (7.5 cm) cinnamon sticks or cassia bark

2 teaspoons allspice berries

8 cloves

3 star anise pods

½ cup oloroso sherry

One 1-inch- (2.5 cm) wide strip of orange zest

⅛ teaspoon salt

1. Place all of the ingredients in a medium, heavy saucepan and bring to a boil over medium heat, stirring to dissolve the sugar. This should take about 20 minutes. Reduce the heat to low and simmer until the mixture reduces to the thickness of light molasses, about 15 minutes. Remove from the heat and allow to cool.

2. Strain into a glass or plastic container and use immediately, or store, tightly covered, in the refrigerator for up to 3 months.

Adapted from a recipe by MARICEL E. PRESILLA

LEMON PARSLEY VINAIGRETTE

THIS LEMONY VARIATION of a traditional vinaigrette adds a little extra spice to salads with its hints of red pepper and garlic. Arbequina olive oil can generally be used whenever olive oil is called for in a Spanish recipe.

MAKES 1½ CUPS

6 tablespoons lemon juice

2 tablespoons champagne vinegar

2 tablespoons Dijon mustard

2 teaspoons minced garlic (about 2 cloves)

1 tablespoon minced shallots

½ teaspoon salt, or as needed

½ teaspoon freshly ground black pepper, or as needed

1 ½ teaspoons crushed fennel seeds

½ teaspoon red pepper flakes

1 cup extra virgin olive oil

2 tablespoons chopped flat-leaf parsley

⅓ cup chopped oregano

1. Combine the lemon juice, vinegar, mustard, garlic, shallots, salt, pepper, crushed fennel seeds, and red pepper flakes in a medium mixing bowl.

2. Whisk in the oil and reserve.

3. Whisk in the parsley and oregano just before serving. Adjust seasoning with salt and pepper, if necessary.

Recipe by THE CULINARY INSTITUTE OF AMERICA

GREEN PARSLEY OIL

THIS METHOD OF INFUSING OIL works with other leafy herbs such as basil, sage, thyme, and rosemary. Vary the quantity of herbs according to whether they are more or less strongly flavored than parsley. Flavored oils make a wonderful addition to salad dressings.

MAKES 2 CUPS

2 cups flat-leaf parsley leaves or other leafy herbs
2 cups extra virgin olive oil

1. **Blanch** the parsley leaves in salted water for 10 to 15 seconds. Shock the leaves in a bowl of ice water and drain on paper towels.

2. **Combine** the blanched herbs with half of the oil in a blender and purée until very fine. Add this purée to the remaining oil. Strain the oil through a cheesecloth, if desired.

3. **Transfer** the oil to a bottle or other storage container. Store in the refrigerator or a cool, dark area and use within 3 to 4 days.

Recipe by THE CULINARY INSTITUTE OF AMERICA

ÑORA-INFUSED OIL

THIS MAKES A WONDERFUL SPICY ADDITION to a vinaigrette, or try drizzling it over steamed or boiled vegetables. You may want to save the leftover strained chile flakes for use in other recipes. Handle the ñora peppers with care—the oil in capsicum can be very dangerous to your skin and eyes. You may even want to wear plastic gloves when handling them.

MAKES 2 CUPS

½ cup dried ñora chile peppers
2 cups extra virgin olive oil

1. **Cut** off the stems of the dried chiles and remove the seeds. Chop the chiles into coarse flakes. It's easiest to do this by processing them in a blender for about 20 seconds. Place the chile flakes in a heat-resistant jar with a seal.

2. **Heat** the oil in a heavy skillet over medium-high to high heat until it is starting to smoke. Remove the skillet from the heat. Wait 3 minutes, or until the oil has cooled down to about 225°F to 240°F (105°C to 115°C).

3. **Pour** the oil over the flakes. Allow to steep for 1 hour.

4. **Cool** and strain the oil. Store in the refrigerator or in a cool, dark area and use within 3 to 4 days.

Recipe by THE CULINARY INSTITUTE OF AMERICA

PAPRIKA OIL

THIS PUNGENT, COLORFUL OIL can be used in any number of ways, from salad dressings and marinades for grilled meats and fish to dips such as allioli. Try this recipe with different types of paprika to customize the flavors in your dishes.

MAKES 2 CUPS

2 cups extra virgin olive oil
½ cup paprika

1. Heat the oil in a small saucepan with the paprika until approximately 150°F (65°C). Remove from the heat and allow to cool to room temperature.

2. Strain the oil into a bottle or other clean container. Store in the refrigerator or in a cool, dark area and use within 3 to 4 days.

Recipe by THE CULINARY INSTITUTE OF AMERICA

DESSERTS

DESSERTS

Spain's sweet tooth

Desserts in Spain range from the traditional sweets that are a legacy of the Moors, to classic French, to *nueva cocina*. Traditional sweets such as marzipans and almond nougats (*turróns*), rich eggy confections, almond cakes and ices, fried pastries (*churros*), candied fruits in sugar syrups, sponge cakes, rice puddings, custards (*natillas*), and flans, date back to the time of the Moors. It was, in fact, the Arabs who brought sugarcane to Andalusia in the 15th century.

Mission Fig Flan, a classic Spanish dessert. Here a rich and creamy flan is laced with sherry and topped with a sweet fig sauce.

DESSERT TIME

Typically the Spanish enjoy cakes, pastries, and other sweet treats not after a meal, but at breakfast, mid-morning, or late afternoon. They may be accompanied by a cup of hot chocolate, tea, or coffee. And on Andalusian summer nights, the lines are long outside the ice cream shops, where icy granitas are a balm against the heat.

PASTRIES AND CHOCOLATE

The Spanish were not about to give up sweets when they reconquered the country and expelled the Moors and the Jews (who shared a love of sweets). Convents became repositories of pastry recipes, their execution perpetuated by nuns to this day. In addition to the many sweets that they inherited from the Arabs and Jews, the nuns developed a whole category of confectionary made with large amounts of sugar and egg yolks (*yemas*; the sweets are also called *yemas*). These evolved because the sherry houses in Andalusia used vast quantities of egg whites to clarify their wines, and sent the yolks to the local convents.

Spain was the door through which chocolate entered Europe. The Aztecs (and the Mayans) whom Cortés's army conquered in 1521 so valued chocolate, which they made into a savory, energizing drink, that they used cocoa beans as currency. The Europeans had little taste for the muddy drink, which the Mesoamericans seasoned with achiote and chiles. But they did recognize its value as currency. Eventually they tried sweetening the drink with sugar and serving it hot and beaten so that it was frothy on top—then it caught on. By the first half of the 17th century it was firmly established in the Spanish court; indeed, the upper class ladies in particular were addicted to chocolate. Its popularity soon swept through Europe. Thick, dark, frothy hot chocolate remains one of the most popular drinks in Spain, especially when it's accompanied by a cruller-like fried pastry called a *churro*. See pages 244–245 for a decadent modern take on hot chocolate with cinnamon *churros*.

SWEET INNOVATION
Spain's food revolution has had a tremendous impact on pastry. A new generation of creative pastry chefs, such as Oriol Balaguer and Paco Torreblanca, have made their mark in the last ten years, opening extraordinary pastry and chocolate shops in cities across Spain and Europe. Rigorous in their approach to pastry yet constantly questioning and experimenting with new concepts, they are true artists. Until about ten years ago, patisserie was relegated to sweet shops and

Churros, Spain's answer to donuts. These sweet pastries are eaten at any time of day. In Spain, vendors sell them from street carts.

Oriol Balaguer's many-layered concept cake. Surprisingly, it is garnished with shaved cheese and fresh arugula leaves.

bakeries, and restaurants had fairly simple dessert selections. Now pastry chefs work hand in hand with restaurant chefs, creating impressive tours de forces that blur the lines between sweet and savory, hot and cold, solid and liquid.

THE BALAGUER CONCEPT CAKE
Every month Oriol Balaguer and his team at Estudi Xocolata (The Chocolate Studio) in Barcelona develop a new prototype cake for the store. If the cake is successful, it makes the next season's collection of new cakes. One particular concept cake showcased the perfect symbiosis between cooking and pastry. Assembled in an 8-inch (20 cm) frame, the first layer of the cake was a streusel made with almond flour, brown sugar, flour, and butter, seasoned with salt, vanilla powder, anise seed, and coffee. The streusel was baked, then coated with a mixture of white chocolate and cocoa butter to prevent it from becoming soggy. The frame was then filled with a baked apple purée, and briefly frozen. Next, the surface of the purée was sugared and caramelized with a hot iron to impart a more intense smoky flavor. Over the caramelized purée went a "couscous" layer, made with ground toasted broad beans. The cake was finished with a line of six cream cheese ice cream quenelles and garnished with shaved semi-cured cheese, Maldon sea salt, cracked pepper, and arugula leaves. This is a classic play on sweet and savory flavors on the same plate together; tasting such a creation is an experience of a lifetime.

HAZELNUT PASSION FRUIT
ICE CREAM

HERE IS A SPANISH/LATINO fusion dessert. Hazelnuts are much loved in Spanish cuisine; they find their way into both savory and sweet dishes, and here they add texture and nuttiness to this tropical fruit ice cream. The original recipe called for jabuticaba purée, a grapelike fruit native to Brazil, but you can substitute passion fruit purée, as shown here. Frozen passion fruit purée is available at most gourmet markets.

SERVES 8

1⅔ cups heavy cream

⅔ cup milk

⅓ cup sugar

⅓ of a vanilla bean, split and scraped

4 egg yolks

½ cup passion fruit purée

16 edible flowers, such as nasturtiums or pansies to garnish (optional)

¼ cup hazelnuts, roasted, skinned, and roughly chopped, plus additional to garnish

1. Combine the cream, milk, half the sugar, and the vanilla bean and scraped seeds in a heavy, medium saucepan and bring to a simmer over medium heat, about 10 minutes. Remove from the heat, cover the pot, and let steep for 15 minutes.

2. Prepare an ice bath in a large bowl. Beat together the egg yolks and remaining sugar in a medium bowl. Bring the cream mixture back to a simmer over medium heat. Ladle out ½ cup and slowly whisk into the egg yolks to temper. Whisk the egg yolk mixture back into the cream and return to a medium-low flame. Heat, stirring constantly with a wooden spoon, until you have a custard that leaves a trail when you run your finger down the middle of the spoon, about 5 minutes.

3. Place a stainless-steel bowl in the ice bath and strain the custard into the bowl. Whisk in the purée. Cool over the ice bath, stirring constantly, until it is completely cooled. Refrigerate for at least 4 hours and up to overnight.

4. Place a 1-quart (1 liter) ice-cream container in the freezer. Freeze the custard in an ice-cream machine, following the manufacturer's instructions; add the chopped hazelnuts during the last 5 minutes of freezing. Transfer to the chilled container and freeze for 2 hours or longer before serving. Scoop ½-cup portions into small bowls and garnish with 2 edible flowers, if using, and a sprinkling of chopped hazelnuts.

Adapted from a recipe by VICTOR SCARGLE

HAZELNUT TUILES

THERE IS A LOT OF CLASSIC French pastry in Spain. Inspired by the Catalan taste for hazelnuts, these tuiles are made with hazelnut butter, which is available at gourmet food stores. If made in advance, tuiles will keep in an airtight container for up to 1 week.

SERVES 8

For the tuiles

¼ cup hazelnut butter

7 tablespoons confectioners' sugar

2 tablespoons honey

¼ cup egg whites (about 2)

¼ teaspoon vanilla extract

1 cup less 1 tablespoon (2 ounces or 60 g) sifted all-purpose flour

For the topping

3 cups fresh fruit, such as raspberries, blueberries, and strawberries

1½ cups whipped cream

1. Preheat the oven to 350°F (175°C). Line two baking sheets with Silpats.

2. Combine the hazelnut butter, confectioners' sugar, and honey in a standing mixer fitted with the paddle attachment. Cream on medium speed until fluffy, about 2 minutes. Add the egg whites and vanilla and beat on high speed until smooth, about 4 minutes. Turn off and scrape down the sides. On low speed, add the flour and beat until just incorporated, another minute. Remove the beater and scrape down the bowl.

3. Spoon 1½ teaspoons of the batter onto the baking sheet, and using an offset metal spatula, spread it out to 3 inches (7.5 cm) in diameter. Continue with 3 more spoonfuls, making sure there is an inch (2.5 cm) between each cookie to allow the batter to spread. Prepare and bake only 4 cookies at a time to allow time for shaping them while they're still warm.

4. Place in the middle of the oven and bake for 4 minutes. Rotate the baking sheet front to back and bake another 2 minutes, or until golden. (You may prepare the next batch while the first pan bakes.)

5. Remove the baking sheet from the oven and cool for 30 seconds, until the cookies can be lifted without tearing but are still flexible. If any of the cookies become too stiff to form, return them briefly to the oven to soften. Shape the cookies into shallow cups using muffin tins or other cup-shaped vessels and set aside to cool. To serve, arrange about 2 tablespoons of a selection of fruit in each tuile cup and spoon 1 tablespoon of whipped cream on top. Repeat with the remaining tuiles, allowing for 3 tuiles per person.

Adapted from a recipe by VICTOR SCARGLE

CHOCOLATE

THE FIRST CUPS OF FROTHY HOT CHOCOLATE took hold in the Spanish court some 350 years ago. The beverage was so popular among the Mayan Indians of the New World that the beans from which it was derived were used as currency. The Europeans only caught on when it occurred to them to sweeten the mix with sugar. Then it achieved cult status.

THE NEW SPANISH CHOCOLATIERS

These days you never know what you're going to find in the middle when you bite into a Spanish bonbon. It could be as unexpected as an anchovy, a black olive, a chile, balsamic vinegar, Parmesan cheese, or rosemary. These fillings might sound strange, but Spanish pastry chefs and chocolatiers are taking their notions about their basic raw material to the limit. "We all associate chocolates with sweets, whether we fill them with fruit or nuts, dried fruit, spices, liqueurs, or aromatic herbs," says master pastry chef Paco Torreblanca. "But chocolate is so versatile that it can lend itself to other applications, as long as we maintain a balance of flavors, and consider the context in which the bonbons will be served. If we think about serving chocolates as aperitifs, for example, then a world of possibilities opens up." So Torreblanca makes chocolate bonbons with crispy onion and Maldon salt, with saffron, with goat cheese, with praline, peanut, and curry, with cocoa nibs and salt.

Other pastry chefs follow suit. Ramon Morató sells nine different "collections" at his Cacao Sampaka chocolate boutiques. These include one with different types of chocolate, one with dried fruits and nuts, and one with liqueurs and eaux-de-vie. Then they begin to get a little more far out: Collección Nº3, American Chocolates and Spices, includes vanilla, curry, saffron, coffee and cardamom, ginger and lemon, chicory, curry, and allspice. Collección Nº4, Flowers, Herbs, and Herbal Teas, includes violet, rose, lavender, peppermint, rosemary, and jasmine tea, among others; Collección Nº8, "Gastronomic Innovations," offers bonbons filled with balsamic vinegar, with anchovy and hazelnut, and with Parmesan cheese. The other flavors in this collection are peanut, black truffle, black olive, olive oil, and "smoke."

"HEALTHY" CHOCOLATE

Several of the new pastry chefs have combined olive oil and chocolate in their confections. Paco Torreblanca, in his quest to create a healthier, natural chocolate that allows the essence of cocoa butter to shine through, developed a formula for ganache that uses olive oil in place of butter. The olive oil chocolates are extremely velvety and smooth; they are deeply chocolaty, yet they have less saturated fat than traditional chocolates because they contain no butter. The chefs have managed to make these olive oil chocolates without altering the structural balance of their ganaches. The olive oil, Torreblanca observes, adds to the chocolate's shelf life, because it delays oxidation.

THE CHOCOLATE STUDIO

Among the new Spanish pastry chefs, there is probably no figurehead greater than Oriol Balaguer, a self-described obsessive when it comes to chocolate. His Barcelona boutique, Estudi Xocolata (the Chocolate Studio), is both a chocolate shop and patisserie, with a number of classic and new-age chocolate selections. One need not look farther than his "Nippon Collection," with wasabi, yuzu, soy sauce, and green tea fillings to see that Balaguer is a cutting-edge chocolatier.

Balaguer is perhaps best known for his series of chocolate eggs that rest on solid chocolate squares. These sculptural works of art are made by coating half-egg-shaped molds with a thin layer of couverture, white or dark, and joining the halves together. Sometimes the chocolate is spread onto the molds with a spatula, using irregular strokes, so that there are open spaces on the surface. Often you'll see something fanciful inside these spaces—a chocolate cube ("Cubist Egg") or many spheres ("The Atomic Egg") or an assortment of bonbons, stuck here and there onto the shell. Other eggs in the collection are decorated on the outside. "Egg and the Hand" is a solid white chocolate egg with a dark chocolate hand attached to it. "Pineapple Egg" is covered in cocoa berry-shaped bonbons.

Balaguer and his cohorts are fascinated by the range of flavors, intensities, and textures inherent in chocolate. He displays this range in a dessert called Chocolate Texture Dessert, in which he tops a strip of chocolate-coated chocolate almond biscotti with five quenelles made with different types of chocolate crème anglaise: one with 70 percent dark chocolate, one with 40 percent dark chocolate, one with 40 percent milk chocolate, another with gianduja, and another made with white chocolate. He sprinkles a cocoa "streusel couscous" over the quenelles, drizzles a mango-passion fruit sauce around the plate, and serves the dessert with Valencia orange sorbet and candied lemon. The sorbet brings the dessert together, providing a refreshing, acidic counterpoint to the chocolate and cleansing the palate between each different taste. This is a far cry from hot chocolate, which nonetheless remains one of Spain's most popular hot drinks, a favorite of schoolchildren and adults alike.

XOCOPILI HOT CHOCOLATE

INSTEAD OF MILK AND COOKIES, try chocolate and *churros*. These fried dough sticks sprinkled with cinnamon and sugar are dipped in spicy chocolate. Xocopili is a Valrhona product that has 72 percent cocoa, and a little salt, piment d'Espelette, curry, and cardamom in it. A similar mix can be made by adding the flavoring ingredients to melted dark chocolate of your choice.

SERVES 8

For the xocopili hot chocolate

2½ cups milk

¾ cup heavy cream

1¾ cups Xocopili or chopped dark chocolate

For the churros

1 cup milk

¼ cup (½ stick) butter

¼ teaspoon sugar

¼ teaspoon salt

¾ cup bread flour

2 to 3 eggs

5 cups vegetable oil, or as needed

1 teaspoon cinnamon

½ cup sugar

1. Make the hot chocolate. Bring the milk and cream to a simmer over low heat in a medium saucepan. Place the chocolate in a stainless-steel bowl and pour the milk mixture over it. Cover the bowl with plastic wrap and allow to sit for 5 minutes. Whisk until thoroughly combined, then set aside.

2. Make the churros. Bring the milk, butter, sugar, and salt to a boil over medium heat, stirring constantly with a wooden spoon. Remove from the heat, add the flour all at once, and stir vigorously to combine. Return the pan to medium heat and cook, stirring constantly, until the mixture starts to stick to the pan, about 3 minutes.

3. Transfer the mixture to the bowl of a 5-quart (5 liter) stand mixer and beat on medium speed with the paddle attachment. Add the eggs one at a time, beating until the mixture is smooth after each addition, 6 to 7 minutes.

4. Place the mixture in a piping bag fitted with a No. 6 star tip.

5. Bring the oil to 325°F (165°C) in a medium saucepan. Pipe 2-inch (5 cm) lengths of dough into the oil (you can fry 6 to 8 of them at a time). Fry until golden brown, about 6 minutes. Remove from the oil, drain briefly on paper towels, and roll in the cinnamon and sugar.

6. Reheat the chocolate mixture over low heat for 1 to 2 minutes, or until just simmering. Serve ½ cup of the hot chocolate with 4 of the churros.

Recipe by THE CULINARY INSTITUTE OF AMERICA

ORANGES AND SAFFRON
WITH COCONUT FOAM

THIS IS A CONTEMPORARY INTERPRETATION of oranges and coconut, a classic combination. The dessert is typical of today's Spanish haute cuisine. The basic ingredients are quite simple, but they are transformed into foam and garnished with a savory saffron infusion.

SERVES 8

For the saffron infusion

2 cups flat mineral water

½ teaspoon saffron powder

For the coconut foam

¼ cup sugar

¼ cup water

1 package gelatin (¼ ounce or 7 g)

Two14-ounce (400 g) cans coconut milk (3½ cups)

For the oranges and the sorbet

10 navel oranges

4 cups orange or blood orange sorbet

16 edible flowers, such as nasturtiums or pansies
   to garnish

1. Make the saffron infusion. Heat the water to 150°F (65°C) in a medium saucepan and add the saffron. Remove from the heat, cover, and infuse for 4 hours. Strain the saffron out of the infusion and reserve. This can be done the day before serving.

2. Make the coconut foam. Bring the sugar and water to a boil, then remove from the heat and allow to cool to room temperature. Dissolve the gelatin in ½ cup of the coconut milk for 2 minutes. Warm the simple syrup to 200°F (95°C) in a medium saucepan and add the gelatin mixture. Stir until it dissolves, about 1½ minutes. Mix with the remaining coconut milk in a pitcher or measuring cup with a pourable spout. Pour into a 1-pint (480 ml) siphon using a funnel and charge using 1 nitrous oxide (N2O) cartridge. Shake well, then place in the refrigerator to chill for 1 hour.

3. Prepare the oranges while the foam is chilling. Peel, section, and cut the oranges into ½-inch (1 cm) dice. Place in a medium bowl and allow to sit for 1 hour to release their juices.

4. Place ½ cup of the chopped oranges on each plate. Top with a number 12-sized scoop (⅓ cup) of the orange sorbet, then spoon over 2 tablespoons of the saffron infusion. Cover the sorbet with about ¼ cup of the coconut foam and decorate with 2 nasturtiums or other edible flowers.

Adapted from a recipe by MARÍA JOSÉ SAN ROMÁN

SPANISH FIG CAKE

THIS "CAKE" is really more of a fig pâté. It can stand in for quince paste and goes nicely with Manchego cheese. Note that the cake must sit for 2 days at room temperature before serving so that it melds into a solid cake.

SERVES 8

2 cups stemmed and quartered dried figs
¼ teaspoon ground cloves
½ teaspoon ground cinnamon
1 tablespoon honey
⅔ cup toasted slivered almonds
2 tablespoons plus 1 teaspoon sherry, divided use
Sixteen ¼-inch- (5 mm) thick slices Manchego (about 6 ounces or 170 g)

1. Place the figs in a food processor fitted with the steel blade and chop finely, pulsing for about 1 minute. Add the spices and honey and blend until combined, about 30 seconds, or until the mixture forms a ball. Add the almonds and process until coarsely chopped and combined with the figs, about 1 minute. Add 2 tablespoons of the sherry and process until the mixture sticks together, about 1 minute.

2. Moisten your hands with 1 teaspoon of sherry and shape the fig mixture into a 5- by 3-inch (13 by 8 cm) log. Wrap in a 12- by 12-inch (30 by 30 cm) sheet of parchment paper, then plastic, and place in a 5- by 3- by 2-inch (13 by 8 by 5 cm) loaf pan, or another nonreactive container that will accommodate the fig mixture. Place a second loaf pan on top of the log to compress it into a firm cake, and allow to rest for 2 days at room temperature.

3. Slice the cake into thin slices about ¼ inch (5 mm) thick. Serve with the slices of Manchego.

Adapted from a recipe by SONDRA BERNSTEIN

RICE PUDDING
WITH CIDER RAISIN SAUCE

THIS IS A DELICIOUS VARIATION of traditional rice pudding. Raisins, a common ingredient in Spanish rice pudding, are combined with reduced brandy and apple cider to make a very sweet sauce. Drizzle the sauce sparingly to avoid overwhelming the citrus hints in the pudding. The sauce may be prepared in advance and stored in the refrigerator for up to 8 days.

SERVES 8

For the rice pudding

6 tablespoons short-grain Spanish rice

¾ teaspoon cornstarch

7 tablespoons sugar, divided use

2 eggs

4 cups milk

Pinch salt

One 3-inch (8 cm) cinnamon stick

2 teaspoons thinly sliced orange zest

1 teaspoon vanilla extract

For the cider raisin sauce

1 cup raisins

3 tablespoons brandy

2⅓ cups apple cider

1 tablespoon cornstarch

½ teaspoon lemon juice

1. Make the rice pudding. Wash the rice under cold water to remove some of the starch. Sift the cornstarch and half of the sugar into a medium bowl. Add the eggs and whisk until thoroughly combined with the sugar mixture.

2. Combine the milk, the remaining sugar, the salt, cinnamon, and orange zest in a medium saucepan. Bring the milk to a boil over medium heat. Add the rice to the milk and simmer until the rice just begins to get tender, about 10 minutes.

3. Whisk 2 cups of the hot milk into the egg mixture to temper. Mix well and whisk the egg mixture back into the remaining hot milk.

4. Bring to a simmer over medium-low heat and simmer for about 7 minutes, or until the rice is tender. Remove from the heat and add the vanilla.

5. Divide the rice pudding evenly between eight ¾-cup glasses or bowls, cover, and refrigerate until needed.

6. Make the sauce. Combine the raisins, 1 tablespoon of the brandy, and enough apple cider to cover the raisins (about ⅔ cup) in a small saucepan. Bring to a simmer over medium heat and remove from the heat. Plump the raisins for 20 minutes, then drain them, reserving the liquid separately. While the raisins are plumping, reduce the remaining cider by half in a large sauté pan over medium-high heat, about 25 minutes. Lower the heat to a simmer.

7. Mix the cornstarch with the remaining brandy and the lemon juice to form a slurry. Add the slurry and plumped raisins to the cider. Simmer until the sauce thickens, about 1 minute. Thin it out with ¼ cup of the reserved raisin liquid, if needed.

8. Spoon about 2 tablespoons of the cider raisin sauce over each serving of rice pudding.

Recipe by THE CULINARY INSTITUTE OF AMERICA

SPICED ALMOND BRITTLE

CLASSIC ALMOND BRITTLE fuses with Latin flavors in this sweet, salty, and spicy confection. It can be enjoyed as a sweet on its own, or it makes a wonderful accompaniment to Mission Fig Flan (pages 256–257).

SERVES 8

½ cup sugar

2 tablespoons corn syrup

1 tablespoon brandy

1 teaspoon salt

¼ cup (½ stick) unsalted butter

⅛ teaspoon baking powder

¼ teaspoon smoked paprika (pimentón)

¼ teaspoon chipotle powder

½ cup toasted slivered almonds

1. Line a baking sheet with a Silpat. In a heavy, medium saucepan combine the sugar, corn syrup, brandy, and salt and stir together with a wooden spoon. Cover the pot and bring to a boil over medium-high heat. Uncover the pot and brush down any stray sugar crystals with a wet pastry brush. Turn the heat to high, insert a thermometer, and cook until the mixture is golden brown and has reached 325°F (165°C), 10 to 15 minutes. Remove from the heat and wait until the caramel stops bubbling.

2. Add the butter and baking powder and stir until incorporated. Add the spices and almonds and combine well.

3. Pour the mixture out onto the prepared baking sheet and spread to an ⅛-inch (3 mm) thickness. Allow to cool thoroughly, then break into pieces. Store in an airtight container, with wax paper separating each layer of brittle, for up to a week in a cool, dry place.

Adapted from a recipe by SONDRA BERNSTEIN

CARAMELIZED GOAT CHEESE
WITH BRUNOISE PEACHES IN CIEZA SYRUP

THIS DESSERT BRINGS TOGETHER PRODUCTS from the province of Murcia. Peaches are grown around the town of Cieza, and Jumilla, in the northeastern part of the province, is known for its sweet red wines.

SERVES 8

½ cup Jumilla sweet wine

One 12-ounce (340 g) log goat cheese

2 tablespoons sugar

10 ounces (285 g) peaches in syrup, drained and cut into ¼-inch (5 mm) dice (about 1 cup)

2 teaspoons crushed pink peppercorns

8 arugula leaves or sprigs of fresh herbs, such as lemon balm, lemon thyme, or mint to garnish

1. Bring the wine to a boil over medium heat in a small saucepan and reduce to 2 tablespoons, about 10 minutes. Remove from the heat and set aside.

2. Slice the cheese into sixteen ½-inch- (1 cm) thick medallions, using a knife frequently dampened with hot water, and place on a sheet pan. Sprinkle the sugar evenly over the goat cheese slices. Using a butane torch, caramelize the sugar, moving the flame quickly and evenly across the surface of the cheese until lightly browned.

3. Place 2 tablespoons of the peaches on each plate and top with a couple of the caramelized goat cheese rounds. Decorate with the ground pink peppercorns, an herb sprig, and ¾ teaspoon of the Jumilla sweet wine reduction.

Adapted from a recipe by JUAN ANTONIO PELLICER

PAPARAJOTES

PAPARAJOTES ARE A SIGNATURE CONFECTION from the province of Murcia. Lemon tree leaves are coated with a batter and fried, which gives the pastry a wonderful citrusy flavor. The leaf is not eaten.

SERVES 8

1 cup warm milk

1 cup warm water

2 teaspoons instant yeast

8 eggs, separated

2 cups all-purpose flour

1 cup sugar

½ teaspoon salt

1½ teaspoons finely chopped lemon zest

3 cups extra virgin olive oil

24 to 32 lemon tree leaves

2 teaspoons ground cinnamon mixed with 2 tablespoons sugar, for dusting

ice cream (optional)

1. Combine the milk and water in a medium bowl and stir in the yeast. Allow the yeast to proof until bubbly, about 5 minutes. Stir in the egg yolks until thoroughly combined. Sift together the flour, sugar, and salt and whisk into the milk mixture. Stir in the lemon zest. Cover tightly with plastic and allow to proof for 1 hour.

2. Beat the egg whites in the bowl of a 5-quart (5 liter) stand mixer with a whisk attachment on low speed until the whites become opaque and foamy, about 30 seconds. Increase the speed to medium high and beat until medium (not stiff) peaks form when you lift the beaters out of the whites, 1½ to 2 minutes (the whites will have the texture of shaving cream). Gently fold one-third of the whites into the batter, until blended thoroughly, then gently fold in the remaining two-thirds of the egg whites.

3. Heat the oil to 350°F (175°C) in a large sauté pan. Clean and dry the leaves and dip a quarter of them into the batter. If the batter doesn't stick, dust the leaves with a little flour first.

4. Deep fry the leaves until golden, turning often, about 2 minutes per batch, and drain on paper towels. Dust with the cinnamon sugar. Repeat with the remaining leaves, frying three more batches. Serve 3 or 4 of the leaves with ice cream, if desired.

Adapted from a recipe by JUAN ANTONIO PELLICER

MISSION FIG FLAN
WITH SPICED ALMOND BRITTLE

VANILLA AND SHERRY add complexity and sophistication to the traditional flan. Here it is served with spiced almond brittle, with its smoky taste of chipotle and sweet pimentón. Note that the caramel sauce can be prepared in advance and refrigerated for up to 2 weeks.

SERVES 8

For the caramel sauce

1½ cups heavy cream

¾ cup plus 2 tablespoons sugar

⅓ cup plus 2 tablespoons corn syrup

2 tablespoons (¼ stick) soft butter, cut into cubes

For the flan

6 tablespoons oloroso sherry

½ cup small-dice dried Mission figs

½ cup Caramel Sauce (from above)

1⅓ cups heavy cream

1 cup milk

1 vanilla bean

4 large eggs

3 large egg yolks

⅓ cup maple syrup

⅓ cup sugar

7 ounces (200 g) Spiced Almond Brittle
  (pages 250–251)

1. Make the caramel sauce. Place the cream in a medium saucepan and bring to a boil over medium heat. Keep warm over very low heat.

2. Prepare an ice bath large enough to accommodate the medium saucepan you'll use to cook the caramel. Combine the sugar and corn syrup in a medium heavy-bottomed saucepan and slowly cook over medium heat, stirring constantly, until the sugar has dissolved, 3 to 4 minutes. Stop stirring and continue to cook until straw colored, about 10 minutes. Reduce the heat to very low and cook for 1 to 2 minutes, until the mixture is a chestnut brown caramel color and is just beginning to smoke. Remove from the heat and carefully stir in the butter until completely incorporated. Gradually stir in the hot cream. Place the saucepan in the ice bath to stop the cooking, stirring for 30 seconds. Remove the pot from the ice bath and reserve until needed.

3. Make the flan. Place the sherry and figs in a small saucepan and cook over low heat until the sherry has been absorbed, 5 to 6 minutes. Mix together with ½ cup of the caramel sauce. Adjust the oven rack to the center position; preheat the oven to 325°F (165°C).

4. Pour the cream and milk into a medium saucepan. Split open the vanilla bean and scrape the contents into the pan, along with the pod. Bring to a boil over medium-high heat, then turn off the heat. Let the mixture steep for 15 minutes to absorb the flavor, then strain to remove the vanilla bean.

5. Beat the eggs, yolks, maple syrup, and sugar in a medium bowl until smooth. Slowly whisk in the milk mixture until incorporated.

6. Butter eight 4-fluid ounce (120 ml) ramekins. Cover the bottom of each ramekin with 1½ tablespoons of the fig-caramel mixture. Ladle in the milk and egg mixture, dividing it evenly among the ramekins. Place the ramekins in a 2-inch- (5 cm) deep baking pan or casserole and fill it with enough hot water to come halfway up the sides of the ramekins. Bake for 30 to 35 minutes, or until the custards are just set, rotating the pan every 15 minutes to ensure even cooking.

7. Remove the ramekins from the water bath and let the custard cool to room temperature. Individually wrap the ramekins in plastic and refrigerate for at least 24 hours and up to 2 days.

8. Unmold the custard by running a small sharp knife between the custard and the ramekin. Invert onto a plate and tap lightly to release. Garnish each plate with 1 to 2 pieces of the spiced almond brittle.

Adapted from a recipe by SONDRA BERNSTEIN

CREMA CATALANA

THIS SMOOTH, LIGHT CUSTARD has orange and lemon zests added to it, which gives it a wonderful citrusy flavor. Use a powerful blowtorch to get a glass-like crust of sugar on top of this dessert. Or use the traditional crema catalana irons to get an evenly browned crust.

SERVES 8

4 cups milk
½ teaspoon thinly sliced orange zest
½ teaspoon thinly sliced lemon zest
One 3-inch (8 cm) cinnamon stick
1¾ cups sugar
3 tablespoons cornstarch
18 egg yolks
1 tablespoon vanilla extract

1. Combine 3 cups of the milk, both zests, the cinnamon, and ¾ cup of the sugar in a saucepan. Bring to a boil over medium heat, stirring constantly to dissolve the sugar. Remove from the heat and allow the mixture to steep for 10 minutes before straining out the zests and cinnamon.

2. Combine the cornstarch with ¾ cup of sugar. Whisk in the remaining cup of milk. Add the egg yolks and vanilla, whisking the mixture until it is completely smooth.

3. Temper the egg mixture by adding about one-third of the hot milk, stirring constantly with a whisk. Return the mixture to the remaining hot milk in the saucepan. Continue cooking, stirring vigorously with the whisk, until the custard just begins to come to a boil and the whisk leaves a trail in it.

4. Divide the custard between eight 4-fluid ounce (120 ml) shallow round ramekins. Cover the surface directly with plastic wrap and cool over an ice bath.

5. Sprinkle 1½ teaspoons of the remaining sugar evenly over each ramekin and caramelize with a blowtorch or iron.

Recipe by THE CULINARY INSTITUTE OF AMERICA

GLOSSARY

Abadejo: Spanish for cod.

Adobo: A paste or sauce typically made from ground chiles, herbs, and vinegar that is used to season and marinate.

Aji: A long, thin, tapering chile with thin flesh and a very hot, somewhat tropical flavor; it can have a green or red color when fresh and is yellow when dried and known as *aji mirasol*. Aji is also the term commonly used in Latin America to describe various members of the chile family Capsicum baccatum and is also called the aji crystal pepper.

Albóndiga: Spanish for meatball.

Al dente: Literally "to the tooth," this term usually describes pasta or vegetables that have been cooked until tender but still firm, not soft.

Allioli: A Spanish sauce similar to the French aïoli (garlic mayonnaise). It is often used as a condiment with fish and meat.

Artisanal cheese: An approach to cheese-making that showcases cheese-makers' skill and intuition, and also places great importance on the high quality of raw ingredients.

Asado: Spanish for roasted or broiled meat.

Asturiana: Blood sausage from the Asturia region.

Bard: To cover an item with thin slices or sheets or strips of fat, such as bacon or fatback, to baste it during roasting. The fat is usually tied on with butcher's twine.

Béchamel: A white sauce made of milk thickened with a light roux (cooked butter and flour mixture) and flavored with white mirepoix vegetables.

Bivalve: A mollusk with two hinged shells. Examples are clams, scallops, oysters, and mussels.

Black beluga lentils: Small legumes that cook quickly and glisten like beluga caviar when cooked. French green lentils may be substituted, however they will not have the same shiny appearance. They are available from online sources and from specialty grocery stores.

Black rice vinegar: An Asian (usually Chinese) vinegar made from glutinous sweet rice. It has a dark color and a rich, mild flavor. It is typically used for braising. Available at most Asian grocery stores and from online sources.

Blanch: To cook an item briefly in boiling water or hot fat before finishing or storing it. Blanching preserves color, lessens strong flavors, and helps remove the peels of some fruits and vegetables.

Blood sausage: Also called morcilla, black pudding, or blood pudding, a sausage where the main ingredient is liquid blood.

Bouquet garni: A small bundle of herbs tied with string. It is used to flavor stocks, braises, and other preparations. It usually contains bay leaf, parsley, thyme, and possibly other aromatics wrapped in leek leaves.

Braise: A cooking method in which an item, usually meat, is seared in fat, then simmered, covered, at a low temperature in a small amount of stock or other liquid for an extended period. The cooking liquid is then reduced and used as a base for sauce.

Broil: To cook by means of a radiant heat source placed above the food.

Broth: A flavorful, aromatic liquid made by simmering water or stock with meat, vegetables, and/or spices and herbs.

Brunoise: Dice cut of ⅛-inch (3 mm) cubes. The item is cut first into julienne, then cut crosswise. A fine brunoise is a dice cut of 1/16-inch (2 mm) cubes, with the item being cut first into fine julienne.

Calçot: A Spanish spring onion similar to a scallion or small leek.

Caramelize: To heat sugar to very high temperatures, usually 310°F to 360°F (155°C to 180°C), causing it to brown and develop a full, rich intense flavor.

Casing: A synthetic or natural membrane (if natural, usually pig or sheep intestines) used to enclose sausage or forcemeat.

Caul fat: A fatty membrane from a pig or sheep intestine that resembles fine netting; used to bard roasts and pâtés.

Causa: A traditionally Peruvian dish of potatoes that have been mashed with onions, dried chiles, and oil, molded into a dome, and garnished with hard-boiled eggs, olives, cheese, shrimp, avocado, and corn on the cob.

Cava: Spanish sparkling wine made by the *méthode champenoise*. Cava must remain in a cellar for a minimum of 9 months.

Cazuela: An earthenware casserole dish that is normally wide and shallow, glazed on the inside, and has a rough and unfinished exterior. Cazuelas are treasured by many cooks because they heat evenly and retain heat long after the dish has been removed from the stove.

Cèpe mushroom: Pale, brown mushroom that ranges in size from 1 to 10 inches (2.5 to 25 cm) in diameter and has a meaty texture and pungent flavor. Most commonly available dried.

Ceviche (also spelled seviche): A seafood salad that originated in Latin America. To prepare it, raw fish is marinated in citrus (usually lime) juice, and sometimes onions, tomatoes, chiles, and cilantro. The acid in the citrus juice "cooks" the proteins in the fish and turns the flesh opaque and firm.

Cheesecloth: A light, fine mesh gauze used for straining liquids and sauces, wrapping poultry and fish for poaching, and making sachets.

Chorizo: A slightly spicy Spanish sausage made from lean pork, garlic, paprika, red bell peppers, and red pepper flakes. It is not to be confused with Mexican chorizo.

Clarified butter: Butter from which the milk solids and water have been removed, leaving pure butterfat. It has a higher smoking point than whole butter, but less butter flavor.

Coagulation: The curdling or clumping of protein, usually due to the application of heat or acid.

Cocido: A Spanish term for cooked or boiled, cocido describes a variety of soupy, stewlike dishes containing meats, vegetables, and especially chickpeas.

Confit: Preserved meat (usually goose, duck, or pork) cooked and preserved in its own fat.

Consommé: Broth that has been clarified using a mixture of ground meat, egg whites, and other ingredients that trap impurities, resulting in a perfectly clear broth.

Croquettes: These may be made from meat, fish, vegetables, eggs, or cheese that has been puréed and/or bound with thick sauce (usually a béchamel), then formed into small shapes, breaded, and deep-fried. Spanish *croquetas* are typically served as tapas.

Cure: To preserve a food by salting, smoking, pickling, and/or drying.

Custard: A mixture of milk, beaten egg, and possibly other ingredients, such as sweet or savory flavorings, cooked in gentle heat, often in a bain-marie, double boiler, or water bath.

Debeard: To remove the shaggy, inedible fibers from a mussel. Originally, these fibers anchored the mussel to its mooring.

Deglaze: To use a liquid, such as wine, water, or stock, to dissolve food particles and/or caramelized drippings left in a pan after roasting and sautéing. The resulting mix then becomes the base for the accompanying sauce.

Demitasse: A small cup with a single handle; used for coffee.

DO (Denominación de Origen): Comprehensive Spanish laws that govern every aspect of grape cultivation and wine production. The laws also regulate the production of items such as cheeses, oils, meats, and beans.

DOCa (Denominación de Origen Calificada): The highest legal designation for wines in Spain. Specific wine production areas are considered DOCa and produce wines of superior quality.

Dredge: To coat food with a dry ingredient such as flour or breadcrumbs prior to frying or sautéing.

Dutch oven: A kettle, usually of cast iron, used for stewing and braising on the stovetop or in the oven.

Espardeña: Sea cucumber. An invertebrate saltwater animal; it has an elongated cylindrical shape with a leathery, velvety, or slimy body tube and a mouth surrounded by short tentacles. The body is generally boiled, sun-dried, then smoked and used in Japanese and Chinese cuisines as a flavoring; also known as a sea slug.

Fabes: *Fabas* in Spanish and fava beans in English, these large, flat, kidney-shaped bean have a tough pale green skin when fresh, which turns brown when dried. The skin is usually removed before cooking; the interior is light green when fresh and cream-colored when dried.

Five-spice powder: A Chinese seasoning that usually consists of powdered Chinese cinnamon, star anise and anise seed, ginger root, and ground cloves. It is available from Asian grocery stores and from online sources.

Fumet: A type of stock in which the main flavoring ingredient (usually fish) is allowed to cook in a covered pot with wine and aromatics.

Gazpacho: A cold Spanish soup made from vegetables, typically tomatoes, cucumbers, peppers, and onions.

Gelatin: A protein-based substance found in animal bones and connective tissue. When dissolved in hot liquid, then cooled, it can be used as a thickener and stabilizer.

Gratin: A dish with a cheese or breadcrumb topping that has been browned in an oven or under a salamander.

Grill: A cooking technique in which foods are cooked by a radiant heat source placed below the food. Also the piece of equipment on which grilling is done. Grills may be fueled by gas, electricity, charcoal, or wood.

Ice bath: A mixture of ice and water used to chill a food or liquid rapidly.

Infusion: Steeping an aromatic or other item in liquid to extract its flavor. An infusion is also the liquid resulting from this process.

Jabuticaba: A grapelike fruit native to Brazil. The cherry-sized spherical fruit grows on the trunk, limbs, and branches of the tree; it has a maroon or purple skin with white to pinkish flesh and tastes similar to a grape.

Julienne: Vegetables or other items cut into thin strips usually ⅛ by ⅛ inch by 1 to 2 inches (3 by 3 mm by 2.5 to 5 cm).

Kaffir lime leaves: Popular in Thai cooking; the leaves from the kaffir lime plant impart a pleasant citrus flavor and are generally not eaten whole. They are available from specialty grocery stores and online sources.

Kosher salt: Also known as coarse salt or pickling salt, this purified, coarse rock salt may be used for pickling because it does not contain magnesium carbonate and thus does not cloud brine solutions. Also used for general seasoning and to prepare kosher items.

Maldon salt: A remarkable sea salt that is hand harvested, which results in soft white, flaky crystals that have a distinctive crunchy texture.

Marinade: A seasoned liquid, usually containing an acid, herbs and/or spices, in which raw foods (typically meat, poultry, fish, shellfish, or vegetables) are soaked or coated to absorb flavors and become tender before cooking or serving. Marinades may also be dry, in which case they are usually salt-based.

Mirin: A Japanese low-alcohol, syrupy, thin, golden-colored rice wine used to sweeten and flavor glazes, sauces, and a variety of dishes.

Mirepoix: A combination of aromatic vegetables (usually two parts onion, one part carrot, and one part celery) used to flavor stocks, soups, braises, and stews.

Mojo: A type of hot sauce that originated in the Canary Islands. Mojos are uncooked and blended or pounded to a fairly smooth consistency. Basic ingredients usually include olive oil, garlic, paprika, and cumin.

Morcilla: Blood sausage stuffed with rice, paprika, onions, garlic, and spices. Commonly used in the Asturias region.

Mortar and pestle: A tool, usually made of stone, wood, or ceramic, used for grinding foods; the bat-shaped pestle presses and rotates the food against the sides of the bowl-shaped mortar.

Nigella: A mild peppery spice commonly known as black cumin and typically used in Indian and Middle Eastern cuisines or in baked goods and sweet dishes. Cumin can be substituted, but the dish will lack nigella's distinctive sweetness.

Ñora pepper: This small, red bell pepper is used dry to add a distinctive earthy flavor to soups, stews, and rice dishes such as paella.

Padrón pepper: A small green pepper grown in Galicia. Although the peppers are generally strong in flavor, it is said that of every batch of fifty, one is very hot.

Parboiling/parcooking: To partially cook a food in a boiling or simmering liquid before finishing and storing.

Pasteurization: A process in which milk products are heated to kill microorganisms that could contaminate the milk.

Pebrella: Wild Spanish thyme grown in the region of Spain between Valencia and Alicante. Traditional oregano or thyme may be subsituted.

Pectin: A thickener used in foods such as jams and jellies.

Pequin pepper: A hot, flavored pepper that may be found dry or fresh. Dried cayenne pepper or fresh Thai bird chile may be substituted.

Picual olive: A medium-sized Spanish olive that has an elongated, pointed shape and shiny black flesh when fully ripe. It is most often used to produce olive oil that is blended with other oils to enhance their flavor.

Piment d'Espelette: A thin red pepper associated with the Basque region of France that is generally sold dried and ground. Hot paprika or New Mexico red chili powder may be used as substitutes.

Pimentón: Spanish for paprika, this ground sweet red pepper powder can be made from many different varieties of red pepper.

Piquillo: Long, red, tapering, triangular Spanish peppers. Canned varieties may be used in lieu of fresh peppers and are available from Spanish specialty stores or from online sources.

Pisto: A Spanish vegetable dish of chopped tomatoes, red or green peppers, zucchini, and onions stewed together. This dish is associated with La Mancha region in Spain.

Plum wine: A femented alcoholic beverage made from plums; popular in Japanese cuisine.

Poach: To cook gently in simmering liquid that is 160°F to 180°F (70°C to 80°C) in temperature.

Quenelle: A light, poached dumpling based on a forcemeat (usually chicken, veal, seafood, or game), bound with eggs, and shaped into an oval by using two spoons. It may also refer to a small scoopful of ice cream, whipped cream, or soft cheese.

Ramekin: A small, ovenproof dish, usually ceramic.

Rayu: Chili-infused sesame oil used in Japanese cooking.

Rocoto: A small chile with an orange-yellow to deep red color skin, a thin flesh, and a very hot, somewhat fruity flavor.

Roe: Fish or shellfish eggs.

Saffron: Known as *azafrán* in Spanish, saffron consists of the stigmas of a purple crocus flower. It adds color and a distinct flavor to Spanish rice dishes as well as to other main-course meals. Most of the world's saffron comes from Spain, and because of the extraordinarily labor-intensive process necessary to collect it, it is the most expensive spice in the world.

Salmorejo: A thick vegetable soup typical of the Córdoba region. Similar to gazpacho, it is served cold and traditionally incorporates tomatoes, olive oil, and sherry wine vinegar. Variations may include green peppers and garlic. It may also be used as a sauce for poultry, fish, rice, or vegetables.

Salt cod: Cod that has been salted, possibly smoked, and dried to preserve it. In most cases, it is desalted before use in cooking.

Score: To cut the surface of an item at regular intervals to allow it to cook evenly, to allow excess fat to drain, to help the food absorb marinades, or for decorative purposes.

Sear: To brown the surface of food in fat over high heat before finishing by another method (e.g., braising or roasting) in order to add flavor.

Sea salt: Salt produced by evaporating seawater. Available refined or unrefined, crystallized or ground.

Serrano ham (jamón serrano): Cured mountain ham from Andalusia but used in regional cooking everywhere. Generally, slightly less salty than its Italian counterpart, prosciutto.

Sherry: A fortified wine made mainly from Palomino grapes grown in southern Spain near Jerez de la Frontera. They range in color from pale gold to dark brown and in flavor from dry to sweet. Varieties include amontillado, brown sherry, cream sherry, fino, manzanilla, and oloroso.

Sherry vinegar: A nutty brown-colored vinegar made from sherry and with a full, round flavor. It is aged in wood barrels, similar to the sherry-making process.

Siphon: Used in food science, the siphon canister is loaded with N2O cartridges and creates foams. Also associated with clams (the thick fleshy tube through which the clam takes in and expels water).

Sous-vide: A food-packaging technique; fresh ingredients are combined into various dishes, vacuum-packed in individual-portion pouches, cooked under a vacuum, and chilled for storage or served.

Spanish dry chile pepper: A small, dry, red chile pepper from Spain. It is mild in heat. Guajillo chile peppers or guindilla peppers may be substituted. They are available from specialty grocery stores and from online sources.

Spider: A long-handled skimmer used to remove items from hot liquid or fat and to skim the surface of liquids.

Steep: To allow an ingredient to sit in warm or hot liquid to extract flavor or impurities, or to soften the item.

Stew: A cooking method nearly identical to braising, but generally involving smaller pieces of meat and hence a shorter cooking time. Stewed items may also be blanched rather than seared to give a paler color. Also, a dish prepared by using the stewing method.

Stock: A flavorful liquid prepared by simmering meat bones, poultry bones, seafood bones, and/or vegetables in water with aromatics until their flavor is extracted. A stock may be used as a base for soups, sauces, and other preparations.

Suckling pig: Baby pig. The smallest classification of whole swine. The meat should be tender and very fatty due to the young age of the animal.

Tannins: Phenolic compounds that lend density and richness to wine. Organic compound foods found in the seeds, stems, and skins of grapes. Creates astringent character in wine, and is an important preservative for the proper aging of selected red wines.

Tapas: Spanish hors d'oeuvres and appetizers (sometimes called "small plates") that may be served hot or cold.

Tartare: This term describes nearly any dish that features a raw ingredient.

Temper: To heat gently and gradually. The term may refer to the process of incorporating hot liquid into a cooler one to gradually raise its temperature, or to the proper method for melting chocolate.

Tempranillo: A red wine grape that is widely planted in Spain's Rioja region and from which a well-balanced, deep-colored red wine is made.

Tortilla: A thick potato and onion open-faced omelet. Ubiquitous in Spanish tapas bars and on family tables.

Tuiles: Literally, "tile." A thin, wafer-like cookie (or food cut to resemble this cookie). Tuiles are frequently shaped while warm and still pliable by pressing them into molds or draping them over rolling pins or dowels.

Vanilla paste: Also referred to as vanilla purée. Liquid extract from vanilla beans is mixed with ground vanilla beans and sometimes sugar. It is available from specialty grocery stores and from online sources.

Verjus: The unfermented juice of unripened grapes. It has a very high acid content and is sometimes used as a substitute for vinegar.

Vinaigrette: A cold sauce of oil and vinegar, usually with various flavorings. It is a temporary emulsion. The standard proportion is three parts oil to one part vinegar.

Zest: The thin, brightly colored outer part of a citrus rind. It contains volatile oils, making it ideal for use as a flavoring.

SOURCES

Some of the ingredients in this cookbook may not be available in grocery stores in the United States. Try asking your local grocer to special-order items for you, or order from an online vendor. The companies listed below specialize in excellent-quality Spanish ingredients and stock most produce, meats, grains, spices, and herbs listed in this book.

ONLINE VENDORS OF SPANISH INGREDIENTS

BULK FOODS.COM | www.bulkfoods.com
Large selection of dried spices and peppers.

CASA OLIVER | www.casaoliver.com
Large selection of fine foods and cookware from Spain.

DESPAÑA | www.despanabrandfoods.com and www.despananyc.com
Order by phone only
Large selection of fine foods from Spain including artisanal cheeses, meats, ñora peppers, saffron, and olive oil. Also sells cookware.

LA ESPAÑOLA MEATS | www.laespanolameats.com
Good selection of meats, cheeses, legumes, and sweets.

MARKYS | www.markys.com
Specialty foods including mushrooms, caviar, and Spanish, Italian, and French cheeses.

THE SPANISH TABLE | www.spanishtable.com
All varieties of meats, cheeses, fruits, vegetables, and hard to find herbs, spices, and beans.

LA TIENDA ONLINE | www.tienda.com
Stockists of traditional Spanish foods such as salt cod, paella rice, saffron, and meats. Also sells Spanish wine.

OTHER ONLINE VENDORS

AMAZON.COM | www.amazon.com
Varied selection of chili pastes and spices as well as South East Asian ingredients such as kaffir lime leaves.

AMIGO FOODS | http//store.amigofoods.com/saypasapa.html
Good source for Spanish cheeses, meats, and rice, and Latin American ingredients such as Peruvian yellow chili paste.

ASIA FOODS | www.asiafoods.com
Good source for South East Asian spices, herbs, and seasonings such as five-spice powder.

ASIAN WOK | www.asianwok.com
Extensive stock of South East Asian spices, herbs, seasonings, and other ingredients such as chili pastes.

DEAN AND DELUCA | www.deandeluca.com
Good variety of gourmet and imported foods.

IGOURMET.COM | www.igourmet.com
Large selection of ingredients and food products from around the world, from Spanish cheeses to wasabi powder.

KALUSTYAN'S | www.kalustyans.com
Varied selection of chili pastes and spices.

MARKET HALL FOODS | www.markethallfoods.com
Large selection of food products from around the world, including Spanish olive oil and pimentón.

PENZEYS SPICES | www.penzeys.com
Large selection of spices, including chili powders and two grades of Spanish saffron.

PERUCOOKING.COM | www.perucooking.com
Peruvian gourmet cooking products, including rocoto chili paste.

SUR LA TABLE | www.surlatable.com
Large selection of food products from around the world, including Spanish olive oil, saffron, and paella rice.

CONTRIBUTORS

JOSÉ ANDRÉS is the chef/owner of Café Atlántico, Jaleo, Zaytinya, and Oyamel restaurants in the Washington, DC, area. Chef Andrés is the host of the popular daily television show "Vamos a Cocinar" in Spain, author of *Tapas: A Taste of Spain in America*, and was conference chairman of the 2006 Worlds of Flavor International Conference & Festival at The Culinary Institute of America. Chef Andrés was the 2003 winner of the James Beard Foundation Award for Best Chef, Mid-Atlantic region, and received the Silver Spoon Award from *Food Arts* in December 2005. (Washington, DC)

PATXI BERGARA and his wife **BLANCA AMEZTOY** run the Bar Bergara in San Sebastián, Spain, which has been in Mr. Bergara's family for 56 years. Under their management the Bar Bergara has focused on a more sophisticated *pintxo* (bite-sized snacks on bread or a cocktail stick). Bar Bergara has been named "Best Pintxos Selection" at the Best of Gastronomy conference in San Sebastián-Kursaal, and has been named an honorary member of the Pintxo Association and the Anchovy Association. (San Sebastián, Spain)

TERESA BARRENECHEA is a chef and cookbook author. Her books include *The Cuisines of Spain: Exploring Regional Home Cooking* and *The Basque Table*, which was awarded the National Gastronomy Prize in Spain in 1998. Previously, for 13 years Chef Barrenechea was the chef/owner of Marichu restaurant in New York, one of the city's top traditional Spanish restaurants. (Madrid, Spain)

SONDRA BERNSTEIN is the proprietor and CEO of the girl & the fig, LLC, which is comprised of the girl & the fig restaurant in Sonoma, CA and the fig café & winebar in Glen Ellen, CA. Sondra is also the author of *the girl & the fig Cookbook*. Her gourmet food product line is available nationwide under the girl & the fig label. (Sonoma, CA)

CÁNDIDO LÓPEZ CUERDO is the chef of Mesón de Cándido in Segovia, Spain. Chef Cuerdo began working in his family's historic restaurant at the age of 15; he eventually became an attorney. He also manages the Cándido Mesonero Mayor de Castilla Foundation, which honors gastronomic innovation, social-minded endeavors, and the promotion of Castile-Leon, and was created to mark the centenary of the birth of his legendary grandfather, Cándido, "Mesonero Mayor de Castilla." (Segovia, Spain)

MANOLO DE LA OSA is the chef of Las Rejas in Las Pedroñeras, Spain, which holds one Michelin star. Inspired by the food his mother and grandmother cooked for local weddings, Chef de la Osa studied at Vid School in Madrid before returning to his hometown and opening an eight-table restaurant specializing in authentic regional cuisine. He was honored with the "Best Chef" award from the Spanish Gastronomic Association. (Cuenca, Spain)

ROBERT DEL GRANDE is the executive chef and owner of Café Annie and partner in the Schiller-Del Grande Restaurant Group. He received his undergraduate degree in biology and chemistry from the University of San Francisco and his Ph.D. in biochemistry from the University of California at Riverside. Chef Del Grande joined Café Annie in 1981 and was instrumental in the development of Southwest cooking in America. He has received a James Beard Award for Best Chef, Southwest region, and been inducted into Who's Who in American Cooking. (Houston, TX)

JOAQUÍN FELÍPE is the chef of the Europa Decó restaurant at the Urban hotel in Madrid, Spain. Chef Felípe began his career studying under Chef Luis Irizar, and later became head of the kitchen at the Catering Paradís Madrid. Later he moved on to the Madrilenian restaurant El Chaflán and the Hotel Real Villa, where he began to study tuna and codfish. In 2005 he joined the Europa Decó, and has since been awarded the "Best Chef Metropoli Prize." (Madrid, Spain)

KISKO GARCÍA is the chef at Choco in Córdoba, Spain. Chef García trained at the Tourism and Catering School of Córdoba, Spain, and in the kitchens of famous restaurants such as Café de Paris, Casa Marcial, and El Celler de Can Roca. Returning to the city of his birth, he became chef at Choco, his family's restaurant. In 2006 Madrid Fusión awarded him the "Andalusia Restaurant Revelation Prize." (Córdoba, Spain)

JOYCE GOLDSTEIN is a food industry consultant, food writer, and prolific cookbook author. Her books include *The Mediterranean Kitchen*, *Cucina Ebraica: Flavors of the Italian Jewish Kitchen*, and *Mediterranean the Beautiful Cookbook*. A former chef at Chez Panisse and chef/owner of Square One in San Francisco, Chef Goldstein is a founding member of Women Chefs and Restaurateurs. (San Francisco, CA)

CHEFA GONZÁLEZ-DOPESO is a chef and restaurant adviser. She has received numerous honors, including being named "Champion of Spain" at the Best of Gastronomy conference in San Sebastián-Kursaal, and being acknowledged by the Academy of Gastronomy of Galicia and the Chamber of Commerce of La Coruña. Chef González-Dopeso was in charge of the Mama-Manuela restaurant opened by her sister Mª Fernanda González-Dopeso. She was also gastronomic adviser to Mama-Manuela Pinchos, El Rincón de Mama-Manuela, and Casa Dopeso. (La Coruña, Spain)

NANDO JUBANY is the chef/owner of Can Jubany in Vic, Catalonia, Spain. A third-generation restaurateur, Chef Jubany began working in his family's establishment at the age of 10. At 18 he started as a chef, and 9 years later opened Can Jubany, which holds one Michelin star and specializes in local ingredients prepared in a contemporary Catalan way. He is the author of *A Taula Nando Jubany*. (Calldetenes, Spain)

MARIA MURIA LLORET is the cofounder of Ca'Sento in Valencia, Spain. What started as a small establishment serving beer and sandwiches slowly became the prestigious restaurant that it is today as a result of Chef Lloret's cooking and her recipes for rice and seafood dishes. Their son Raúl Aleixandre manages the kitchen today. (Valencia, Spain)

MARILÚ MADUEÑO is the executive chef at Huaca Pucllana Restaurant in Lima, Peru. A graduate of Le Cordon Bleu in Paris, Chef Madueño furthered her studies by working in a number of renowned restaurants, including La Rosa Nautica Restaurant in Lima and Taillevent in Paris. At Huaca Pucllana she works with native ingredients, creating and reinterpreting traditional and contemporary Peruvian dishes. (Lima, Peru)

KEVIN MARQUET is the executive chef at The 9th Door in Denver, Colorado where he focuses on using authentic ingredients to masterfully create Spanish tapas. He worked with the American Lamb Board to develop recipes for the Spain and the World Table Worlds of Flavor conference in 2006. He worked as the executive chef at Mona's and was the sous chef at MODA. (Denver, CO)

JANET MENDEL is an American-born journalist who has lived in southern Spain for more than 30 years. She is the author of the newly released *Cooking from the Heart of Spain: Food of La Mancha*, as well as *My Kitchen in Spain*, *Cooking in Spain*, and *Traditional Spanish Cooking*. (Andalusia, Spain)

KIYOMI MIKUNI is the chef/owner of Hôtel de Mikuni, one of Tokyo's most acclaimed restaurants. Chef Mikuni's first exposure to the international culinary world started at the age of 20 at the Japanese Embassy in Switzerland; he has since traveled around the world to find new flavors to complement his style. Recently his interest has focused on Spain and exploring the natural flavors and conceptual affinities between Japanese and Spanish foods, with a special emphasis on seafood, rice, and umami. (Toyko, Japan)

PEDRO MORÁN is the chef/owner of Casa Gerardo in Prendes, Spain. Casa Gerardo, which holds one Michelin star, was founded in 1882 by Chef Morán's great-grandfather, and has remained in the family ever since. In 1983 the restaurant, which specializes in up-to-date traditional cuisine, received the National Prize of Gastronomy from the Academia Nacional de Gastronomía. (Asturias, Spain)

DANIEL OLIVELLA is executive chef/partner of San Francisco's B-44 Catalan Bistro. Born in Catalonia, Spain, Chef Olivella got his start in his family's restaurant in Vilafranca del Penedes. Before founding B-44 in 1999, he was the executive chef at Thirsty Bear restaurant in San Francisco. In 2001, *San Francisco* magazine selected Chef Olivella as its rising chef of the year, and *USA Today* lauded one of his paellas, "Arros Negre," as one of the best 20 dishes in the United States. (San Francisco, CA)

FRANCIS PANIEGO is the chef of Echaurren in Ezcaray, Spain. Chef Paniego studied at the Escuela Superior de Hostelería y Turismo de Madrid and later trained at El Bulli. He has received a number of honors, including being named "Best Cook of La Rioja." He is currently readying a new restaurant in Rioja Alavesa, built by Frank Gehry. (Rioja, Spain)

JUAN ANTONIO PELLICER is a restaurant and catering technician and cookery teacher at the Cartagena Tourism and Catering School in the Murcia region of Spain. He collaborates with the University of Murcia's Department of Bromatology and Nutrition, and with the Department of Agriculture, Fisheries, and Cattle Farming of the Murcia region. (Cartagena, Spain)

ROBERT PETZOLD collaborated with Gilroy Foods to create dishes for the Spain and the World Table Worlds of Flavor conference in 2006. He was the chef de cuisine at Bocadillos restaurant in San Francisco, CA, where he oversaw the tapas that were created for the restaurant. He has also worked at La Folie and Beaucoup in the San Francisco Bay Area. (San Francisco, CA)

MARICEL E. PRESILLA is a chef, author, and culinary historian specializing in the cuisines of Latin America and Spain. She is the chef/owner of Zafra and Cucharamama restaurants in Hoboken, NJ, which specialize in traditional Pan-Latin cooking. Chef Presilla, who holds a doctorate in Spanish history, is also the author of *The New Taste of Chocolate* and a forthcoming book on the culinary traditions of 21 Latin American countries. (Weehawken, NJ)

JESÚS RAMIRO is the chef/owner of Ramiro's in Valladolid, Spain. After apprenticing in various restaurants, Chef Ramiro opened a restaurant in his hometown of Valladolid. He then traveled throughout South America, and later opened restaurants in Puerto Rico, Mexico, and the United States. In 2006 he opened his newest restaurant, Ramiro's, in the Science Museum of Valladolid. Chef Ramiro is known for his conceptual cuisine, and Ramiro's includes a workshop specializing in innovative dishes. (Valladolid, Spain)

MARÍA JOSÉ SAN ROMÁN is the chef/owner of the Restaurant Monastrell in Alicante, Spain. Chef San Román studied with Jean Louis Neichel of Barcelona and Joan Roca of Girona prior to opening her restaurant. She also teaches cooking and is involved with an exploration of saffron and its applications, a collaboration with the University of Castilla-La Mancha. Chef San Román is a member of Euro-toques. (Alicante, Spain)

VICTOR SCARGLE is the executive chef of the restaurant Go Fish in St. Helena, CA, where he uses the harvest from his extensive restaurant gardens to augment his deliveries from local farms and complement the fish he and sushi chef Ken Tominaga receive fresh daily. Chef Scargle honed his skills in the fast-paced kitchens of Michael Mina, Traci Des Jardins, and Doug Rodriguez. (St. Helena, CA)

MARIE SIMMONS is an award-winning cookbook author, a popular cooking teacher, and a food writer. Her recipes and food articles have appeared in hundreds of magazines. For over 15 years she wrote a monthly column for *Bon Appetit* magazine, and a weekly column for the *Los Angeles Times Syndicate*. Simmons has written eighteen cookbooks including *Fig Heaven*, *Fresh & Fast*, and *The Amazing World of Rice*. She currently writes a bi-monthly column, Simmons Sez, for the *Contra Costa Times* and the Bay Area News Group. (Richmond, CA)

GABINO SOTELINO is the vice president and executive chef of Ambria, Mon Ami Gabi, and Cafe Ba-Ba-Reeba in Chicago, IL. He is also part owner of all seven restaurants with Lettuce Entertain You Enterprises, Inc. (LEYE). In 1974 Chef Sotelino moved to Chicago and became executive chef for Le Perroquet. Three years later he joined LEYE as chef for its recently acquired restaurant, the Pump Room. In 1980 they opened LEYE's first fine-dining restaurant, Ambria. Chef Sotelino was named "Chicago Chef of the Year" by the Chefs of America in 1990, and Gault Millau's The Best of Chicago gave Ambria a rating of three toques, the highest possible—an honor shared with only three other restaurants. (Chicago, IL)

NORMAN VAN AKEN is the executive chef/owner of Norman's in Miami, FL, in Orlando, FL, at the Ritz Carlton, and in Los Angeles, CA. He is one of the few chefs in America to have won the James Beard Award, the Robert Mondavi Award, and *Food Arts* magazine's Silver Spoon Award. Chef van Aken is the author of four cookbooks: *Feast of Sunlight*, *The Exotic Fruit Book*, *Norman's New World Cuisine*, and *New World Kitchen*. In 2006, van Aken received the "Founders of the New American Cuisine" award from Madrid Fusión, recognizing his exceptional talents that have changed and influenced cooking and dining in the United States. (Miami, FL)

MARI CARMEN VÉLEZ is the co-owner and head chef of La Sirena Restaurant in Petrer-Alicante, Spain. Coming from a mostly self-taught background and having completed many specialized restaurant-related courses, Chef Vélez has been collaborating for some years with different organizations with the aim of publicizing and promoting Alicante cuisine and the Mediterranean diet. She also teaches cooking to the Valencian community, and for the past seven years has taken part in the gastronomic program "Costa Blanca," broadcast on Radio Alicante-Cadena SER. (Alicante, Spain)

RAFAEL VIDAL is the chef of Levante in Benissanó, Spain. Chef Vidal is the third generation of his family in the kitchen, which now also includes his children and other relatives. The restaurant is known for its paella, which Chef Vidal has prepared for the king of Spain. Levante is listed in numerous gastronomical guides (Michelin, Gourmetour, CAMPSA) and has received many honors. (Benissanó, Spain)

ANYA VON BREMZEN is a contributing editor and food columnist for *Travel & Leisure* magazine. She is also the author of *The New Spanish Table*, *The Greatest Dishes!*, *Fiesta! A Celebration of Latin Hospitality*, *The Terrific Pacific Cookbook*, and co-author (with John Welcham) of the James Beard Award-winning *Please to the Table: The Russian Cookbook*. She has written for *Gourmet*, the *Los Angeles Times*, *Condé Nast Traveler*, and *Elle*. (New York, NY)

SUSAN WALTER is a private chef and a consultant to restaurants, commodity boards, and manufacturers. She has developed Spanish and Asian menus for the Alaska Seafood Marketing Institute at the Culinary Institute of America. She was owner and executive chef of the acclaimed Ristorante Ecco in San Francisco and partner and Executive Chef of Cheese Please Catering. She has authored three cookbooks, including *Seasonal Vegetarian Cooking* and the James Beard Award-nominated *Entertaining Made Easy*. (Santa Rosa, CA)

PARTICIPATING SPEAKERS AND GUEST CHEFS AT THE 2006 SPAIN AND THE WORLD TABLE CONFERENCE

CARLES ABELLÁN Chef/owner of Comerç 24 (Barcelona, Spain)

FERRAN ADRIÀ Chef/owner of El Bulli (Roses, Spain)

ANDONI LUIS ADURIZ Chef of Mugaritz (San Sebastián, Spain)

RAÚL ALEIXANDRE Chef of Ca'Sento (Valencia, Spain)

CLARA MARÍA GONZÁLEZ DE AMEZÚA Founder/Owner of El Alambique (Madrid, Spain)

JOSÉ ANDRÉS Chef/owner of Café Atlantico, Jaleo, Zaytina, and Oyamel (Washington, DC)

COLMAN ANDREWS Author of *Catalan Cuisine, Flavors of the Riviera*, and *Everything on the Table* (New York, NY)

RAFAEL ANSÓN Ph.D., founder/president of the Spanish Gastronomic Academy (Madrid, Spain)

RICHARD ARAKELIAN Senior Director of Culinary for Sodexho (Morris Township, NJ)

ORIOL BALAGUER Pastry chef and owner of Estudi Xocolata (Barcelona, Spain)

PEDRO BARBA GIL Butcher and manager of Asprofes (Valencia, Spain)

TERESA BARRENECHEA Chef and author of *The Cuisines of Spain: Exploring Regional Home Cooking* and *The Basque Table* (Madrid, Spain)

MICHAEL BATTERBERRY Editor-in-chief of *Food Arts* (New York, NY)

PATXI BERGARA Owner of Bar Bergara (San Sebastián, Spain)

SANTIAGO BOTAS Consultant and olive oil expert (Madrid, Spain)

ENRIC CANUT Cheese maker and author (Barcelona, Spain)

CÁNDIDO LÓPEZ CUERDO Chef of Mesón de Cándido (Segovia, Spain)

GERRY DAWES Writer and photographer (Suffern, NY)

ANDREA MASSARO DEBERNARDI Pastry chef of Huaca Pacllana Restaurant (Lima, Peru)

ROBERT DEL GRANDE Executive chef/owner of Café Annie (Houston, TX)

MANOLO DE LA OSA Chef of Las Rejas (Cuenca, Spain)

GREG DRESCHER Executive Director of Strategic Initiatives for The Culinary Institute of America (Napa Valley, CA)

MARK ERICKSON C.M.C., Vice President of Continuing Education for The Culinary Institute of America (Napa Valley, CA and Hyde Park, NY)

JOAQUÍN FELÍPE Chef of Europa Decó (Madrid, Spain)

DOUG FROST M.S., M.W., author of *The Far From Ordinary Spanish Wine Guide* (Kansas City, MO)

CARLES GAIG Chef/owner of Gaig Restaurant (Barcelona, Spain)

DANI GARCÍA Chef of Calima (Málaga, Spain)

KISKO GARCÍA Chef of Choco (Córdoba, Spain)

MARCO ANTONIO GARCÍA Chef/owner of Mannix (Campaspero, Spain)

JOYCE GOLDSTEIN Food industry consultant, food writer, and author of *The Mediterranean Kitchen* and *Cucina Ebraica: Flavors of the Italian Jewish Kitchen* (San Francisco, CA)

CHEFA GONZÁLEZ-DOPESO Chef, restaurant advisor (La Coruña, Spain)

NANCY HARMON JENKINS Food writer and author of *The Mediterranean Diet Cookbook* and *The Cooking of Puglia: Traditional Recipes from the Heel of Italy's Boot* (Maine, U.S., and Tuscany, Italy)

CHARLES HENNING C.H.A., Managing Director of The Culinary Institute of America at Greystone (Napa Valley, CA)

AMADO ALONSO HEVIA Manager of La Venta del Jamón (Madrid, Spain)

NANDO JUBANY Chef/owner of Can Jubany (Calldetenes, Spain)

PETER KAMINSKY Food writer and author of *Pig Perfect: Encounters with Remarkable Swine* (New York, NY)

THOMAS A. KELLER Chef/owner of The French Laundry, Bouchon, Bouchon Bakery, and Per Se (Napa Valley, CA and New York, NY)

MARIA MURIA LLORET Co-founder of Ca'Sento (Valencia, Spain)

JUAN JOSÉ LÓPEZ Chef/owner of La Tasquita de Enfrente (Madrid, Spain)

KAREN MACNEIL Wine and food educator, author, and chair of Professional Wine Studies at The Culinary Institute of America (Napa Valley, CA)

MARILÚ MADUEÑO Executive chef of Huaca Pucllana Restaurant (Lima, Peru)

SANTIAGO MARTÍN Head of Embutidos Fermín (Salamanca, Spain)

ENRIQUE MARTÍNEZ Chef of El Hotel Restaurante Maher (Navarra, Spain)

MAX MCCALMAN Maître fromager of the Artisanal Restaurant Group, dean of curriculum at the Artisanal Cheese Center, and author (New York, NY)

HAROLD MCGEE Writer and author of *On Food and Cooking* (Palo Alto, CA)

JANET MENDEL Journalist and author of *Cooking from the Heart of Spain: Food of La Mancha* (Andalusia, Spain)

KIYOMI MIKUNI Chef/owner of Hôtel de Mikuni (Tokyo, Japan)

PEDRO MORÁN Chef/owner of Casa Gerardo (Prendes, Spain)

DANIEL OLIVELLA Executive chef/partner of B-44 Catalan Bistro (San Francsico, CA)

STEVEN OLSON Wine writer and restaurant consultant (New York, NY)

MIGUEL PALOMO Chef/owner (Sevilla, Spain)

FRANCIS PANIEGO Chef of Echaurren (Rioja, Spain)

JUAN ANTONIO PELLICER Restaurant and catering technician/cookery teacher at Cartegena Tourism and Catering School (Cartegena, Spain)

LLORENÇ PETRÀS Owner of a mushroom shop in La Boquería market (Barcelona, Spain)

MARICEL PRESILLA Author, culinary historian, and chef of Zafra and Cucharamamma (Weehawken, NJ)

JESÚS RAMIRO Chef/owner of Ramiro's (Valladolid, Spain)

JOAN ROCA Chef of Cellar de Can Roca (Girona, Spain)

DAVID ROSENGARTEN Editor-in-chief of *The Rosengarten Report* (New York, NY)

ARTURO RUBIO Founder/promoter/manager of Huaca Pucllana Restaurant (Lima, Peru)

TIM RYAN C.M.C., Ed.D., M.B.A., President of The Culinary Institute of America (Hyde Park, NY)

MARÍA JOSÉ SAN ROMÁN Chef/owner of Restaurant Monastrell (Alicante, Spain)

SUVIR SARAN Chef/owner of Devi, author, and contributing authority to *Food Arts* (New York, NY)

BRUCE SCHOENFELD Contributing editor for *Wine Spectator* magazine (Boulder, CO)

JULIAN SERRANO Executive chef of Picasso (Las Vegas, NV)

MARIA JOSÉ SEVILLA Author of *Life and Food in the Basque Country* and *Spain on a Plate* (London, England)

GABINO SOTELINO Vice president/executive chef of Ambria, Mon Ami Gabi, and Café Ba-Ba-Reeba (Chicago, IL)

NORMAN VAN AKEN Author and executive chef/owner of Norman's (Miami, FL)

MARI CARMEN VÉLEZ Co-owner/head chef of La Siren Restaurant (Alicante, Spain)

RAFAEL VIDAL Chef of Levante (Benissanó, Spain)

ANYA VON BREMZEN Contributing editor/food columnist for *Travel & Leisure Magazine* (New York, NY)

PAUL WAGNER Founder of Balzac Communications & Marketing (Napa Valley, CA)

ARI WEINZWEIG, Founding partner of Zingerman's Community of Businesses (Ann Arbor, MI)

CLARK WOLF Founder and president of Clark Wolf Company (New York, NY)

RICHARD WOLFFE Senior White House correspondent for *Newsweek* (Washington, DC)

ANTONI YELAMOS Director of Operations/Beverage Director for THINKfoodGROUP (Washington, DC)

INDEX

Page numbers in *italic* refer to photographs.

ACKNOWLEDGMENTS

The Culinary Institute of America

HYDE PARK

president DR. TIM RYAN C.M.C. '77
vice-president, continuing education MARK ERICKSON C.M.C. '77
director of intellectual property NATHALIE FISCHER
managing editor KATE MCBRIDE
editorial project manager MARGARET WHEELER '00
production assistant PATRICK DECKER '05

GREYSTONE

executive director of strategic initiatives GREG DRESCHER
associate director of strategic initiatives and corporate relations
  HOLLY BRIWA
associate director of strategic initiatives JOHN BARKLEY
communication manager CATE CONNIFF-DOBRICH
curriculum designer KAREN FORNI
photographer TERRENCE MCCARTHY

This book, which is based on "Spain and the World Table," the CIA's 9th Worlds of Flavor International Conference & Festival, owes its success to a wonderful group of collaborators. First and foremost, I want to thank our conference chairman, chef and author José Andrés, for his vision and leadership on this program; his passion for Spain and its food culture; and his dedication to bringing together such an impressive team of chefs and partners that made this unprecedented program a reality.

Thank you to all of the Spanish chefs and other food authorities who joined our gathering from Spain and across the United States. We very much appreciate all that you did to make this conference such a memorable event.

Of course, none of this would have been possible without the vision and support of our many sponsors, most notably the incredible team at The Spanish Institute for Foreign Trade in Madrid, and the talented individuals that lead Foods from Spain and Wines from Spain in New York. Thanks also to the many Spanish regional governments and private companies as well as the many American companies and organizations who not only supported our Spanish event but also many other conferences at the CIA.

I am especially grateful to our agency team in Barcelona—Grup GSR-Produccions de Gastronomia—that coordinated all the chefs and other experts from Spain, and who were true partners in making this program a reality. Bravo! A heartfelt thanks to Roser Torres, Manu Caballero, Sergio Pérez, Chus Barranchina, and Santi Mas de Xaxàs.

Over the years The Worlds of Flavor Conference series has evolved into one of the most influential conferences in the foodservice industry. For this I am grateful to CIA President Tim Ryan CMC, Vice President Mark Erickson CMC, and, more recently, CIA at Greystone Managing Director Charles Henning for their strong support and for believing very early on that the future of American food would be dramatically reinvented due to the explosive growth and appreciation for the vibrant flavors of world cuisines.

This conference series—part Carnegie Hall showcasing top world culinarians, from celebrated chefs to village cooks, and part dazzling spectacle of meals, tastings, and marketplaces—could only have been made possible with the support of our talented staff and faculty at CIA Greystone. I'm especially grateful to the longstanding contributions and leadership efforts of Holly Briwa, Associate Director of Strategic Initiatives, and Chef Instructor Toni Sakaguchi for making every one of our conferences successful. My heartfelt thanks also goes to the entire CIA at Greystone team, and especially the Education staff and faculty, including Christina Adamson, Dalia Banerjee, John Barkley, William Briwa, Aaron Brown, Tucker Bunch, Adam Busby, CMC; Cate Conniff-Dobrich, Diana Delonis, John Difilippo, Stephen Durfee, Joseba Encabo, Robert Jörin, Lars Kronmark, Brenda LaNoue, Tom Wong, and Ken Woytisek. Thank you all!

-GREG DRESCHER, The Culinary Institute of America

Thank you to all the chefs and experts who agreed to close their restaurants and shops and come over from Spain to make this conference a success, especially my friend and mentor Ferran Adrià.

Thanks to Roser Torres, Santi Mas de Xaxàs, Manu Caballero, and the rest of the team at Grup GSR who made this event happen. Finally, thank you to my team: Ruben Garcia, JohnPaul Damato, Terri Cutrino, Rodolfo Guzman, Nico Guardado, and Laura Trevino, who supported me during the long process of putting this event together.

-CHEF JOSÉ ANDRÉS of THINKfoodGROUP

THE CIA'S ACKNOWLEDGMENTS

Thank you to Chefs Olivier Andreini CMC, John Reilly, and Theo Roe for their expertise in the preparation and presentation of the recipes for photography. Thank you to Creative Foodworks for recipe testing.

PUBLISHER'S ACKNOWLEDGMENTS

DK Publishing would like to thank Alexander Velez at Despaña in New York City (www.despananyc.com) for the kind loan of props for photography.

PICTURE CREDITS

The publisher would like to thank Terrence McCarthy for his kind permission to reproduce his photographs of the 2006 Worlds of Flavor conference: pages 6, 7, 8, 12, 86, 91, 237. 59. All other photography by Ben Fink, except: pages 59, 87, 117: DK Images; page 155: Jupiter Images; page 191: Atlantide Phototravel/Corbis.